OUTSTANDING PRAISE FOR *TAKING FIRE*
by Ron Alexander and Charles W. Sasser

"A gripping combat memoir . . . honest and exciting . . . a rousing tale, full of sharp detail and told in the harsh language of soldiers baptized in fire."

—Kirkus Reviews

"Everybody who survived ground combat in Vietnam had his life saved at one time or another by helicopter crews. We were in awe of them. You will be too after reading *Taking Fire*."
—Jim Morris, author of *War Story* and *The Devil's Secret Name*

"An honest and exciting narrative of the stress of war."

—Library Journal

"[Sasser and Alexander] succeed quite well in evoking the Vietnam War from the point of view of a helicopter pilot who served bravely and with distinction."

—Publishers Weekly

RAIDER

The True Story of the Legendary
Soldier Who Performed More POW Raids
than Any Other American in History

RAIDER

CHARLES W. SASSER

ST. MARTIN'S GRIFFIN
NEW YORK

www.stmartins.com

Library of Congress Cataloging-in-Publication Data

Sasser, Charles W.
    Raider / Charles W. Sasser.—1st St. Martin's Griffin ed.
        p.   cm.
    ISBN-13: 978-0-312-36065-8
    ISBN-10: 0-312-36065-7
    1. Kittleson, Galen Charles.   2. United States. Army—
Non-commissioned officers—Biography.   3. United States.
Army. Special Forces—Biography.   4. Raids (Military science).
5. Prisoners of war—United States.   6. World War, 1939–1945—
Concentration camps—Philippines—Cabanatuan.   7. Sontay
Raid, 1970.   I. Title.

U53.K58 S27 2006
356'.16—dc22

                                                    2006050644

10   9   8   7   6   5   4   3   2

This book can be dedicated only to
Sergeant Major Galen Kittleson,
an American hero

"I never saw a man who looked
With such a wistful eye
Upon that little tent of blue
Which prisoners call the sky."

Oscar Wilde

Preface

One of the greatest tragedies of war for the United States in the twentieth century has been the suffering of American military servicemen seized and held captive by the enemy. Those prisoners of war who miraculously survived internment and escaped, were released, or were rescued brought back tales that stunned and horrified the nation. American POWs from WWI to Vietnam experienced almost unendurable atrocities ranging from sadistic torture and deliberate starvation to brainwashing and execution.

"Death camps" such as the Cabanatuan hellhole, which held the survivors of the Bataan Death March during World War II, and the "Hanoi Hilton" in North Vietnam became infamous for their maltreatment of American prisoners. In them, POWs daily confronted starvation, disease, despair, abuse, and brutal death.

Experiences described by U.S. Air Force Captain Howard Rutledge, pilot of an F-8 Crusader shot down over North Vietnam on 28 November 1965, and caged for seven years behind the cold stone walls of the Hanoi Hilton, are representative of those endured by American POWs in this century.

"[The guard] shackled me to my slab in rear cuffs and irons," Rutledge wrote in his memoirs. "For five days I couldn't move. It was summer and very hot. The humidity must have been in the 90s, the temperature in the 100s. I developed one of those severe heat rashes where the red welts turned to blisters and ultimately to boils. . . . They wouldn't come to a head, so I had to pick them to stop the swelling. . . . In a few days, I counted at least sixty boils about one inch in diameter over my entire body—under my arms, in my nose, in my hair, on my ears, legs, arms, hands and fingers. . . .

"Our intestines were crawling with worms that would work their way through our systems in surprising ways. One night Harry (another American POW) woke up with what he thought was a piece of string in his mouth. He pulled out a six-inch worm . . ."

Some 20,000 American fighting men are still listed as POW or MIA (missing in action) from the four major wars of this century in which the United States has been involved: 1,250 from WWI; 7,751 from WWII; 8,177 from Korea; and 2,266 from Vietnam. Many of this number remained captive in POW camps for years after the wars in which they were captured ended. Behind bars and barbed wire they waited, year after year, looking to the skies in hopes of release or rescue. Many died still waiting.

While America made a number of attempts to rescue her imprisoned warriors during the course of these conflicts, most failed. The man who holds the distinction of having participated in more raids to free POWs than any other American in history—*four* raids during two separate wars— is virtually a legend in U.S. Army Special Forces.

Galen Charles Kittleson, who retired as Command Sergeant Major of the U.S. Army's 7th Special Forces Group (Airborne), went on his first raid during World War II in the South Pacific when he was nineteen years old. Months later, he was among a force of famed Alamo Scouts and U.S. Army Rangers that launched another raid to free the survivors of the Bataan Death March.

Two and a half decades passed before Master Sergeant Kittleson, now a crusty combat veteran, twice more penetrated enemy lines in rescue attempts of Yank POWs. His raid of 21 November 1970 on a POW camp only twenty-three miles from Hanoi in North Vietnam is undoubtedly the most daring and famous in American history.

Raider is the story of those four raids and the extraordinary farmer-warrior from Iowa who participated in them. Chances are slim that any of the 20,000 Americans listed as captured or missing in action remain alive at this late date. However, if even one prisoner is still in captivity and looking to the skies day after day for salvation, he deserves to look up one day and see, dropping out of the clouds, brave saviors like Sergeant Major Galen Kittleson—*The Raider*.

Acknowledgments

The information in this book is based upon a variety of sources: Personal observations and the observations of witnesses; official U.S. Army documents and After Action Reports; diaries; newspaper and other published accounts; extensive taped interviews with Sergeant Major Galen Kittleson, U.S. Army, whose autobiographical accounts form the nucleus of this book; interviews with soldiers such as Lieutenant William Nellist of the famed World War II Alamo Scouts and Lieutenant George Petrie, Sergeants Tom Kemmer, Lorenzo Robbins, Dave Adams, and Kenneth E. Mc-Mullin (U.S. Army Special Forces), who participated in the daring Son Tay Raid to rescue American POWs from the North Vietnamese; a long talk with U.S. Airman Dave Ford, who was held prisoner for five and a half years at the notorious Hanoi Hilton in North Vietnam; and a lecture/question-and-answer session given by Major Nick Rowe, who was also held POW for five years by the North Vietnamese.

I would like once more to extend my personal thanks to those brave men and to the dozens of others who cooperated with me and assisted me in writing this book. Without their guidance this book may never have been completed.

I would also like to express my gratitude to the following authors and their published works, from which I also drew in writing this book—*The Great Raid on Cabanatuan* by William B. Breuer (New York: Wiley Books, 1994); *I Came Back from Bataan* by Sergeant James Donovan Gautier, Jr., with Robert L. Whitmore (Greenville: Blue Ridge Publishing, 1997); *Corregidor* by General E.M. Flanagan, Jr. (Novato: Presidio Press, 1995); *The Raid* by Benjamin F. Schemmer (New York: Harper, 1976); *Five Years to Freedom* by James N. Rowe (New York: Ballantine, 1971); *Silent Warriors of World War II* by Lance Q. Zedric (Ventura: Pathfinder Publishing, 1995); and *Tan Phu: Special Forces Team A-23 in Combat* by Leigh Wade (New York: Ivy Books, 1997).

Actual names are used throughout except in those rare instances where names were lost due to either memory loss or lack of documentation, where privacy was requested, or where public identification would serve no useful purpose and might cause embarrassment.

In various instances dialogue and scenes have necessarily been re-created. Time has a tendency to erode memories in some areas and selectively enhance it in others. Where re-creation occurs, I strive to match personalities with the situation and the action while maintaining factual content. The recounting of some events may not correspond precisely with the memories of all involved. In addition, all data has been filtered through the author. I must therefore apologize to anyone omitted, neglected, or somehow slighted in the preparation of this book. I take responsibility for such errors and ask to be forgiven for them.

While I am certain to have made interpretational mistakes, I am just as certain that the content of this book is accurate to the spirit and reality of Sergeant Major Galen Kittleson and all the brave men who participated in the events described in this book. My objective was to present a true account of one man's selfless duty to country and to his fellow soldiers captured by enemy forces.

Charles W. Sasser

PART I

". . . And bringeth the prisoners out of captivity."

The Prayer Book

CHAPTER 1

There was no moon at the moment, but there would be one later. It would be red and menacing like the Japanese Rising Sun, and it would ride low on the watery horizon of the wartime Pacific, building a bloody shimmering boulevard across the sea to the two PT boats whose navy crews would await the outcome of the raid. Aboard the PT boats in the near-total pre-moon darkness, two teams of 6th Army Alamo Scouts—thirteen elite soldiers—prepared to slip over the PT gunnels into a pair of rubber boats. Dark-skinned native New Guinea guides in khaki shorts lay on their bellies, one guide on each patrol boat, and attempted to steady the rubber craft that bounced alongside on a roughening sea. Dutch Coastwatcher Louie Rapmund, a skinny sunburned man wearing an Aussie hat with one side of the brim turned up, stepped back and braced himself against the PT cockpit. He rebelled against being among the first into the unsteady rubber boats.

"Mate, I never been much at riding bucking brumbies," he whispered to the dark shadow of the Scout next to him.

"You get used to it," the Scout replied.

"Like a toothache?" the Dutchman said.

There was no further conversation. Rapmund stayed out of the way of the Scouts' preparations and watched. He accompanied the raiding party only because he spoke the local native lingo and because it was to him the native had come after escaping from the Japanese. The man told of how a former Dutch governor, his family, and their Japanese workers—sixty-six men, women, and children in all—were being held by the Japs at slave labor in the village of Maori on Cape Oransbari in the Vogelkop area of northwestern New Guinea.

General Douglas MacArthur's headlong rush of island-hopping to retake New Guinea and keep his promise to return to the Philippines had resulted in isolating more than 200,000 Japanese troops in pockets of resistance throughout northern New Guinea. Within these pockets, Japanese soldiers retained "prisoners of war," most of whom were Melanesian, Dutch, and Australian planters and their families—forced labor for the Emperor's army.

"We have a good chance to rescue at least one batch of them," Lieutenant Bill Nellist had explained in a premission briefing to his Scout team six days earlier at the Navy PT boat base on Woendi Island.

Nellist bent over a map of the Vogelkop, his tall figure resembling a stork's intent on pouncing on a fish. A kerosene lamp burned on a map table, around which gathered the other six members of the team. Their shadows loomed on the tent walls.

"This is Maori," he said, jabbing a finger at the map. "PT boats will insert our team and Rounsaville Team on Cape Oransbari about three miles from the village. Guides will take us there through the jungle. We expect about thirty Japs at the village. But, fellas, there's a Jap garrison about twenty miles away with two thousand other heavily-armed Nip troops. We can't afford to screw up. We have to get in fast, kick ass, and get out of there with the prisoners."

It was 28 September 1944. The Nellist and Rounsaville Teams had graduated from 6th Army's Alamo Scouts on 6 September. For the past three weeks, Scout operations officers like John M. "Jack" Dove had used the new teams sparingly to break them in—overnighters reconnoitering areas of light occupation by the Japanese, quick missions to contact Coastwatchers or to question natives. The fledgling Scouts chafed at the bit, eager to stretch their legs and run. They had been trained and trained hard to infiltrate and operate behind enemy lines in small six- and seven-man guerrilla elements: reconnoitering Jap installations; blowing up barges and truck convoys; sabotaging enemy movements; training natives to spy, sabotage, and raise hell with the Nips. They were ready to get on with their part of the war.

Jack Dove was a husky six-foot two-hundred-pounder from Hollywood, California. Handsome enough to be a movie star—say, a John Wayne type—he flashed a constant boy-next-door grin. "You'll all get your chance to fight the Japs," he reassured the new Scouts.

The Oransbari raid promised to test the Nellist and Rounsaville Teams. It was their first *real* mission.

"We're going to lose our virginity," hooted Willie Wismer.

"You are too *ugly* to lose yours," big Gilbert Cox hooted back.

Twice before during the past four nights the raiders had attempted landings. The first time a sudden squall prevented the teams from departing Woendi. On the second attempt, one of the PT boats tasked with transporting the raiders struck a floating palm and twisted its screws.

Tonight, however, looked to be a "go."

The PT boats' big Packard engines idled almost without noise, their exhausts underwater and therefore muffled. The boats were grungy, battle-scarred, rat-ridden, cockroach-infested 80-footers with high prows, each armed with four torpedo tubes, a .50-caliber mounted machine gun and an antiaircraft gun. Waves pounded and sucked against the plyboard hulls. Wave action tossed each rubber boat high and against its mother ship with a slithering sound.

Private First Class Galen Kittleson knelt on the deck of his PT and reeled in the rubber raft by its painter. *For Christ's sake, where is it?* It was that dark. He flopped out on his belly next to the native guide and reached over the side to find the raft. He felt wet rubber and made out the little boat's outline.

No more hesitation. He grabbed his .45 Thompson submachine gun and sprang with it into the rubber boat. Waves bounced it up to receive him. He sprawled backwards, but sponged to his feet and steadied the boat against the PT for the others to board.

"Move it!" hissed team leader Lieutenant Nellist. The five other soldiers of Nellist Team—Tech Five Willie Wismer, Corporal Andy Smith, Staff Sergeant Tommie Siason, Private First Class Gilbert Cox, Private First Class Sabas Asis—pounced in with Kittleson, using his body to steady themselves while they found positions. The native guide nimbly piled in on top, while Rapmund the Coastwatcher would have gone overboard had Nellist not grabbed his battle harness. Big Gilbert Cox took over and wedged the Dutchman between Asis and Wismer at the bow. Lieutenant Nellist and a private named Hill were the last aboard. Hill and Jack Dove in the other boat would return the rubber rafts to the patrol boats.

By this time Rounsaville Team had loaded its rubber raft. Kittleson grabbed a paddle and pushed off from the PT boat. It disappeared almost instantly into the darkness. The two rafts bobbed low in the water, rising and falling together, their occupants paddling almost side by side to maintain contact.

Kittleson peered ahead into the South Pacific night. He either saw the darkened inkline of land dead ahead or it was his imagination. He dipped his paddle deep and threw his shoulders into the resistance. The Tommy gun rested across his thighs, always within reach.

Kittleson was a diminutive soldier, barely five-four on a tall day. At nineteen years old, he was the youngest fighter in the elite Alamo Scouts. Despite his age and size, however, the farmer kid from the Iowa cornbelt had already won a Silver Star for Valor by single-handedly knocking out a Jap machine gun on Noemfoor.

The kid had volunteered for the army and had volunteered for the paratroops. Now, in volunteering for the Alamo Scouts, he had volunteered for the most hazardous missions the army could throw at him in the fight against the Japs. Before, while he was in action with the 503d Parachute Regiment, U.S. 6th Army, the other GIs treated him almost as a good luck amulet. "Kit" Kittleson, they said, only half jokingly, lived a charmed life, and that charm protected his buddies.

Kittleson knew better. It wasn't charm; it was faith. His was a simple and direct faith. On the PT boat en route, he had bowed his head and silently asked the protection of God for himself, the other raiders, and the prisoners they were attempting to rescue.

And now he was ready. Ahead, breakers shallowed into shimmering white foam, creating an eerie phosphorescent effect in the black night. The rafts together shot into a small protected cove. Their bottoms scraped on coral. Looking like a child's stick figure, Nellist sprang from the boat into the surf. The others followed. The hulking figure of Gilbert Cox slapped Kittleson on the butt as the team waded quickly ashore.

Even the night birds went silent for the landing. The beach was only about a yard wide, one step between the saltwater and the beginning of tropical rain forest. A black wall. Kit dropped to one knee with Cox at arm's reach on one side and Asis on the other; he was damp from the ocean spray. No one spoke, not even a whisper. Voices carried long distances at night. Even *sweating* when you were behind enemy lines seemed deafening. It was up to Rapmund and the natives to find the footpath.

Kit asked God to have mercy on the souls of those who must die tonight.

CHAPTER 2

This was Rounsaville's show; he was calling the shots as mission leader. Lieutenant Thomas "Stud" Rounsaville was a long man, all legs and shoulders. He dropped to his knees next to Kittleson. Kit shifted his ear close to the officer's lips.

"Take point with the Melanesian when they find the trail," he said, then melted away with Nellist to check on the other men. It wouldn't do for anyone to become separated from the others on a night like this.

The natives located the trail after a short search. It started at the beach near the mouth of the Wassoenger River. It was not much of a trail, more a faint footpath slippery and sticky with mud from the afternoon's rain. Trees dripped water. In the distance, back from the beach, night birds began calling again as from a Tarzan movie.

Kittleson and the two natives took point. Kit used a night lens on his flashlight. It emitted a faint red glow hardly visible from fifty feet away, but was sufficient to keep the trail underfoot. The little force lined out caterpillar-style on the path, while Lieutenant Dove and Private Hill lashed the rafts together and returned to the PT boats to man the communications net and wait out the hours until the rescue attempt.

The trail led dark, wet, and silent through heavy foliage, south across the Oransbari Cape to its south shore and the village on the Maori River. Although the escaped native New Guinean insisted the Japanese occupiers felt comfortable in their little jungle redoubt and that security was therefore lax, only potentially dead men took anything for granted in enemy country. Kittleson sweated from tension and effort. He tested each footstep for the crack of a twig or the scraping of a rock before trusting his weight to it. He paused frequently to listen to the dark and sniff the dank air, his eyes all but useless underneath the overhanging forest canopy. No words were spoken or needed.

The red moon climbed out of the sea as the two Scout teams snail-paced through the jungle toward the target, but the forest canopy squeezed all light out of the atmosphere before it reached the jungle floor. Rotting vegetation produced foxfire—phosphorescent eyes glowing balefully in the darkness, watching the movement of the intruders as though resenting it. Great glowworms appeared to float in an ocean of black.

Tropical jungle at night is a threatening and alien world—especially if it conceals men whose desire is to kill you in the quickest and most savage manner possible.

The raiders had departed the PTs at 1700 hours, shortly after nightfall. They had until dawn to cover the three miles to Maori.

Kit focused all his senses into the blackness ahead.

A rifle shot barked somewhere ahead, so suddenly and unexpectedly that Kittleson's war-honed instincts dropped him face down into the mud even before he thought about it. A second shot following immediately after the first registered more rationally in his brain. The shots came from farther off than he first supposed, but they were still near enough to pose a possible threat. Japs weren't shooting at them, though. But what the hell were they shooting? Prisoners trying to escape?

No one moved for a quarter-hour, not even to scratch his nose or brush away the swarms of mosquitos that covered him like a living cloak. Gradually, Kittleson's heart stopped thumping so heavily against the mud. He strained his senses to penetrate the unknown distance ahead.

Lieutenant Nellist crept forward to the pointmen, startling Kit with his silent approach.

"Damn, Bill," Kittleson breathed. "You trying to give me a heart attack?"

"We're getting close," the lieutenant whispered. "The natives think the Japanese were shooting wild pigs. They hunt them at night. Let's move out. But take it slow."

They couldn't have gone much slower.

The raiders crossed the Maori River upstream of the village an hour before the first smear of dawn. The river was more like a shallow creek heavily wooded on both sides. Kittleson waded across. It was knee deep. He pushed his way silently into a thick copse of undergrowth. The teams quickly formed a perimeter. It was still so dark, the red moon having sunk now beyond the forest, that the Scouts set up within arm's reach of each other. Kittleson smelled cooking fires from the village still hidden ahead but now so near that the crowing of a rooster and a dog's barking sounded almost within the tight perimeter. He hoped the fires were last night's and that the Japs were not yet stirring. Surprise was a necessary prerequisite of the assault.

Rounsaville dispatched the escaped prisoner to scout the enemy camp for last-minute intelligence. Only seven days had passed since the man's break for freedom. Sending him back in was risky business, but riskier still lurked the possibility that the Japanese may have reinforced the village's defenses during the intervening week.

By the time the spy returned, gray morning twilight had crept into the blackness of the night. Day birds were awakening in the jungle, muttering sleepily, and a brown hen with its ass worn bare clucked nearsightedly past not ten feet from where Kittleson lay. It surprised him that he could see it. He glanced to his left and made out the tall prone form of

Andy Smith. Smith looked back. He was 6th Army's top athlete and its most valuable basketball player. He was also something of a good-natured bullshitter who let the other men *know* he was 6th Army's top jock.

The Melanesian slipped back into the perimeter wearing a broad grin on his swarthy face and carrying three Jap rifles he had relieved from their sleeping owners. Team members huddled close in the bushes around the spy and the Coastwatcher to receive the report and finalize assault plans.

"Nothing change," the former POW whispered in pidgin English. "I count so many, this." He held up splayed hands and flashed off the number 23 on his fingers. "This many"— eighteen fingers—"him sleep now in this one house."

He drew in the dirt with a stick.

"This many"—five—"him in this house. Here. Dutch peoples and other peoples, him in this house and this house . . ."

Using Rapmund as an interpreter, Rounsaville quickly drew a schematic on the ground. A long nipa hut barracks on stilts against rainy season flooding apparently housed the main body of the Japanese—the eighteen from whom the native had stolen the rifles. It was set nearest the jungle and farthest from the beach and the mouth of the Maori River. A smaller stilted hut nearby housed five Jap *Kempeitai*, Japanese intelligence specialists, and the native chief who was being held hostage.

Between these two structures and the beach rose several smaller huts and another long stilted bamboo building into which the prisoners were herded each night for sleeping. There were no guards over them, but any captive caught outside after lockdown was subject to execution on the spot.

The only defenses appeared to be along the beach where the Japs had dug shallow emplacements and set up a Dutch heavy machine gun and a Japanese light machine gun. The sentries there occupied a small, hastily-built palm-and-bamboo hut.

The Japs felt so secure they hadn't bothered establishing night sentries.

They were making it too easy.

Stud Rounsaville gave the attack its final polish. As soon as it was light enough to avoid stumbling around in the brush like clumsy carabao, Nellist, along with three soldiers in his team—Kittleson, Gilbert Cox, and Tom Siason—would follow the river to the beach and take out the machine guns. Andy Smith, Willie Wismer, and Private Sabas Asis from Nellist Team had the responsibility of charging the *Kempeitai* quarters, where they were to rescue the native chief and capture the *Kempeitai* intelligence officer if possible. The remaining bulk of the attackers led by Rounsaville would target the main Jap barracks, after which they would release the POWs and escort them to the secured beach for pickup by arriving PT boats.

"I'll fire the shot to initiate the assault," Rounsaville said. "Any questions? Good luck, Scouts."

If everything continued according to plan, some sixty-six men, women, and children who had been virtual slave labor to the Japs for months would find themselves breathing free air.

Rounsaville gave the signal to move out. Soldiers rose like silent ghosts in the thin silvery fog seeping in off the ocean. Excitement cloyed around them even thicker than the fog. Kittleson drew a deep breath to ease the pounding of his heart and fell in with Nellist, Cox, and Siason. Less than a year ago he had been milking cows, growing corn, and playing baseball back in the farm country of Iowa. The war had been so far away it seemed almost unreal. Since then, however, the kid who once harbored the notion of becoming a high school coach and a farmer had been honed by training and combat into a deadly weapon of destruction. He turned off all emotion in order to meet the cold hard demands of action.

God, after all, had done His share of smiting in the Old Testament when it came to conquering evil.

CHAPTER 3

The Kittleson family had numbered an even dozen. Galen Charles Kittleson was the eldest of the eight surviving barefooted offspring struggling through the Great Depression in an old white two-story farm house through the cracks of which a skinny cat might squeeze without leaving hair. He was the eldest of the children who *lived*, not the first born. The first two had died at birth, attended by a midwife. Galen lived, but his dad took one look at him, then stared, twisting his straw hat in his hands.

"Kind of scrawny," Floyd Kittleson murmured.

"He'll grow," said his mother, Caroline.

"Hardly as big as a little catfish." Floyd was of old-school Norwegian stock. A man of clipped, accented words—and few of those. Action, he always said, spoke much louder than words.

"Floyd, you have yourself a son," Caroline scolded. "Thank God this one lived. You'll be proud of him, you will."

The firstborn grew up running—always running. He loved the feel of the family farm west of tiny St. Ansgar in northern Iowa. He liked the feel of morning dewfall on his bare feet when he raced into the pastures to collect the cows for milking, the feel and slightly musky scent of the breeze rustling the leaves of the rolling fields of corn that stretched into distance and memory.

"I'm going to be an Iowa farmer, just like my pops," he would chirp brightly.

He was a skinny little kid who weighed less than a 100-pound sack of feed oats until after he started high school, then gained little in weight and height after that. He was strong, though, for his size. Ploughing with the team of roan Belgians in the corn fields, baling and hauling hay, harvesting corn—it built muscle and, his father said, character.

"A farmer, above all men, must know God," Floyd would say in rare moments of loquaciousness. "He sees the face of God growing around him every day."

It was a simple, deeply ingrained faith the Kittleson children were to carry with them for life.

Times were tough for the family before the war; the Depression lingered on. There was always food on the table, but not always shoes to wear to school. Clothing had patches on top of patches. Galen decided to quit school when he was fifteen years old, to get a job and help with the family finances. To his surprise, his father merely nodded at his son's decision. Floyd was a deep believer in sons of first- and second-generation immigrants obtaining education.

"I'm going to be a farmer," Galen reasoned. "I can read and write already. Why do I need to know where Norway or Sweden is on the map or who this guy Hitler is?"

"I already have a job for you," Floyd said, further astonishing his son. Galen had expected resistance.

Floyd worked at the railroad unloading coal cars to bring in a little extra income during the farm offseason. Galen quit school the next day and accompanied his father to the railhead where a string of gondolas sat on a side track, each mounded with coal. Floyd handed his son a scoop shovel.

"Let's go to work, boy," he said. "Strong arms, strong back, and a weak mind. That's what it takes."

Galen returned to school the next day. His father merely smiled.

Pearl Harbor occurred during basketball season at St. Ansgar Independent High. It was a distant thing, akin to a revolution in India or a famine in Africa. The war fever that swept the nation barely touched the Kittlesons and their neighbors in the corn and hay fields of Iowa. At least, they weren't touched until the area's young men began disappearing into the army. On Saturday nights in downtown St. Ansgar, fewer and fewer young men gathered to walk the streets and appraise young women and girls walking the streets.

"Have you seen Angus?" someone might ask.

"He joined the army, what I hear."

"What for did he do that?"

"What I hear, the Japs are about to invade California."

Gradually, in this manner, through the disappearing of the farm sons, through newspaper and radio reports, and gossip on the streets and around the stove at the feed store, the war came even to St. Ansgar. Galen Kittleson graduated from high school in the spring of 1942 and enrolled for the fall term at nearby St. Olaf College, after the harvest. He was athletic, but far too small to even think of professional sports; he could, however, coach.

He lasted one semester before he felt the call of duty and, like many young men, the call of adventure. U.S. involvement in the war had been raging for a year when he marched into his local draft board in Osage. After all, he was eighteen years old and there was nothing in St. Ansgar to hold him. He had escorted a pretty junior named Darlene Bruggeman of nearby Toeterville to his high school graduation banquet, but it was a casual relationship. The farm would be there when the war was won and the Yanks came marching home.

"I would like to go as soon as possible," Galen informed Mrs. Nellie Riersen, who ran the draft board.

"Are you sure you're old enough?" Mrs. Riersen asked suspiciously, eyeing the diminutive youth.

"Yes, ma'am, I shore am."

"Better you start packing then, young Galen. Bring your birth certification, if you have one."

CHAPTER 4

A Santa Fe Trailways bus transported Uncle Sam's skinny new recruit to the induction center in Des Moines, where he and a few hundred other young farm kids from Iowa, Minnesota, and Missouri had their hair sheared and exchanged their baggy overalls and jeans for even baggier khaki uniforms and fatigues. A sense of excitement and purpose permeated the induction center atmosphere. There were *Uncle Sam Wants You!* signs and *Know Your Enemy* posters and war bond ads and painted directional arrows on walls. Rough sergeants and fresh new lieutenants with squeaky voices vigorous from officer drill school herded the fresh meat around like cattle, shouting and cursing. *Head 'em up, herd 'em up, roll 'em out!*

Herded them onto a troop train, all that fresh khaki and shorn heads. Two days later, Kittleson debarked in a light snowfall at Camp Buckner, North Carolina. He looked around at a rough squatters' camp of wooden, white-painted, uninsulated barracks stuck in dress-right-dress rows all over the countryside. Barbed wire encircled them. Companies of recruits marched and ran, chanted Jody calls, and conducted rifle drill under the watchful eyes and unrelenting goading of drill instructors.

"Move it! Move it, you shitbirds. The war'll be over at this rate before you new meat ever gets there."

They were lined up in ragged ranks and assigned training companies, right down the alphabet.

"Georgio, M. . . . Company 184 . . ."

"Harrison, D. . . . Company 184 . . ."

"Isaacs, L. . . . 185 . . ."

"Kittleson, G. . . . Company 185 . . ."

"That's a heavy weapons company, fella," whispered the draftee next to him. His name was Lord and he was from Minnesota. Kittleson recognized the stocky fair-haired Swede from the troop train.

"They always put the little fellas in heavy weapons," Lord snickered, then made a face when the L of his name landed him in the same company.

"Heavy weapons?" Kittleson asked, whispering.

"Don't you know nothing, fella? You know—machine guns, mortars . . ."

The DI caught them talking. "Cut the happy horseshit, ladies," he growled, "or I'll make you sor-r-r-ry."

"I'm already sorry," Lord managed from the side of his lips.

Kittleson didn't make a big smash in boot camp training. He was a quiet, self-effacing, baby-faced kid who did what he was supposed to do and maintained a low profile. He could run and shoot and hold his own during drill. While he wasn't a fuckup, he wasn't a standout either. Doing his time the quiet way. Getting through. Heading for the meat grinder at the end. Companies trained together, then shipped out to the war together.

Placed in the machine gun section, he carried the water-cooled .30-caliber. A ball buster of a weapon with the barrel snugged inside a water-filled radiator. A gunner not only carried the machine gun, which weighed nearly fifty pounds including bipod, he always loaded himself and his assistant down with ammo and water for the radiator. During a break in training, Kittleson set up the gun and was practicing traversing and searching with it when a DI stopped to look him over like he had never seen him before.

"Which platoon are you in, private?"

"I'm in yours, drill sergeant."

"Well . . . hell. Kittleson, huh? I like your gumption and interest. I'm making you the new acting squad leader."

Barracks were always cold. At night, watches had to keep the coal-burning stoves stoked with fuel. Bullshit-and-bull sessions always started around the stoves at night while the inductees prepared their uniforms and equipment for the next day's training. Topics centered on the war, on movements and casualties, battles and heroes. Some of the men, having never experienced combat, were braggadocios. Others got real quiet after a while.

Lord regarded Kittleson with a wise, knowing eye. "Kittleson," he said. "Let's you and me volunteer for the paratroopers."

Kittleson looked up from shining his boots. "What are paratroopers?"

"How far back in the corn did you grow up, boy? Paratroopers jump out of airplanes with parachutes. A real sharp outfit. These boys are tough."

Kittleson shrugged. Why not?

"Are you out of your gourd?" the DI screamed and jerked Kittleson's acting squad leader stripe. "You ain't smart enough to wear this stripe. Paratroopers get their asses shot off."

Lord, as luck had it, failed his airborne physical and shipped out overseas with the rest of the outfit. Kittleson passed, the only one in his company to go into the paratroops. A huge sign greeted him at the front gate of Fort Benning, Georgia: *Through These Gates Pass the Toughest Paratroopers in the World*. That was how the psyching-up began for bailing out of perfectly good airplanes in flight. Kittleson couldn't know it at the time, but Airborne was only the beginning of his association with elite military units and the daring missions they were often called upon to conduct.

"God?" he breathed reverently, stuffed duffle bag balanced on his shoulder. In the distance, a four-engined C-47 troop transport plane cast spores that blossomed into mushrooms in the sky. Nearer, men parachuted from the top of a 250-foot tower. "God, what have I gotten myself into?"

He had never even been *inside* an airplane, much less flown in one and then *jumped out*.

He was a *farmer*, for Christ's sake.

Beyond the gate was Hell Week. Then another Hell Week. Then Jump Week for the survivors.

Airborne shuffle. One mile, two miles, no sweat. Four miles, five miles, not done yet.

> *Two old ladies lying in bed.*
> *One looked over to the other and said:*
> *"I wanna be an Airborne Ranger.*
> *I wanna live a life of danger . . ."*
> *Airborne! Airborne! All the way!*

Torture of the swingline trainers. Dangling from harnesses in the air. Practice PLFs—parachute landing falls. Jumping from the 34-foot tower on a cable again and again. Parachuting from the 250-foot tower. More running and pushups. Yelled at and cuffed by the airborne instructors. Uniforms salt-crusted with sweat. Popping salt tabs.

Everyone was a number, not a name: "Billet 802, what are you?"

"Airborne, Sergeant Airborne! All the way!"

"Can you *kill* Japs, Billet 851? Can you kill Krauts?"

"With my bare hands, Sergeant Airborne!"

Men jumped out of perfectly good airplanes to do battle on the ground. Tough, reckless men with a contempt for death and danger.

Kittleson stood in the door for his first parachute jump. By the numbers. Tips of his fingers outside, touching the skin of the aircraft. Boot toes protruding over the edge. Slip-stream screaming past only an inch from his face. He watched lazily as ponds and green fields and brown fields and cows in pastures and trucks on a farm-market road drifted past precisely 1,250 feet below.

Soon, he told himself, he would be doing this for *real*. Parachuting into battle with either the 82d or 101st Airborne Divisions, or one of the four Airborne regiments constituted the previous year, 1942. The 82d had already made quite a name for itself with paradrops into North Africa, and onto Sicily only two months ago.

The jumpmaster slapped him on the ass. "*Go!*"

And he went.

Kittleson was in training for so long that sometimes he was afraid the war would end before he had a chance to enter the fray and prove himself. These tough young para-troops were all gung ho and spoiling for a fight—the young almost always feel immortal. Kittleson need not have worried, however. The war during the summer and fall of 1942 found Allies moving in agonizing slow motion toward France and Germany in Europe, and island-hopping toward Japan in the Pacific.

Barracks talk analyzed news from the fronts, embroidered it, expanded on it, and speculated on what it meant for those new airborne troops about to graduate. Everyone wanted orders to Europe. Little was known about the South Pacific other than that it was a miserable place to fight a war—boiling heat; an impenetrable jungle hell; diseases that rotted off feet and ate out crotches; blood-sucking leeches; snakes; unfriendly headhunters; and a vicious, fanatical enemy hiding in the jungle and resisting inch by bloody inch, willing to die fighting rather than surrender. The war in Europe was a more *civilized* war, or so it seemed to the young paratroopers contemplating their future.

The parachute training company made its fifth and last qualifying jump and assembled in formation for the issuance of orders. Names were called off this time, not billet numbers. They were called alphabetically.

"These names I call first will be going to Europe," the Jump School commander announced.

The letter K was not quite halfway through the alphabet. Kittleson waited, his attention riveted on the officer standing on the little podium reading from his list. The names sounded in the hush like the tolling of a bell at midnight. *Abrams . . . Albee . . . Bishop . . . Cassidy . . . Delmans . . . Eisner . . . Franklin . . . Grace . . . Harrington . . . Jackson . . .*

The officer paused. He looked up. No one stirred in the ranks facing him. Relief spread slowly across the faces of those whose names had already been called. Anxiety and uncertainty marked the others.

Please don't let him stop now.

"The following sixty airborne troopers will be assigned to 6th Army's 503d Parachute Regiment. In the South Pacific," he added.

"Kincaid . . . King . . . Kittleson . . ."

CHAPTER 5

Troopships were not designed for comfort. That was especially true of USS *Monticello*, a captured Italian merchant ship converted to a sardine can. There were four holds in the rusty gray vessel, two aft and two forward. Each was two decks deep. Kittleson found himself assigned to a canvas cot among a tier of cots at the bottom of the well. Each tier was seven or eight high and spaced like a stack of flapjacks. The only way to lie in a bunk was flat on your back or belly. Otherwise, you bumped the guy above and gave him a thrill.

Lighting consisted of dim lanterns here and there that never quite dispelled the sense of being in a cellar. It was a hot cellar of about 98.6 degrees, the average temperature of all the human bodies crammed into it. Walkways between the tiers of cots were so narrow that inmates had to walk sideways in the aisles while climbing over mounds of duffle bags, packs, and other equipment. One section of each hold was massed with canvas-covered crates filled with war materiel: ammo, weapons, C-rations, etc.

Kittleson took up smoking. C-rats contained minipacks of Lucky Strikes in green. Soldiers couldn't smoke above decks at night once *Monticello* departed San Francisco Bay in late January 1944, because prowling Jap subs might see the cigarette glows. Everybody smoked in the bays; smoke swirled in the dimness. Men belched, farted, talked, laughed, snored, sweated, played cards, cursed, and occasionally had a tension-clearing fist fight. None of them knew specifically where they were going except that their destination was *somewhere* in the South Pacific. That could mean almost anywhere from New Zealand or Australia to New Guinea or the Philippines—except the Japs still held most of everything and were still fighting General MacArthur to keep holding on.

In the morning, while it was still cool, Kittleson made his way topside and leaned against the railing, smoking a Lucky Strike and quietly watching the sun turn white hot as it rose out of the sea. There was nothing but water as far as he could see in any direction. Water and sky and tufts of cloud that resembled cotton jerked from its bolls.

"You'd think our escort would stay within sight," he mentioned to another 503d replacement, a green kid not much older than himself. Morrison, from California, was one of the sixty paratroopers unlucky enough to have a name falling in the lower part of the alphabet at Fort Benning.

Morrison gave a wry laugh. "Ain't you noticed, Kittleson?" he asked. "We ain't got no escort."

Kittleson looked at him as it slowly dawned on him. "You mean . . . ?"

"There's just us. One ship crammed with all these new guys. If a Jap sub spots us . . ." He made a downward jabbing motion with his thumb.

Monticello zigzagged her way south, covering twice as much water as the distance actually gained. The ship ran without lights at night and the troops stayed crammed below decks, listening in the dead of night to the slightest ping or the subtlest change in the sound of the engines that might indicate a Jap sneak attack. Kittleson wondered if it was possible to swim to some island if they were sunk.

He never saw an island.

He began keeping a daily journal in a small green pocket diary. Stoic and reserved like his Norwegian father, like most farmers who spent long hours in the fields within themselves, he jotted down merely a line or two at the close of each day—something, he thought, that would jog his memory in later years about what the World War was really like from a common private's point of view.

January 29. Crossed international date line.
January 31. Changed courses. Getting pretty disgusted.
February 2. Won $20 playing Five Card Stud.
February 3. Sighted land. Don't know where we are.

Green hills loomed over the horizon one morning to end the horrible journey. Troops hated *Monticello* by this time and wanted only one thing—*off*! Combat had to be better than the boat. The former merchant ship slipped into New Guinea's Milne Bay. Cheering troops lined her rails as *Monticello* weaved through anchored warships, rusted merchants, and other troopships. The shore was even more crowded—a slum of tents, bamboo huts, metal Quonset buildings, and mountains of war materiel in crates all jumbled and stacked and eating into the surrounding jungle.

There was a war going on, but the war was somewhere else. Accustomed to more than a week at sea without lights, Kittleson blinked in surprise at how the harbor was lit up at night. Work continued twenty-four hours a day, as though a city were being built overnight from scratch. Apparently, the Japs weren't so very aggressive after all, at least not on New Guinea's northeastern coastline. Kittleson was mildly disappointed.

Disappointment changed to frustration. As a green trooper he didn't know exactly what to expect from war, but certainly expected more than what it had turned out to be so far. Incoming replacements set up pup tents and squad tents and became laborers in the construction of an airstrip, concrete bunkers, and other defenses.

February 9. Put on work detail.
February 11. Worked on detail digging ditches.
February 12. Mixed cement until Feb. 15.

On the morning of 17 February, replacements for the 503d were loaded aboard the troopship *Cape Cleare* and sent to a tent city outside Brisbane, Australia, where the regiment was on stand down. It was here that Kittleson received his first impression that the war might not be so far away after all. Inserted into Echo Company, 2d Battalion, to take the place of another GI who had been killed, he began training in earnest: compass courses, bayonet drill, patrolling, practice parachute jumps, rifle instruction. He qualified as Sharpshooter on the range with the M-1 Garand and the M-1 carbine. The quiet little Iowa farmer soon caught the eye of both his company commander, Captain Smith, and Sergeant Stokes, his squad leader.

"You're a pretty good soldier, Private Kittleson," Sergeant Stokes said. He was a big man in his early twenties with a rough pockmarked face. "You keep it up, you'll have my job."

"I'll do whatever job I'm assigned," the kid said in his simple, straightforward way.

The old combat hands talked about the action they had seen prior to stand down for reoutfitting and replacement. The new guys gathered around to listen intently, both intrigued and horrified.

"This sum'bitchin' Jap comes right at me screaming *'Banzai!'* like he had gone completely nuts. A GI next to me lets go with a bazooka round that takes off the Jap's head slick at the shoulder. The Jap must not have realized he was dead right off, because, even without his head, he still took three or four more steps running before he went down . . .

"The yellow bastards had the company surrounded. We set up defenses in the treeline along the beach, but you could hear trucks and tanks bringing in Jap reinforcements. We knew we were going to get hit that night. We did. It was about midnight and we had been hearing sounds in the jungle for over an hour. Everybody was jittery as hell. Somebody would let off a few rounds now and then and the officers would have to go around and calm them down.

"Along a little after midnight, this Jap yells out in clear English that you could hear all around the perimeter. 'Yankees? Yankees? We are coming to kill you now.' He must have had a sense of humor because when the attack started all the Japs were singing 'Deep in the Heart of Texas. . . . ' "

Rumors circulated with the air. The 503d was going to combat-jump at Hollandia, wherever that was. . . . MacArthur would use the 503d to spearhead his return to the Philippines. . . . Always rumors. Always the bridesmaid, the men complained, but never the bride. The goddamned war would be over before the 503d made a name for itself.

"Your *grandchildren* may still be fighting this same war," Sergeant Stokes said, adding, "if you live long enough to have grandchildren."

One evening after a training patrol into the bush, Stokes approached Kittleson.

"Private Kittleson, you're our new First Scout," he said. "You're promoted to PFC—private first class."

Kittleson nodded sagely, accepting the assignment with only one question: "What's a First Scout?"

Each squad had two scouts. They were the pointmen for the squad, its eyes and ears in combat. They ranged out ahead to check the trail for enemy or other dangers. They were the first men to die if they missed something.

"You know," the sergeant said. "Like Kit Carson."

From then on, the other men shortened "Kittleson" to "Kit." He was never exactly sure why he was selected as First Scout, nor was he immediately aware that his progression in the army was leading him step by step into increasingly elite units and positions. He was a quiet kid, almost withdrawn, but he possessed a kind of phlegmatic self-assuredness, a deep confidence. Whatever he had, his leaders seemed to notice it after a period of overlooking him.

He picked up his gear along with the .45 Thompson submachine gun issued to scouts, and moved into a tent with his second scout, another ex-farmer, named Olsen, from Florida. Olsen was slim, broad-faced, and of average height, which made him several inches taller than the Iowan. They quickly developed a close working relationship that depended more upon instinct and understanding of each other than upon spoken communication. Together they won the regimental scouting competition.

"I happened to overhear the longest conversation ever heard between Kit and Olsen t'other evening," went a standing joke in the company. "Kit says, 'Let's go to chow,' and Olsen says, 'Okay.'"

On 29 April, all furloughs were canceled and the 503d went alert for movement.

"We're going to New Guinea," Sergeant Stokes said. "From there, to the Philippines and then to Japan to kick Tojo in the balls. The mighty 503d is on the move again."

Kit Kittleson, First Scout for Second Squad, Echo Company, 2d Battalion, felt his heart hammering in his chest. He was thinking about the Jap who kept running even after his head was shot off.

CHAPTER 6

It was up to Douglas MacArthur and the other generals to plan the sweeping strategies to win the war; the grunts merely employed tactics great and small day by day to make the strategies work. General MacArthur, commander of all forces in the Southwest Pacific, had retaken the Admiralty Islands and now proposed to bypass Hansa Bay and Wewok and make a 500-mile leap directly to Hollandia on the coast of New Guinea. That would bring him closer in time and distance to realizing his greatest aim—returning to the Philippines where he had been so soundly defeated by the Japanese in December 1941, his army destroyed and some 70,000 American and Philippine soldiers taken POW via what had come to be known as the Bataan Death March.

On 22 April 1944, the most ambitious amphibious operation yet undertaken in the Southwest Pacific—217 ships carrying 50,000 combat troops and 30,000 support personnel—invaded Hollandia, the largest anchorage on the north coast; Tanahmerah 22 miles to the west; and the Japanese airbase at Aitape, 120 miles east of Hollandia. The 11,000-man Japanese garrison at Hollandia faded away with little resistance. Some 7,000 enemy soldiers fled into the jungles to the west.

Attack forces had included 6th Army's 41st Division, and the 41st Division's 163d Regimental Combat Team. Although the 503d Airborne was on alert for the invasion, it was not summoned to the battle. The operation went more smoothly and quickly than the Allies had anticipated. A total of only 152 Americans lost their lives while 3,300 Japanese were killed. By the time C-47s airlanded PFC Kittleson and the 503d on the former Japanese airstrip at Hollandia on 2 May, most of the invasion forces had spearheaded west along the New Guinea coast to knock out Japanese bases on the way to the huge Vogelkop "Bird's Head" Peninsula and the Philippines beyond. The Hollandia area was being turned into a gigantic Allied air base. The sides of mountains were being sheared to widen trails into roads, bridges and culverts strengthened and thrown across rivers, docks constructed, and pipeline laid to feed gasoline to the airfields. What had once been native villages, primeval forest, and crude Japanese garrisons was quickly becoming a city of 140,000 men.

War for the 503d Parachute Regiment, U.S. 6th Army, consisted mostly of mopping up what advancing forces had left behind. The jungles around Hollandia still teemed with Japanese. Fighting them was nothing like the big battles at Iwo Jima or Tarawa. It was more skirmishing than set-piece battle. At least, PFC Kit Kittleson's part of the war was like that—and what a common GI saw of war, his personal part of the war, that *was* the war.

Let the generals work with the global "Big Picture." The Big Picture kept getting cut down as it passed from higher echelon to lower. By the time it reached the grunts in their foxholes it had been reduced to little more than mud, mosquitos, and drudgery.

It seemed to Kittleson that a combat soldier's entire time was spent *looking* for the enemy, not fighting him. This miserable experience was what gradually turned wide-eyed, scared-shitless recruits into soldiers: Shuttling here and there in landing craft to be thrust ashore on quiet, sandy beaches that the Japs didn't want either, because of the goddamned sand fleas and mosquitos, especially the hated anopheles; slogging caterpillar-like through the sauna of forests set on slow simmer; climbing hills so steep and slippery with vegetation that every two steps forward meant one step back.

Blistering sun. Rainwater down the back of the neck and the crack of the ass. Freezing and wet at night. Crawling into muddy holes and attempting to sleep until guard duty, the jungle alive in the dark with its own shadows and silence. Swarms of bugs biting and sucking. Too dead tired to lift an arm to slap at them.

Sweat-drenched. Gasping for breath. Exhausting treks through solid jungle. C-rations and D-rations, if you were lucky, and candy bars that tasted like Ex-Lax. Always craving fresh water, a break from that treated in canteens to kill germs. Treated water tasted of salt and iodine and made the stomach rebel.

Conversations narrowed to: "Oh, no! I've shit my pants again."

"You already stink. Who cares?"

"I've crapped nine fuckin' times today. Make way, make way. I gotta go again."

"Nine times ain't *shittin'*. I got the company record. I shit twenty-seven times in one day. Now, *that's* shittin'."

Where were the goddamned Japs?

May 12. 2d Platoon, E Co. ordered on combat patrol. I was lead scout. Beginning to think war is getting close.
May 13. No Jap encounter. Spent night on hillside. Slept in poncho. Didn't sleep. Scared. Thought heard Japs.
May 14. Sent to reconnoiter lake. Could not find. Jungle too dense. Bad sago swamps. Eating K rations. Lost way back. Finally found bivouac at 1800.
May 15. Returned to camp after sleeping in poncho night before. Miserable, dirty, unshaven, hungry, no dry cigarettes.

May 17. Crossed Tamie River. Platoon leader almost drowned. Lost all his equipment. Reached village 1800 hours after 7 miles through mud ankle deep.

May 18. Rested. Food dropped by parachute. Had no food since breakfast of 17th. A welcome sight, those C-47s.

June 8. Put on latrine orderly.

Weeks passed before Kittleson spotted his first enemy soldier, even a dead one. Nips killed during the Hollandia fight had been tossed in piles at the bottoms of holes, which were then soaked with chemicals and covered with dirt to prevent disease.

Second Battalion's three companies were sent on a slow combat patrol into the interior to investigate enemy activity in the area. Echo Company took battalion point, Second Platoon assumed point for the company, and Kittleson was lead scout: first man in a battalion-sized operation. Young Kittleson felt the responsibility settling on his shoulders as he checked his .45 Thompson and packed dry socks and a couple of C-rats with his poncho in his combat pack. Travel light, freeze at night.

Sergeant Stokes took his two scouts, Kittleson and Olsen, aside. "Just follow that trail," he said, pointing where it began and then disappeared into the dense green. "The lieutenant will be directing any changes. Keep open a sharp eye. Nips have been seen."

Kittleson nodded as he actually *felt* his senses sharpening and coming alive. He could never seem to explain the process, so he didn't try. He simply realized he had a knack for the job. It was like he dissolved out of himself and became an ephemeral mist in the forest, a part of the mud and the trees and the very air he breathed. It was an acute awareness of sound and scent and sight. He may have gone so unnoticed stateside during training that even his DI didn't know who he was, but here where danger lurked with a careless footfall or an overlooked dead tree branch, he was high profile and trusted to be the unit's eyes, ears, nose, and primordial survival instinct.

The jungle trail serpentined beneath thick foliage. It was dank and dim on the trail and the canopy absorbed sound so that any noise not dampened became louder than reality. Olsen followed his lead scout by ten to twenty yards, covering him, moving nearer or farther back as terrain dictated.

He saw Kittleson flinch and pause to look into tropical growth alongside the trail. Sprawled in it lay a Jap skeleton, its bones picked clean by insects and scavengers, and yellowed and green-scummed from moisture and lack of bleaching sunlight. It still wore scraps of uniform. Kittleson kicked curiously at the bones, but there was no weapon and any other souvenirs had been picked from the body. It was the first enemy soldier he had seen, if he didn't count Japanese Zeroes dogfighting in the skies with Yank Hellcats.

The skeleton was only bones and hollowed eyes and death-grinning teeth. Alive, he had had one tooth missing. It must have affected his smile. Kit wondered if he had had a lisp.

Oddly enough, the nineteen-year-old scout felt nothing at the sight of the dead man except a mild curiosity. Olsen gestured questioningly before halting the column. Kittleson pointed at the skeleton.

"God have mercy on your soul," he murmured, then moved off down the trail, Tommy gun slung ready for use, right hand on the pistol grip, finger laid alongside the trigger guard.

It required mere days for the tropical forest to reclaim dead flesh.

The terrain opened up into a wide grassy area splashed with sunshine at the base of a rise in the trail. Kittleson spotted movement. The scout thrust out a warning hand and dropped to one knee to become motionless. Olsen passed along the warning and the column froze. Most of Echo remained in forest shadow.

Kittleson watched as the top of a gray-brown crush cap appeared, bouncing with the head underneath as it gradually appeared above the rise. Then the shoulders with a long rifle slung around the back. The Jap, who looked no older than the American scout silently watching his approach, bopped along as merrily as Little Red Riding Hood on her way to Grandma's house. He had everything except a picnic lunch and a summer's song on his lips. Probably a runner delivering a message from one unit to another, with the woods all to himself—at least that must have been what he thought.

Kittleson crouched in the open, as visible as a tree trunk. The Jap failed to see him. Kit pressured the Tommy's trigger, his left hand hard on the forward grip to control muzzle rise.

The submachine gun burped. Little Red Riding Hood died without seeing the wolf. It was so sudden he didn't even look surprised. Heavy .45s stitched him from his stomach to his face. He still had his head. *He* didn't keep walking.

The first *live* enemy soldier the scout had ever seen—and he killed him cleanly.

It was war. He had been trained for it. The only emotion he felt was that continuing mild curiosity. He approached the body cautiously, his eyes on the trail beyond. The jungle was quiet and again motionless, not even a breeze. The dead Jap lay on his back. Most of his face was gone and there were bloody ragged holes in his guts and chest. A short little kid.

Kittleson made a circle around the fresh corpse, concerned that more enemy might have heard the shots and set up an ambush. Second Squad's platoon leader, Lieutenant Abbott, came forward and motioned the scout to continue down the trail.

It was Echo Company's first kill. Kittleson became something of a hero. He wondered how long it would take for the jungle to polish the Jap's bones.

"How does it feel to kill a man?" Olsen asked him later.

Kittleson thought about it. He said, "Are you going to eat them peaches?"

What he felt was between God and him. He would deal with all this in his soul after the war ended.

Shortly after 6th Army secured Hollandia's airfields, MacArthur learned that the nature of the soil underneath them made them unsuited to handle heavy bombers. More than six hundred miles of Japanese-occupied territory lay beyond Hollandia on New Guinea's north coast before MacArthur could turn north toward the Philippines. The Japanese bases had to be knocked out to prevent a serious threat from the rear during the Allied thrust forward. MacArthur also needed new airfields that could launch bombers for the Philippines and, eventually, Japan.

On 17 May, a Tornado Task Force landed 125 miles west of Hollandia to seize Japanese airfields bordering Maffin Bay and to take the tiny island of Wakde, which contained an excellent Jap airfield. It took Americans until early September to secure Maffin Bay with savage fighting that claimed the lives of four hundred Yanks. Wakde Island fell after four days of equally savage fighting in which the enemy had to be flushed out of coral caves and killed.

The island of Biak in Geelvink Bay some two hundred miles to the northwest was MacArthur's next target, which he attacked on 27 May. Biak proved to be a hilly natural fortress of coral densely covered by tropical rain forest and jungle undergrowth. Coral ridges and terraces were honeycombed by hundreds of large caves. The island's three airfields all lay on the southern coast, protected by 11,000 Japanese soldiers. Attackers poured hundreds of barrels of gasoline into networks of crevices and ignited them with TNT, burning and blowing the enemy out of the ground like cornered rats.

Americans secured one of Biak's airfields on 7 June, then the other two eleven days later. It would not be until 20 August, however, that General Walter Kreuger, commander of 6th Army, declared the Biak campaign officially over.

The island of Noemfoor was next even as the battle for Biak continued. Noemfoor lay sixty miles west of Biak and about midway to the Vogelkop Peninsula. Like Biak, Noemfoor had three Japanese-built airfields, but they were larger. One of them was 5,300 feet long and surfaced.

Not a shot was fired as 6th Army's 158th Regimental Combat Team landed. The fight started back of the beaches where the defenders waited. The Americans sent out a hurried call for reinforcements.

This was "Big Picture" stuff. All a private like Kit Kittleson knew was that the 503d Parachute Infantry was quickly withdrawn to the Hollandia airfields and placed on alert for a combat jump onto Noemfoor. Kittleson's Second Battalion was scheduled for the second wave behind First and Third Battalions. He waited, calm but anxious, watching as paratroopers laden with battle gear and equipment loaded other C-47s. The first planes lifted with the rising sun on 20 June.

It was finally going to happen. A parachute jump under fire to equal what the 82d Airborne was accomplishing in North Africa and Italy. Kittleson, carrying his Thompson, stepped off to himself, dropped to his knees, and offered a simple prayer. "God, take care of our men. Protect them in Your name and, if we should die, look after our souls. Amen." Then he was ready.

It didn't surprise him that over half the men prayed openly, while most of the others at least closed their eyes and offered a standing prayer. The old adage about there being no atheists in foxholes actually applied.

During the next two days, C-47s dropped 1,400 503d paratroops onto Kamiri Drome, the island's main airstrip. The troop planes thundered in at less than four hundred feet above the ground. No one wore reserve 'chutes; at that altitude a reserve wouldn't have had time to deploy anyhow if the main malfunctioned. Troopers landing on hard coral suffered 10 per cent casualties, including 59 serious fractures. General Kreuger canceled the second airborne wave. Kittleson couldn't make up his mind whether he felt relieved or disappointed.

June 20. First Battalion jumped. Injuries high. Third Battalion left for airport at 1800.
June 21. Third Battalion jumped. Injuries higher. Jumped on Kamiri Strip.
June 22. Second Battalion moved to airport.
June 23. Planes grounded. Bad weather.
June 24. Flew to Biak. Spent night 500 yards from Jap positions. Planes divebombing Japs.

June 25. Loaded on LCI (landing craft). Left for Noemfoor at night.

June 26. Unloaded at Namber Strip. No opposition. Spent night in foxhole.

June 27. *0800.* Battalion started for Inasi to wipe out Japs. Second Battalion killed seven Japs along trail. Spent night at water hole.

June 28. Moved on. No resistance.

June 29. Killed sniper in cave, burst from Tommy gun.

June 30. Moved on to Inasi. Excellent springwater. Jap killed inside perimeter by D Company.

Whatever the global grand strategy, the GI's war remained a war of mud, bugs, and drudgery. Now, there were Japanese dead around with their terrible stench. Previous Yank riflemen left them where they fell. But there were live ones too. Kittleson felt them everywhere, peeking from tree tops . . . from the jungle . . . watching their every move. . . .

Second Battalion with Kittleson on point for Echo in the lead came to a waterhole just before dark. The battalion pulled into a tight perimeter for the night. Banks of black cloud from the west blew over and dumped water. Somewhere there had to be a rule that you couldn't have a war without mud.

Word came down via the squad leader, Sergeant Stokes: "Don't fire unless you're fired upon. I don't want anybody getting trigger happy. Understand?"

Olsen and Kittleson huddled together for warmth in their foxhole. About an inch of water at the bottom of the hole seeped into the scouts' boondockers. Kittleson shivered.

"Malaria?" Olsen asked.

"Just wet and shaking."

"Fuckin' miserable. Kit, ya' ever think about home?"

"Sometimes."

"Ya' ever think about how we used to take little things for granted? Like dry feet and a warm bed? Like standing up and walking without being afraid of getting shot?"

"Get some sleep. I'll take first watch."

Hiding in a hole in the middle of a foreign jungle, wet and hungry and scared dry-mouthed, surrounded by demons: the things living nightmares are made of. It was no problem keeping awake.

"The goddamned Japs'll crawl up on you in the middle of the night and slit your throat," the older hands warned.

After two hours staring round-eyed into blackness, Kittleson ended his watch and shook Olsen awake. Olsen was only dozing.

Something dropped out of the tree above and landed heavily across Kittleson's legs. He knew his throat was about to be cut. Instinctively, he grabbed and flung the intruder as far from him as he could. His own strength astounded him.

The flying iguana crashed into bushes next to the .30-cal machine gun crew. The nervous gunner yelled and laid on the trigger, lighting up the night with muzzle flash. That set off the next position. The entire perimeter lit up. The jungle rattled with rifle and machine gun fire. Bullets cut the air, grenades exploded with brilliant flash-bangs. Men ran wildly and aimlessly in the dark, weapons spitting flame in all directions.

Officers and sergeants yelled and shouted and somebody shrilled on a whistle. The shooting ended as suddenly as it began.

"What the hell is the matter with you fuckin' people?" Sergeant Stokes demanded, stomping from hole to hole. "You're acting like a bunch of greenhorn boots. The front line is 200 miles that way. Kittleson, Olsen, check to see if anybody got hurt. Now go to sleep, goddamnit. But not *all* of you. Fifty percent alert."

"Lieutenant Abbott, I tell you. I *seen* them Japs," Private Suddeth insisted.

It was 100 percent alert for the rest of the night.

When morning came, Lieutenant Abbott and the company commander came around. "Who the hell started that shit last night?"

No one knew.

"I wonder if they killed the lizard?" Kittleson whispered to Olsen, and they both snickered.

Second Platoon was ordered to link up with Third Battalion at Hill 670. Kittleson and his Tommy took point with Olsen covering. The jungle world absorbed sound as a cemetery absorbs souls. Then the undergrowth thinned out some so that sunlight coming through the canopy in golden nuggets actually reached the faint people trail.

After two or three hours on the move, Kittleson detected movement about thirty yards ahead on a low knoll. He signaled *Danger!* to Olsen to halt the column. A Japanese strongpoint. One Jap stood up and stretched, yawning. Kittleson counted two more heads almost merging with the foliage. They were sitting in the open around a heavy machine gun. They had not dug in or anything.

The scout circled silently to the left to take cover behind a forest giant. He knew he had only moments before the Japs sensed they were no longer alone. That machine gun could raise hell and inflict damages unless it was destroyed promptly.

He took bead with faithful ol' Tommy and eased in the trigger. The deep-throated *Brrrrp!* of the weapon seemed to explode the jungle. Standing spread-legged and purposeful, bracing himself into the recoil, Kittleson sprayed the machine gun nest with .45s, raking a deadly hail of lead back and forth and hearing the meaty *Thunk! Thunk! Thunk!* of bullets smacking flesh.

The Japs crumpled, mowed down like scythed wheat.

There were other Japs beyond the machine gun nest, concealed in the trees, a large patrol on a rest break. The enemy pointman had not been nearly as cautious and observant as the American. Caught by surprise, the Japanese nonetheless opened up with a terrific crescendo of rifle fire that tore into foliage all around Kittleson and his platoon. Leaves and branches rained down on the scout's head. He slammed in a fresh clip and shifted his fire to the right.

Lieutenant Abbott shouted orders. A .30-caliber machine gun squad led by a corporal squad leader called Manos maneuvered toward the fighting scout's position. Manos ran up to Kittleson's big tree.

"Where the hell are they, Kit? I got the .30-cal right behind—"

Hot lead popped into the big tree like a hailstorm gone supersonic. Manos screamed in the middle of a sentence and dropped like God had reached down with a baseball bat and clobbered him. He rolled screaming on the forest floor, hugging his bleeding stomach while his heels drummed in agony.

A Jap grenade struck the big tree and bounced. It landed within a foot of Manos, its fuse hissing. Kittleson saw every detail of it, the C-ration-like can of the little bomb itself, the handle, the hiss of smoke . . .

Manos was going to die. No time for contemplation, only action. Kittleson lunged from cover while Jap riflemen zeroed in on him. He snared the downed squad leader's battle harness. He expected the grenade to go off in his face. He snatched Manos off the ground with such force that the momentum carried them both to cover behind a jagged outcropping of rock. Shrapnel from the exploding grenade whizzed overhead and splintered the rock outcropping.

"Manos? Manos . . . ?"

Manos groaned in agony.

By now, Lieutenant Abbott was forward and directing fire. Then came a yell that the officer was down.

The fight ended as suddenly as it had begun. The Japs faded away, leaving behind the corpses of the three machine gunners Kittleson had killed and the stench of burnt gunpowder and fresh blood. Second Platoon suffered two WIA, Lieutenant Abbott and Corporal Manos. Medics patched them up and built litters out of ponchos and chopped tree branches. The platoon withdrew with its wounded.

"Kit, it could have been much worse if you hadn't spotted the machine gun and taken it out," Lieutenant Abbott commended his lead scout. He lay on his litter, bloody bandages covering one leg. He would be evacuated, but he would survive. "I saw what you did for Manos. That took guts."

Manos, whose life Kittleson saved during the fight, died on his makeshift stretcher before the platoon reached an evacuation point. He was moaning and crying out in pain as men took turns carrying the stretcher. Then he seemed to sink into rest and he was quiet and seemed so much smaller.

"I'm going to stick to you like stink on shit," Olsen said to Kit. "You got a charmed life. I hope it rubs off on me."

Kittleson knew it was more than *charm* that protected him.

Two weeks later the scout was cleaning his weapon at a waterhole battalion base camp when Lieutenant Diehl, Abbott's replacement, approached.

"You'll be receiving the Silver Star medal Abbott recommended you for," he said.

Kittleson nodded.

"Kit," he said. "You and I are volunteering for the Alamo Scouts."

"What are Alamo Scouts?" Kittleson asked.

CHAPTER 7

By its very nature, intelligence work often shrouds itself in over-secrecy and suspicion. Commanders are sometimes reluctant to share information with other commanders. General MacArthur so distrusted the Office of Strategic Services (OSS), which answered to the Combined Chiefs of Staff in Washington rather than directly to him, that he refused to allow OSS intelligence gatherers south of the equator. Instead, he used a number of other intelligence sources such as the Allied Geographical Section, the Allied Intelligence Bureau, Australian Coastwatchers, Naval Commando Demolition Units (NCDUs), and the Amphibious Scouts.

It was out of such an atmosphere of suspicion, secrecy, frustration, and anger that the famed Alamo Scouts were born. Theirs was one of a number of difficult births then and during the Cold War that followed the World War and propelled American armed forces into unconventional warfare, leading to the formation of elite special forces units such as the U.S. Navy SEALs and the U.S. Army Special Forces (Green Berets).

The 6th Army was activated for service in the Southwest Pacific on 22 January 1943 and shipped to Camp Columbia,

Australia, on 16 February under the command of General Walter Kreuger, a whipcord-like Texan. Because of Kreuger's origins, the 6th would operate under the code name *Alamo Force.*

MacArthur used the Alamo Force to initiate the Papua phase of his offensive against the Japanese. After landings on Woodlark and Kirkwina Islands in the Solomon Sea on 30 June 1943, Kreuger prepared for the next phase of the offensive—Operation Dexterity—to retake New Guinea beginning in the fall. He required prompt and accurate intelligence on enemy strengths and locations on the island continent. Admiral Daniel Barbey, commander of 7th Amphibious Force, and Kreuger turned to the newly formed joint Army, Navy, Marine, and Australian Amphibious Scouts, otherwise known as the 7th Amphibious Force Special Services Unit, to provide this information. It would be shared between 6th Army and Barbey's 7th Amphibs.

Trouble began when poor communications between the 7th Amphibs' landing party and the PT boat that was supposed to exfiltrate it forced the recon scouts to remain an additional eleven days in enemy jungle. They barely eluded capture and starvation before they were recovered.

Lieutenant Milton Beckworth, an army member of the scouting party and later an Alamo Scout, was supposed to report directly to Kreuger's G-2 section after the mission. Instead, the navy snatched him and took him to Milne Bay, where navy intelligence specialists debriefed him first. Inexplicably, the navy then held him incommunicado on a small navy craft anchored in the bay. He finally jumped ship after four days and made his way to Kreuger. The general was furious.

"To hell with this," he raged. "I'll form my own intelligence unit."

On 28 November 1943, less than three months before Private Kit Kittleson arrived by troopship USS *Monticello,* Kreuger issued orders establishing the Alamo Scouts Training Center (A.S.T.C.) to "train selected volunteers in reconnaissance and raider work." He pulled training programs from proven elite outfits like 1st Special Service Force ("Devil's Brigade"), the U.S. Army Rangers, the Navy's Scouts and Raiders, and the NCDUs. His objective was to train highly motivated soldiers to infiltrate enemy lines in six- to seven-man teams, gather intelligence or conduct other special missions, and then escape undetected.

Volunteers had to be proven combat veterans in excellent physical condition. They didn't have to be big men, nor muscle-bound, but they had to be capable of enduring long, arduous marches with little or no food and rest; capable of swimming well in rough surf and jungle streams; and emotionally stable with a developed sense of duty, confidence, and self-discipline. Men not only brave but also endowed with intelligence and common sense. Men who put mission and team first. General Kreuger demanded *elite*, adventurous men for difficult and dangerous missions.

The A.S.T.C.s conducted eight six-week training classes between 27 December 1943 and 2 September 1945. Although the school graduated approximately 250 enlisted men and 75 officers, only 117 enlisted men and 21 officers were actually retained as members of "6th U.S. Army Special Reconnaissance Unit," better known as the Alamo Scouts. At their peak, they numbered a thin twelve teams in the field with about 65 men and thirteen officers, the smallest elite unit in American military history. Their reputation, however, would far exceed their small numbers. Much of that reputation was built upon two missions—both of them raids to free prisoners of war from the Japanese.

CHAPTER 8

Captain Homer "Red" Williams of Philadelphia used a simple test to aid him in selecting Scout candidates, as the Scouts' first commandant, Lieutenant Colonel Fred Bradshaw, had before him. Scouts had to possess a keen memory and good powers of observation. Williams sat the applicant at a table across from him and began the interview. On the table were arranged about twenty different items—pocket knives, keys, seeds, cigarettes, a watch, a comb. . . . Nothing was mentioned about these items until the session ended and the soldier was dismissed and started to walk away.

"Halt, soldier!" Williams snapped. "Don't turn around. How many items are on the table? What are they? What brand of cigarettes? What kind of watch was it?"

If the GI failed to list most of the items, he was automatically eliminated.

PFC Kit Kittleson passed the selection process. The training camp was, like the rest of the war, a mobile thing that shifted forward with the advance of Allied lines. Deuce-and-a-half trucks picked up the candidates at Hollandia and transported them to a long idyllic stretch of beach punched in deep around a cove. There was a coral reef on the far side of the cove over which waves had crashed century after century. Extending into the sea on the gentle, protected side was a bamboo wharf to which were moored rubber rafts. Square, six-man squad tents had been erected among the palms.

Approximately one hundred nervous GIs reported for training at the camp's athletic field on 1 August 1944. They were a diverse group from all branches of 6th Army—infantry, parachute, armor, signal, artillery, and engineers. They were Caucasians, Spanish, Filipinos, loyal Japanese Nisei, and American Indians. They had one thing in common: they were 6th Army's finest warriors.

"So you volunteered too?" the man in ranks next to Kittleson said from the corner of his mouth. They were at attention, waiting for the commandant.

Kittleson stole a glance at the tall man. He was blond, burly, and possessed of a fair complexion that looked like it never tanned, only reddened and peeled and reddened again.

"Name's Gilbert Cox," the tall man murmured.

"Kit Kittleson."

"Know what this is all about, Kit?"

"Some kind of hotshot recon outfit? Like Airborne, only more so."

"Yeah." He gave a short laugh. "My lieutenant comes up to me and says I 'meet all the requirements' and that, therefore, I'm a volunteer. Next thing I know, here I am. You going to stay, Kit?"

Anything had to be better than slogging around in the green hell chasing Japs one or two at a time.

"Yeah. Me, too," big Cox affirmed. "What the hell. Color me stupid."

It seemed to Kittleson that the longer he stayed in the army, the smaller and more *elite* his outfits became. First there was infantry, then Airborne, then a scout MOS and now an *Alamo Scout*. If this kept up, he wryly observed to himself, he'd be so special that by the time the Allies got to Japan he'd be marching into Tokyo alone.

If God let him live that long.

Captain Red Williams burst from his tent. He was a slab-sided, gruff man with bright carrot hair. Kit had already learned he had a reputation for being a hardass. Other officers didn't much like him, but he was a stickler for detail and good at what he did.

"Welcome, men, to the beginning of the fourth class conducted by the Alamo Scout Training Center," began the captain, standing reed-straight and regarding the troops with hard blue eyes. "You have been selected because you are 6th Army's finest troops. Your mission will be to operate behind Japanese lines with all its danger of capture, interrogation, and death. . . . This work does not call for a bunch of *toughs*. We want you to be just as tough as you can be, but there is no place in this organization for a *tough*. You have to use your brains, your cunning, your skill. You have to depend on your buddies. This calls for the highest caliber of men and the highest quality of soldiering. . . . If we find that you are not mentally, temperamentally, or physically fit and do not meet our required standards, if you don't give it everything you have, you will be returned to your units. . . ."

A slightly built man with big ears, a pointed face, and eyes as dark and mischievous as a raccoon's mimicked the captain's deep voice: "Men, you have to use your brains, your cunt, your skills . . ."

With that, Corporal Willie Wismer joined Cox and Kittleson. They soon gravitated toward the tall lieutenant, Bill Nellist. Almost from the beginning it was understood that those who survived training would form the nucleus of a Nellist Team. At the end of the course, the men themselves would *vote* on who should be retained from those who completed it. Nowhere else in the army did this bit of democracy exist.

Training was even tougher than Airborne and more than Kittleson expected. Training included running, swimming, and calisthenics, followed by daily "man-to-man combat."

Tall Nellist looked around the circle and pointed at the short-est man there—Kittleson. "Step out here, private." He then proceeded to flop the little man around in arm throw and dis-arming demonstrations.

Afterwards, he apologized. "Kittleson, is it? You're a good sport, fella. It's more realistic if the other fellas can see some really dramatic throws and falls on a little guy about the same size as the Japs."

Despite his size, Kittleson turned out to be a scrapper. Nothing was overlooked in hand-to-hand combat: flat of the hand, elbows, head smashes, feet, knees. Scouts made a big circle facing inward and everybody was blindfolded. One man prowled around the outside of the circle and threw a stranglehold on someone at random. The victim had to break the hold any way he could before he passed out.

"You folks are bigger, stronger, and badder than the Jap bastards," instructors encouraged. "Play rough. Gouge out his eyes. Kick him in the balls, throw him on the ground and finish his ass any way you can."

Men attacked each other just for the fun of it. Someone was always lurking in the shadows. The smaller men like Kittleson and Sabas Asis used speed and their knowledge of weak spots to compensate for their lack of brawn. One night, attacked by Lieutenant Nellist, Kittleson swept aside like a cat against a greyhound, upset the taller man, and threw him hard to the ground, knocking the breath out of him.

"Sorry, sir," Kittleson said.

"Nothing to be sorry for, Kit," Nellist gasped. "Damn. Help me up."

Kittleson grinned. "It's more realistic, sir, if the other fel-las could have seen this really dramatic throw . . ."

Scouts had to be good boat handlers and good swimmers, as they would be spending so much time both in the ocean and in the many swift streams, rivers, and swamps of the Pa-cific islands. Rubber boats would be their primary mode of transportation to infiltrate and exfiltrate enemy territory. Teams practiced at least ten hours a week running the boats through the hazardous coral spray on the windward side of the cove. Sometimes trainees were taken a mile or so out to sea and dumped overboard.

"Chow will be ready whenever you get in," an instructor would say.

One afternoon a new ritual was introduced. Teams were ordered to swim out from the beach to an anchored boat, aboard which they climbed to don full combat gear, including packs and weapons. Then, as they started to swim back, an officer appeared on the boat dock with a .45 Thompson submachine gun.

"*Duck!*" he yelled.

That was the signal to dive as fast and as deep as they could. A spray of bullets punched holes in the water where Kittleson had been.

God, this is getting pretty rough . . .

Other training days were crammed with learning radio and Morse code, blinker lights, and other forms of communications. Before the war, Lieutenant Nellist had been the California National Guard's Rifle Champion; he taught shooting. Scouts also practiced with other firearms and weapons—M-1 Garands and carbines; .45 Colt pistols; Thompsons; Browning Automatic Rifles; grenades; knives, garrotes, clubs. Nights were spent on the ocean and in the swamp working with land and water navigation. They learned scouting, reconnaissance, and patrolling; escape and evasion problems; cover and concealment; tracking and survival; and jungle medicine and jungle craft.

The brutal six-week course ended with one of the most unique training problems ever conducted in the history of the U.S. Army. To get a taste of what a real mission would be like, as well as to put into practice all they had learned, teams were boat-inserted into lightly occupied enemy territory to operate for three nights and two days.

"Surviving the training problem," said Captain Williams, only half joking, "is a prerequisite for graduating."

During training, officers and men were constantly rotated

so that everyone got an opportunity to work with everyone else. Lieutenant Orbano, a Filipino-American, took charge of Kittleson's team for the final exercise. Cox wrangled his way onto the six-man team, but Corporal Wismer and Lieutenant Nellist were split up among other teams. The "Big Jap Hunt" started, assisted by native guides.

For Kit Kittleson, it was more of the same thing he had endured during past months as a grunt pointman with Echo Company: humping the boondocks.

The first night the team slept in an abandoned nipa hut containing a Japanese skeleton. It rained during the night and the roof leaked, but it was better than sleeping in the forest. Somebody propped the skeleton up against the wall, stuffed a cigarette between its teeth and crushed a GI bush hat on its head. Lieutenant Orbano said the Jap probably became separated from his buddies during the Hollandia campaign and starved to death.

The next evening the trail followed a stream until it passed through a village of five or six nipa huts, all abandoned and slowly rotting back into the forest. Undergrowth crept across the path once beaten clean by bare feet. Dozens of Japanese skeletons filled the huts. The GIs inspected them out of morbid curiosity.

Some of the enemy soldiers obviously perished from battle wounds inflicted by either Allied soldiers or the long blades and spears of local natives. Others possibly died of starvation and exposure, cut off from their units by the advancing Americans. Some skulls were missing. Cox wondered if headhunters still lived in the New Guinea jungles.

"This is like sleeping in a graveyard," the big Scout observed uneasily.

"The war has turned the whole world into a graveyard," Kittleson replied.

He knew how quickly the remains of men vanished. Three days after he'd shot and killed the courier on the trail, Echo Company happened to pass back through. The elements had already turned the dead man into a yellowed, grinning caricature of himself.

August 28. Returned to beach, met Lt. Beckworth. Disgusted as hell. Tired, unshaven, dirty, stunk like damned native.
August 29. Returned to camp. Cleaned up. Six bottles of beer. Seen show. It didn't seem so bad now. Voted for Scout team.

Out of the original one hundred GIs who began Class Four of A.S.T.C. training, fourteen men—twelve enlisted and two officers, Lieutenants Bill Nellist and Tom "Stud" Rounsaville, in two teams—were retained as Scouts. Kittleson was among them. So were Gilbert Cox and Willie Wismer. Making up the rest of Nellist Team was Sergeant Andy Smith, a big, dark-haired 24-year-old who had been voted 6th Army's top athlete and most valuable basketball player; pug-nosed Filipino-American Sabas "Bob" Asis; and Thomas Siason, also a Filipino-American.

Three weeks following the Scout graduation, Dutch Coastwatcher Louie Rapmund and the Melanesian escapee showed up at the PT base on Woendi Island with their tale of a former Dutch governor, now a plantationer, being held POW by the Japs on Cape Oransbari.

"Him, the Jap, feel safe," explained the native in broken English. "Him think no GI reach him in such far place."

"Shi-*it*," scoffed Wismer. "Him ain't heard about Alamo Scouts."

CHAPTER 9

Lieutenant Nellist, Kittleson, Cox, and Siason made their way swiftly but silently through the thickly growing palms on the beach toward the machine gun nests. The surf murmured against the shore, muffling the sounds of their boots crunching on sand. Enough of the night remained to conceal their movements as long as they held to the trees.

The day quickly acquired color from the coming dawn. A small nipa hut on stilts suddenly materialized ahead out of the thin fog. It was of crude bamboo construct with a palm-thatched roof and a ladder leading up to a little balcony at the open door. Dug in the sand among the palms were three fairly deep fighting holes. At the lip of one about thirty yards to Kittleson's right was the Dutch machine gun. It was unattended at this early hour, fortunately, not sandbagged, and it looked rusted, all signs that the Japs felt secure in their isolated redoubt.

The intruders dropped behind a patch of sea oats as a Japanese soldier emerged from the hut. He wore his crush cap at a jaunty angle and carried his tunic in his hand. Even in the dim light Kittleson discerned the bony outline of the guy's ribs. He climbed down the ladder to the sand and the deep shadows.

A second soldier still drawing on his combat blouse came out. He spoke to the man below as he descended the ladder. They both laughed. They squatted and soon had a small fire going. It emitted a thin trail of smoke and Kittleson smelled it in the air. They put on a pan to heat water for tea and another pan to start rice. Oddly enough, Kittleson felt suddenly hungry; he had not eaten since the previous afternoon.

Neither Japanese was armed, but only a few steps away lurked the machine gun. The light Jap gun was not in sight anywhere. Killing when the time came had to be swift and sure. If even one of the Japs survived long enough to reach either gun, rusted or not, he could throw one hell of a kink into the Scouts' mission planning. A thing like that could ruin a guy's day.

Two more enemy soldiers awoke and leisurely joined the first two for breakfast. Feeling like a voyeur peeping through someone's window, Kittleson listened to the clinking of pans, low talking, and laughter. Shadows were still deep below the hut so that the little fire flickered dimly on the underside of the hut and the figures remained in pantomiming silhouette.

Nellist touched Kittleson's shoulder. He signaled that Kittleson and Siason were to cover while the lieutenant and the big man Cox worked their way to a better shooting position. Kit nodded and took up a stand lying on the sand at the end of the sea oats. Siason knelt behind a fallen palm with his carbine. Nellist and Cox slithered toward a patch of sea grass that carpeted a slight knoll about ten yards closer. They silently disappeared into the grass.

Now there was nothing to do but wait for Lieutenant Rounsaville's rifle shot to initiate the action.

Kittleson sweated even though it was cool. It was a lovely, peaceful morning and it calmed the soldier for what had to be done. It was a killing kind of morning, Siason was to say later, a morning in which departed souls ascended to heaven in peace after the violence that released them from their earthly bonds.

The little soldier was nineteen years old and he had killed at least five men, up close and personal so that he saw their faces and would remember them while not remembering them. He scented the salt in the air from the sea, mixed with the funky odors of the river. He felt his elbows digging into the damp sand. He watched the enemy soldiers and his eyes narrowed like those of a big cat targeting its quarry. Tommy gun was ready to taste fresh blood.

Two of the Japanese sauntered off from the cooking fire in separate directions toward the beach, to take a morning piss or something. A third squatting over his boiling rice suddenly stood up. He listened and seemed to sniff the air. His friend, still shirtless, rose to his feet as well and murmured an inquiry. They conversed in low tones and listened, like they sensed something amiss but couldn't quite isolate what it was. Together, slowly, listening and looking, they took tentative steps toward the patch of sea grass where Nellist and Cox hid.

Andy Smith, Willie Wismer, and their Filipino partner, Sabas Asis, split off from Rounsaville Team and crept toward the smaller *Kempeitai* hut. Rounsaville and his men, plus the Coastwatcher and two guides, a force of ten men, wormed toward the long hut used by the Japanese as an enlisted billet. Palms grew up to and around the building; their fronds would form shade in the tropical afternoons. Darkness remained deep underneath the low stilted floor. There were no sentries. The Japs seemed careless.

A bit of sea breeze rattled the palm tops. Rounsaville heard snoring coming from above his head. The men waited around him, crouching low to keep from bumping their heads on the low floor above, weapons bristling in all directions like an aroused porcupine. Rounsaville checked his watch. He nodded. He touched the man nearest him and the signal was passed.

There was a ladder at either end of the long hut leading up to the bamboo gallery. There were also a door and windows at either end, over which hung mosquito netting. Long-legged Rounsaville crawled out from underneath the barracks and led a contingent of three Scouts and Rapmund to the far ladder. Sergeant Alfred "Opu" Alfonso led the others to the opposite end.

They had heard movement from the building minutes earlier. Now, a dim glow of light from an oil lamp framed a window in Alfonso's section. The invaders eased up the ladders and spread out to cover doors and windows. Men sleeping or just awakening were at their most vulnerable; Alfonso peeped around the eve of the window framing the light and saw a stubby Jap cook yawning and putting tea on a wood stove for breakfast. Alfonso pressed his back against the wall and waited for Lieutenant Rounsaville to start the attack.

The sun rises and sets rapidly in the tropics. Light would flood into the village in another four or five minutes. Alfonso glanced down the length of the hut front to where the shadows of Rounsaville and the others formed dark lumps against the walls. He eased his left hand forward to the switch of the flashlight taped to the side of his twelve-gauge shotgun. It would still be dark inside most of the building, excluding the kitchen. Flashlight beams illuminated targets and provided firing points.

The Japs wouldn't know what the hell hit them.

Twenty-five yards away, the smaller hut outside which Andy Smith, Wismer, and Asis crouched remained in darkness. Sleeping sounds oozed peacefully from it.

And near the beach, one hundred yards away, the two enemy machine gunners looked around suspiciously. They took a few more slow steps toward the hiding Americans. They looked directly at the sea oats field that contained Kittleson and Siason. One said something to the other, who went back to the hut and retrieved his rifle.

Within a few more minutes the sun would pop up and reveal the Americans.

Kittleson steeled himself.

What was holding up Rounsaville's signal?

CHAPTER 10

Lieutenant Nellist and Cox also sweated with tension while awaiting the signal. Then it came with such sudden presence that it seemed to startle the entire world, like a crack across the sky.

The two Japanese flinched, looking momentarily confused, and in that moment came their downfall.

Nellist blasted the one on the left with the heavy M-1 Garand he always carried; Cox took out the other one with his lighter carbine. Bullets slapping into their chests knocked them back. There was a last piteous scream and then they collapsed and rifle fire crackled savagely from farther inside the village as the raid commenced.

Kittleson jumped to his feet. He flicked on the flashlight taped to the Tommy's barrel as he and Siason charged headlong into the fray. They leaped over the Jap corpses. Kit sprang up the ladder to the stilted shanty and dashed inside, submachine gun and flashlight beam sweeping the interior.

The hut was empty except for sleeping cots draped with mosquito netting. Two rifles leaned against the wall near the door.

In the time it took Kittleson to make this assessment,

Nellist and Cox plunged past the hut, weapons blazing at the two remaining Japs. The poor terrified bastards, there they were, unbuttoned and engaged in their morning ablutions when demons burst out of the morning twilight and literally caught them with their drawers down.

Siason glimpsed a figure diving into one of the foxholes. He approached cautiously to find an officer cowering in the bottom of it, pistol in hand and a look of frozen horror on his face. The guy was too scared to shoot. Siason instinctively squeezed his trigger. A burst of deadly lead chewed into the Jap's chest. Little holes in his rib cage released tendrils of smoke and gases with the sound of a punctured tire. He blinked once, disbelieving, and that was all for him.

That was also the end of all the sentries and the machine gun nest. The defenders had not gotten off a single shot. Kittleson was surprised at how smoothly it had gone. He sprang off the hut's low balcony to find five downed Japanese. He had yet to fire a round of his own.

"Check 'em out! Make sure they're dead!" Lieutenant Nellist shouted.

With the possible exception of the *Kempeitai*, no prisoners were to be taken.

"Kit! You and Siason go on down the beach and set up a defense. Cox and I'll handle this end."

Kittleson sprinted off ahead of the Filipino through the palms toward the trail that led to the major Jap encampment farther inland. From the village came the fierce din of battle. The little Scout hoped everything was going as well for Rounsaville as it had for them here. It had to: They had maybe a half-hour, more or less, before two thousand pissed-off enemy troops came pouring down the trail to the rescue of their buddies.

Rounsaville's radioman would already have alerted the PT boats to come in to pick up rescuers and POWs. All Nellist Team had to do now was secure the beach and hold it until Rounsaville finished off his Japs and let the prisoners loose.

A column of black smoke billowed above the palms as

Kittleson dropped to cover behind a palm where he had clear fields of fire to the front. Siason took cover to the other side of the trail. He looked over at Kit and grinned tightly.

Simple plans were almost always the best plans. At precisely 5:30 A.M., as synchronized beforehand, Rounsaville stepped away from the outside wall of the long barracks. He peeled the mosquito net away from the door. He flicked on his rifle light. It pierced the dark interior. A sleeping Jap blinked into the light. Rounsaville shot him.

Shrieking like wild forest spirits, Alamo Scouts blitzed the building. The Japanese soldiers were too surprised and terrified to resist. Carbines spat rapid-fire. Thompsons chewed holes through the walls and through human flesh. It was a slaughtering ground, a butchering pen, made even more hellish by screams of pain and terror, made surreal by clashing smoke-filled beams of dancing light that brought death to whomever they touched.

Most of the Japanese soldiers, naked except for their underwear, died either on their sleeping mats or within a few feet of them, their gory bodies piling up on the floor. Six or seven leaped out windows in desperate attempts to escape. Scouts ran outside on the balcony and pinged at them with carbines as they stampeded for the jungle.

Alfonso shotgunned the Jap cook through the window with double-aught buckshot. He died with a little cup of tea in his hand. Then the Scout pivoted as wounded and naked Japs began leaping out of windows. He sighted in on them, pumping his shotgun, and had the satisfaction of winging two of them. Crying and screaming, they dragged themselves to a ditch and would probably have pulled the ditch in on themselves if they could have. Two other Scouts chased them and blasted them where they cringed.

Three or four wounded made it to the jungle. Their agonizing cries of suffering contributed a Dante-like atmosphere to the crack of gunfire, and now the crackling of flame and the boiling of smoke, as Scouts lobbed concussion grenades into the barracks to finish the job. The long crude hut shook on its stilts, like a rag in the mouth of a bulldog. Flames leapt with macabre glee.

Alfonso and Frank Fox started into the jungle after the surviving enemy soldiers.

"Let 'em go!" Rounsaville called out. "They're finished! Round up the prisoners. Double time. Let's get them the hell out of here!"

Willie Wismer, Smith, and Asis were poised at the *Kempeitai* hut when Rounsaville plugged the awakening Jap in the long barracks. They rushed inside, rifle lights probing the darkness. Five Japs were sleeping on cots beneath draped nets— two to the left of the doorway; two to the right; and the fifth, the officer, at the rear next to the old chief being held hostage.

They startled to a sitting position. Smith's carbine took out the two on the left. Death throes tangled their bodies in their nets. He fired a full clip. All movement ceased.

"Sayonara, assholes!" he roared. "Pleasant dreams."

Asis and Wismer each killed one. Their ears rang from the confined gunfire. The copperish odor of fresh blood almost turned their stomachs.

The fifth enemy twisted in his bunk and came out from his netting with a wicked bayonet clenched in one fist. Flashlight beams targeted him. Smith yelled to take him prisoner and dropped an empty clip from his carbine, reloaded, and edged toward the confused *Kempeitai*. The Japanese, cornered and dangerous, poised blinking and blinded by the lights.

"Give up, you crazy sonofabitch!" Smith yelled.

Instead, the officer sprang toward Smith's voice. Smith parried and vaulted to the side. He slashed at the officer's head with the stock of his carbine, but missed.

Asis's carbine shot flame. The Jap vibrated on his feet. Flashlight beams followed his body as it slid to the floor. He gurgled his last breath.

"Stupid bastard."

The chief was unharmed. The three Scouts seized the bewildered native and hustled him from the hut before Wismer tossed a grenade into it to set it afire.

* * *

Gunfire ceased as suddenly as it started.

At first, the released prisoners were disoriented. Some of them hid. Rounsaville quickly located the family dwelling of the former Dutch governor, who spoke English. He helped Scouts reason with dazed prisoners and collect them from their huts for assembly among the palms to be ready to board the PT boats when they arrived.

Except for the middle-aged Dutchman, his wife, and their even dozen offspring ranging from about seven years old to late teenhood, the freed captives were dark-skinned Javanese or Melanesians with shiny black hair. Most were women and children; the men had been either executed or forced to flee into the jungle when the Japanese invaded. Kittleson noted they appeared well-fed as the first batches of them, carrying their few belongings, streamed out of the inferno onto the morning-lit beach. They huddled fearfully together among the palms, waiting and not quite sure of their fate at the hands of these fierce-looking men who now held them.

Scouts spread out in the village to search every hut, then torch it to prevent its use by the enemy. In one of the simple residences, big Andy Smith found a Japanese windup phonograph on a wicker table with a stack of records next to it. Apparently, the Japanese officer who lived there occupied his time listening to music—American music. Smith sorted idly through the records and found several by Bing Crosby. He placed one on the turntable and wound the machine.

As the village burned around him, the corporal from St. Louis pulled up a chair, planted his muddy boots on the table next to the phonograph, closed his eyes, and rode Bing's smooth voice singing "Melancholy Baby" back to gentler times in another world.

A sound brought him back with a slight start. He opened his eyes as PFC Rufo Vaquilar walked in. At thirty-four years old, Vaquilar was a tough ex-convict from Pontiac, Michigan, who had volunteered for combat duty in order to get out of the penitentiary. He seldom spoke; he didn't speak now. He simply tilted the muzzle of his .45 Thompson toward Smith.

"What the hell . . . ?"

Flame filled the submachine gun's muzzle. Smith dived to the floor and tried to bore through the spaces in the bamboo floor. He looked up into the still-ringing air when the burst ended. Vaquilar stood with a twist of smoke eddying from his weapon.

"Crazy bastard! The damned fight's over!" the outraged corporal yelled when his voice finally returned.

Vaquilar replied with a mere gesture of his head. Smith turned to find a naked Jap soldier sinking slowly to the floor. The guy clawed at the wall in a last desperate attempt to stay on his feet. He dropped his long rifle, to which a bayonet was firmly fixed. Blood streamed from his chest. He collapsed to the floor and moved no more.

"Guess he didn't like 'Melancholy Baby,'" Vaquilar commented drily.

On the beach, Kit Kittleson watched the liberated continue to pour from the village. Rays of golden morning sunlight now slanted nearly horizontally through the palms, as though spotlighting the former prisoners center stage. Their spirits began to pick up as full realization that they were really freed set in. There was whispering here and there. Some of the children grinned at Kittleson and Siason as Scouts hustled them toward the beach. The two PT boats idled their engines offshore in the clear light. Lieutenant Jack Dove paddled ashore with the rubber rafts.

Sergeant Alfonso was leading a bunch out of captivity when he detected movement in the bush. He swung his shotgun, finger on the trigger.

"Halt!"

A skinny white man sprang into view like a Jack-in-the-box, arms stretched as high and wide as they would reach. "No shoot! No shoot! Me no Jap. Me Frenchman. Me got wife, ten chil'run. We go with you!"

Twelve more joined the procession, bringing the total number of rescued prisoners to seventy-eight. A black pall of smoke from the village twisted slowly into the air, like a tamed and tethered typhoon, as Scouts relayed their charges from beach to PT boats with the rubber rafts. Kittleson and Siason were the last two aboard. The PTs kicked in their Packards and steered toward Biak Island and freedom.

It was a strange voyage, made joyous by happy voices of relief kept pent up until now. The rescued POWs sang the Dutch National Anthem. Navy crewmen aboard the boats pounded Scouts on their backs, shook hands, and shouted congratulations. Kittleson and Cox found places for themselves on the forward deck near the starboard torpedo tube. Kittleson lit a cigarette and drew the soothing smoke deep into his lungs while the celebration continued around him. Both PT boats were jammed forward to aft with people.

The operation had consumed twelve hours from kickoff to pickup. Not one raider had suffered so much as a bamboo cut.

Near the boat's bow a pretty young mother with surprisingly fair skin and dark curly hair braced herself and her infant on the deck. She was light-skinned enough to be from Iowa or Minnesota, Kittleson thought, watching her. He hadn't seen a woman in over six months, except the dark native females with their skinny legs, paunches, and sagging breasts like thick flaps of skin. This girl with her baby was *gorgeous*.

Completely unabashed, the girl pulled aside the strap of her thin dress to release one round golden breast. The baby eagerly took the dark nipple into its mouth. Big Cox, a true country boy, bobbed his head downward in embarrassment.

"I wisht that was me," he whispered to Kittleson, nodding at the baby.

"You wouldn't look good with tits," Kit said with his dry humor.

"I wisht I was the *baby*, you little dipshit."

"If anybody ever asks you what it is we're fighting for," Kittleson said, still looking at the pretty girl. "That's what it is right there."

CHAPTER 11

On the same morning that the two PT boats packed with Alamo Scouts and liberated captives set out from Cape Oransbari to Biak Island, some six hundred American POWs were slowly dying of disease, starvation, and atrocities at a Japanese stockade 1,400 miles away near the village of Cabanatuan on Luzon, the largest of the Japanese-held Philippine islands. They were the skeletal survivors of more than seven thousand first penned here less than four years earlier when the Philippines fell to the Japanese. The most prominent feature of the prison camp was the makeshift graveyard adjoining the stockade. There were fresh mounds daily.

A few hours after the surprise attack against Pearl Harbor on 7 December 1941, Rising Sun bombers from Formosa had launched a "Second Pearl Harbor" by bombing and strafing key U.S. air bases on Luzon. Japanese amphibious forces landed on Bataan Island the next day, followed by main assaults during Christmas week against Lingayen Gulf on western Luzon and against the east coast of the island. Trapped between the two advancing enemy forces were

23,000 American GIs and 98,000 Filipino regulars and draftees.

General Douglas MacArthur imposed War Plan Orange 3, which called for American-Filipino forces under Major General Jonathan M. "Skinny" Wainwright to confront the invaders, then pull back south, phase line by phase line, into the mountains and jungles of the Bataan Peninsula forming the western shore of Manila Bay. What neither General MacArthur nor American troops knew was that the maneuver was a ploy to buy time. President Franklin Roosevelt and the Joint Chiefs of Staff had already settled on a plan calling for the defeat of Germany first while abandoning the Philippines to the Japanese. Although Roosevelt kept promising MacArthur relief through reinforcements and supplies, none was ever to arrive. American and Filipino soldiers in the Philippines were *expendable* in the Big Picture of the war.

By 5 January 1942, all Allied troops had been channeled onto the Bataan Peninsula or the fortress island of Corregidor in Manila Bay. The Japanese quickly captured Guam, Wake, and the Marshall and Gilbert Islands, thereby effectively isolating and blockading Luzon. Although the only escape offered Americans on Bataan was capture or death, MacArthur continued to promise hope. On 15 January, he dispatched the following directive to all unit commanders:

> Help is on the way from the United States. Thousands of troops and hundreds of planes are being dispatched. The exact time of arrival of reinforcements is unknown as they will have to fight their way through Japanese against them. It is imperative that our troops hold until these reinforcements arrive. No further retreat is possible. . . .

Without reinforcements and resupply, Bataan defenders weakened daily and rapidly dwindled in numbers. Medical supplies were soon exhausted. Daily rations were cut to one-half, then cut again. Malaria, dengue fever, scurvy, dysentery, and malnutrition downed at least one-third of the force, but the wounded and the ill had no choice but to remain in their foxholes.

All GIs on Luzon, no matter their specialities, were now organized into infantry. The 27th Bomb Group, an Army Air Corps outfit, was thus transformed with a stroke of the pen into the 27th Provisional Infantry Battalion and moved with other similarly constructed units to man the Bazac-Orion line. This main line of resistance (MLR) stretched east to west across the Bataan Peninsula from Orion on Manila Bay west to Bazac on the South China Sea.

The first news the troops received was that rations would be cut to two meals a day. They went to work strengthening defenses: digging spider holes and setting up gun emplacements, patrolling and preparing to repel *Banzai!* charges.

Fighting was heavy during the month of January, followed by a lull from about the first of February to mid March. Random air strikes and artillery shelling continued, however, while the Japanese paused to wait for their own resupply and reinforcement. A lot of their troops had been mowed down in *Banzai!* charges. The defenders' meager supplies of food and medicine continued to dwindle so that by the time the fighting resumed, some 80 percent of the combat troops were unfit for fighting.

Common sense told the GIs they were being abandoned; they were going to be sacrificed. Roosevelt ordered MacArthur to flee his headquarters on Corregidor and escape to Australia to command all U.S. troops in the South Pacific. Wainwright took command of the "Legion of the Living Dead" left behind. Bitter soldiers took to wearing a "V" on their helmets. It stood for "Victim," not "Victory." Poems about "Dugout Doug" circulated among the foxholes.

In Australia's fresh clime
he took out the time
to send us a message of cheer.

My heart, he began,
goes out to Bataan.
But the rest of me's
staying right here.

Knowing the Americans were sick and starving, Japanese planes occasionally bombed the MLR with propaganda leaflets promising food, medical care, and even women—if the Americans would only surrender.

TICKET TO ARMISTICE
Use This Ticket To Save Your Life
You Will Be Kindly Treated
Follow these instructions:
1. Come toward our lines waving a white flag
2. Strap your gun over your left shoulder muzzle down and
pointed behind [sic] you
3. Show this ticket to the sentry
4. Any number of you may surrender with this one ticket
Japanese Army Headquarters
Sing Your Way To Peace
Pray For Peace

Everyone had lost a considerable amount of weight, many of them up to one-third of what they normally weighed. Their hair and beards went uncut and became infested with lice. They were tattered and torn, caked with mud and blood. Men with skeletal frames gnawed on roots. Fifty a day died of disease and starvation. Many hunkered in their own excrement, too weak to climb out of their defensive positions.

That part of the MLR defended by the 27th followed the edge of a jungle. Because all the horses and mules had been eaten, the weak and starving men spent much of their time scrounging for food in a nearby agricultural area that grew sugar cane, rice, peanuts, and other truck crops. Driven by hunger to recklessness, GIs sneaked out under cover of darkness to tie bundles of rice, peanuts, or cane to their backs and crawl back to their lives. They threshed the rice and boiled it into flour. They made peanut butter from the peanuts.

Men chewed on sugar cane, leaving trails of chewed material behind wherever they went. Chewed piles of white sugar cane marked every defensive position. A few of the more creative and industrious made a wooden press with which they extracted juices to boil into syrup to pour over rice-flour hot cakes.

An occasional carabao (water buffalo) wandered into range and was butchered, but these were rare. They, as well as all other food, became even more rare as soon as the Japanese learned what the defenders were doing. They burned the sugar cane fields and killed any buffalo in the area. Americans on line resorted to eating roots, grubs, monkeys, snakes, lizards, and anything else they could catch. Soon, even the wildlife vanished. After that, there was almost nothing to eat.

On 2 April, 50,000 fresh Japanese troops arrived on Luzon to reinforce the siege. The mightiest Jap bombardment of the war began the next day and continued for six hours. The entire Allied front became a blazing inferno in which squads and platoons faced cremation. An earthquake rattled the island, adding to the turmoil.

"It's the end of the world!" one GI screamed.

Japs began their final assault on 3 April, opening a three-mile breach in the line. Japs poured troops through the wedge. Allied units withdrew.

On 7 April, enemy troops broke through on the left flank of the 27th Provisional Infantry Battalion where a Philippine army unit had simply pulled out in the middle of the night. At daybreak, Jap landing barges rammed ashore on the beach below Orion. The battalion commander, a former bread truck driver from New York, ran across the rice paddy yelling, "Hold the line, but prepare to move out. When I ring the gong, retreat. We'll have trucks to take you back."

Japanese swarmed across the rice paddies down below like gray-brown ants. No gong sounded. Finally, a platoon sergeant sent a runner to battalion headquarters to see what was happening. He returned out of breath.

"Headquarters has cleared out. Everybody's gone. They left us here to cover their getaway."

Grim-faced, the platoon sergeant stared at his men for a long minute before he reached a decision.

"Destroy your machine guns," he said. "Break up into small groups and head south until you reach our lines. You're on your own. It's every man for himself. Try to save your own skins."

Voice of Freedom made the radio broadcast that stunned America:

> The Philippine-American troops on the war-ravaged and bloodstained peninsula have laid down their arms. With heads bloody but unbowed, they have yielded to the superior force and numbers of the enemy. . . . The world will long remember the epic struggle that Filipino and American soldiers put up in the jungle fastness. Besieged on land and blockaded by sea, cut off from all sources of help in the Philippines and in America, these intrepid fighters have done all that human endurance could bear.

The Japanese expected to take 25,000 prisoners. Instead, they captured 80,000. They were not signatory to any international agreements governing the taking and treatment of prisoners of war. To their way of belief, surrender was a disgrace. Fighting to the last man or committing suicide was preferable. They looked upon the Americans they captured, therefore, as lower than criminals and deserving of nothing more than contempt. They felt no obligation to treat POWs humanely.

Nearly 80,000 people—about 66,000 Filipino soldiers and 12,000 American GIs—were cornered near Marivales with no way to make it out to Corregidor. There was nowhere else to retreat; it was the end of the line. Jap soldiers arrived on the morning of 11 April, herded their captives down to the national highway, separated them into groups of one hundred and began marching them the sixty-five miles north to Camp O'Donnell in Tarlac Province.

The tone of captivity was set immediately. If a man's ring would not come off his finger, screaming, threatening soldiers simply chopped off the finger. One American possessed Japanese coins, which captors assumed he had scavenged from dead Japanese. They pulled him out of line, bayonetted him, and left him dying on the roadside.

Guards ripped off prisoners' casts, beat them with clubs, and stole the crutches of amputees, who were then forced to crawl or die. Men too weak from wounds, sickness, or starvation to walk received a club, bayonet, or bullet where they fell. Jap troops passing by in trucks made sport of trying to whack prisoners in the head with bamboo poles or rifle butts. Those too injured to get back up were bayonetted.

Other sport entailed compelling a prisoner to stand with his arms extended. The object was to hack off both arms with a sword one at a time before the captive fell. Still other Japanese would bayonet a POW in the stomach and then laugh and mimic his death throes.

The march's first bodies were left strewn along the road. Their numbers grew quickly. They soon littered the road—swollen, monstrous things bloating, stinking, and crawling with maggots and hordes of fat green flies underneath the burning tropical sun. Eyeballs popped out and hung on cords; crows fought over these delicacies.

Endless columns shambled north through this disgusting debris, adding to it. There was boiling sun and choking dust, indescribable thirst exacerbated by temperatures of up to 115 degrees, Japanese soldiers shouting and shooting as their ferocity grew. Prisoners were clubbed for trying to drink filthy water from the footprints of water buffalo. Buzzard squads of Japanese followed along behind the formations to slaughter those too weak to continue. The dead, went one bitter joke, were "the lucky stiffs."

One group came to a bridge over a small river. A guard

gave the POWs permission to drink. They broke and ran. Thick green scum covered the water's surface. Several fly-covered corpses floated in the water like bloated balloons. The men dropped to their knees anyway and thrust their heads into the water.

The march took five days. At night, guards crowded 1,500 to 2,000 men into a barbed-wire enclosure big enough for no more than 500. Japs swatted the prisoners with clubs and tree limbs as they filed into the compound. Behind them in a pile lay the bodies of the men they had killed.

During one night stop, a Jap appeared with a GI's head impaled on his rifle bayonet. The knife went up through the throat and into the brain. Two more Japs followed, each with an American's head on the end of his bayonet. It was a grue-some sight with sightless eyes bulging, mouths gaping, and ragged bloody skin hanging around the necks where they had been severed from their bodies.

More than one thousand Americans died or were mur-dered during what later became known as the infamous Bataan Death March. By the time the survivors reached Camp O'Donnell, the metamorphosis from human to animal was all but complete. Along the way a Filipino girl had tossed a piece of coconut to the pitiful marchers. Two colo-nels dived for it and ended up in a fist fight over it.

Camp O'Donnell was set on a mile-square treeless plain surrounded by tall cogon grass. An unfinished Philippine army base, it was a squalid installation of ramshackle bamboo-walled, thatch-roofed buildings around which the Japanese had strung barbed wire and erected wooden guard towers. Dissipated and broken by the long battle and the Death March afterwards, survivors crammed into barracks intended for half their number soon turned the compound into a gargantuan sewer.

There was no plumbing. There were only two water spig-ots for the entire camp, and they only trickled water. La-trines were open slit trenches buzzing with black flies and stench.

Twice a day each POW received one cup of rice *lugoa*

cooked on clay stoves prisoners constructed themselves. It was hardly enough to keep anyone alive. Soon, the already starving POWs became little more than burnt parchment skin stretched over bones. Hearts weakened from abuse and malnutrition. Men suffered from pneumonia, malaria, tuberculosis, and other diseases. Many toppled over dead while waiting in chow lines. Others slipped and fell into slit trenches and suffocated, too weak to climb out. Some men simply gave up, turned their faces to the walls, and died. Each morning the living had to disentangle themselves from the dead. Bodies were stacked two and three deep in the Double Zero ward—the morgue.

Burial details labored all day, every day, to keep ahead of the dying. A heavy rain would float the corpses out of their graves and they would have to be buried again. During the night, prisoners already miserable on their thin sleeping mats listened to packs of dogs snarling and fighting and digging to reach the rotted bodies in the burial grounds.

Corregidor held out for another month after the collapse of Bataan before it fell on 6 May, feeding seven thousand more GIs and five thousand Filipinos to the Japanese Death March. These prisoners were taken to a former Philippine army recruit training camp forty miles northeast of Camp O'Donnell near the bustling commerce town of Cabanatuan. Like O'Donnell, Cabanatuan camp was set on a plain of tall cogon grass without trees. Treatment there reached and perhaps surpassed the level of brutality at O'Donnell.

The Japanese soon declared Filipino prisoners "reconstructed" and released forty-five thousand of them. Surviving GIs from O'Donnell were transferred to Cabanatuan in June 1942. O'Donnell became a ghost camp while Cabanatuan took over as sewer, holding between seven thousand and twelve thousand POWs, most of whom were Americans.

By October 1944, the month the Alamo Scout raid freed captives of the Japanese held on Cape Oransbari, death, murder, and shipments of POWs to slave labor details in

Formosa, Manchuria, Japan, and other places had reduced the inmate population of Cabanatuan to six hundred or less. Even while General MacArthur continued his push to return to the Philippines, wistful eyes watched the blue skies over Cabanatuan for signs of relief or rescue.

CHAPTER 12

MacArthur was returning to the Philippines. Smooth-faced Willie Wismer brought the news to Nellist Team. He was ever the facilitator, the cooperator who had a way of ferreting out intelligence about missions and movements even before Lieutenant Nellist found out about them. Nellist Team had been mostly cooling its heels at the Woendi Island PT base since the Oransbari triumph.

"It's the real scoop," Wismer insisted. "The Philippines are next. I heard it from a cook who was talking to General Kreuger's driver who said he got it directly from a clerk in G-2 . . ."

He pointed to a rusted bolt-bucket of a PT tender anchored in deeper water out past the PT piers. *Wachapreague* had just returned from some other mission the night before.

"We're going on *that*," Willie said.

He was right, as far as it went. On the night of 12 October, four teams of Alamo Scouts—Nellist, Rounsaville, Littlefield, and Dove—received orders to board *Wachapreague* for immediate movement. All anyone knew was that they were heading for the Philippines—but there were seven thousand *islands* in the Philippines.

Life aboard the tender, as with any troopship, was not designed for comfort. The boat was not crowded, however, and Kittleson found it rather pleasant after living in tents and foxholes. The occasional inconvenience was endured in wry silence or with a tolerant rebuke.

"Boy, if you gotta fart, go topside to fart and let the Japs die from it."

Wachapreague steamed slowly north for days among tropical islands. She seemed to be killing time more than sailing with a purpose. The poker game that never really started and never really ended moved from deck to troop bay and back to deck. Scouts cleaned gear, bullshitted, and wrote letters home. Kit kept his journal.

October 13. Left Woendi Island PT base at 1300 on *Wachapreague* bound for Philippines. Played checkers. . . .
October 16. Entered Palau Harbor. Refueled. . . .
October 18. Set sail.
October 19. Water pretty rough. Played checkers with Gilbert. Kinda homesick.
October 20. Sailing for Philippines. As yet don't know where or what we're heading for. Sub alert . . .

The closest Kittleson had to a sweetheart was the pretty hometown brunette, Darlene Bruggeman, whom he had dated a time or two while in high school. He took her to the Junior-Senior Banquet, but mostly, they were just friends. He had met her at St. Ansgar where she was one grade behind him. She lived in nearby Toeterville, which was little more than a collection of houses in the middle of a corn field.

After Kittleson volunteered for the draft and went away to war, the girls left behind wrote to all the boys they knew; it was their contribution to the war effort. Darlene, attending St. Olaf College, was roommates with Mary Longahough, on whose letter-writing list Kittleson's name appeared.

"You know Galen," Mary said to Darlene. "Why don't you write him too?"

That was how it started: casually. Gradually, however, the little Scout from Iowa began looking forward to Darlene's letters. They brought to him the sound of female laughter and the scent of perfume. They refreshed memories of high school basketball games, hanging out on Main Street and watching the corn fields grow and the pretty girls pass by. A soldier at war lived for mail call; it left him feeling hollow and alone when mail was delayed, as it often was. Mail was his lifeline back to a real world where men were not killing each other.

At night sometimes aboard *Wachapreague*, when it was soft and quiet above decks, someone broke out a guitar and maybe baby-faced Willie Wismer started to sing in his clear tenor. Gilbert Cox's big grin slowly faded into what Wismer called a "sick calf" look. The team joined in.

> *From this valley they say you are going,*
> *And I'll miss your bright eyes and sweet smile . . .*
> *But remember the Red River Valley . . .*

Off-key though it might be sung, "Red River Valley" always flooded Kittleson with home thoughts. It made his chest tight and caused an ache deep in his throat. He walked away from the others and stood at the rail of *Wachapreague*, looking up at the canopy of stars and maybe warplanes screaming north between him and the heavens. He prayed to God for strength and courage and thanked Him for bringing him safely this far.

Scout missions behind enemy lines carried with them a peculiar mixture of excitement and fear. Instinct and training took over once a mission began. It was the waiting beforehand that was toughest, when there was time to think. Thinking was very hard on a GI about to enter combat, whether it was his first time or not. It made him reflect on what *could* happen.

Pug-nosed Tommie Siason said in his crisp English, "It is not so bad if you are killed right away. What is bad is if you lose your legs or your arms."

"Or your balls," Andy Smith put in.

"*Especially* your balls," Wismer agreed, grinning. "I'd rather lose my head than my precious family jewels."

"Why?" Asis asked. "You will never use them anyhow."

"If the Japs capture you," big Gilbert Cox said, "you'll wish you had lost your balls *and* your head. Those poor boys that got caught on Bataan. You can just imagine what they must be going through."

"If they're still alive," Andy Smith said. "Always keep an extra bullet in your pocket."

Lieutenant Nellist looked up from cleaning his .45 pistol. He was the team's heart and head, but at the same time he maintained a slight aloofness. Smith fished a .45 cartridge from his pocket to prove he wasn't bullshitting.

"This last round is to squeeze through your own brain if it looks like you're going to be taken prisoner of war," he said, and Willie Wismer was no longer grinning.

Kittleson never carried a spare bullet, but now he thought about how he would save the last round for himself if it came to that.

From this valley they say you are going.
And I'll miss your bright eyes and sweet smile . . .

CHAPTER 13

At midnight of 19 October 1944, while *Wachapreague* steamed north over the Mindanao Sea to the tune of "Red River Valley," General Douglas MacArthur stared into the night from the darkened bridge of his flagship cruiser *Nashville*. Ships loomed out of the night and then disappeared again almost before their outlines were discerned. Dark waters below and a black sky above wrapped the invasion fleet in a near-impenetrable cloak. Stars were distant and cold and there was no moon.

MacArthur, now 61, with a face like a Samoan wood carving, tapped the bowl of his signature pipe in the palm of his hand. He continued to stare into the darkness, as though using his considerable force of will to penetrate the night. Although Roosevelt had ordered him to escape from Corregidor before it fell, he had never fully forgiven himself for leaving. *Abandoning* Luzon, *deserting* his soldiers. That was what the GIs called it—and they weren't far wrong. The jokes and songs and poems made up at his expense by the men left behind to face the Japanese juggernaut pursued him to Australia. They had stung him then. They haunted his waking and sleeping hours in the years since.

My heart, he began,
goes out to Bataan.
But the rest of me's
staying right here.

But, by God, he was keeping his promise. Tonight. To-morrow. General MacArthur *was* returning to the Philippines. This time he was staying. His first stepping stone on the way back to Luzon was the central Philippine island of Leyte.

He had halted his invasion fleet to wait and prepare for dawn in open water outside Leyte Gulf. It was a formidable armada made up of sixteen fast aircraft carriers, six new battleships, and eighty-one cruisers and destroyers of Admiral Nimitz's Third Fleet. Aboard and preparing for landing were 200,000 soldiers of General Walter Kreuger's 6th Army. Fifth Air Force would provide additional air cover while the U.S. Seventh Fleet was ready to support the beachhead with its small escort carriers and slow, old battleships.

H-hour was dawn. MacArthur had no idea what the Japanese battle plan might be.

Cruisers and destroyers with depth charges patrolled the waters like deadly silent ghosts, looking for enemy submarines. Nervous men lined the rails or paced the decks. Like MacArthur, like their other commanders, they wondered what dawn might bring. Wondering if they had seen their last sunset.

Officers huddled in wardrooms around maps. Troops inspected their weapons, tested their gear, wrote last-minute letters home.

Few slept.

General MacArthur went to his cabin. He read from his Bible. He prayed for his men, for himself, for the nation, and he prayed for victory.

At dawn, the invasion force awoke like a sleeping predator. An enemy periscope broke the sea's surface, but destroyers pounced on it. Depth charges churned up the bottom.

Big naval guns opened up on the beach in the first morning sunlight, pounding it and the jungle-clad hills rising beyond it. Thousands of guns hurled shells with a deafening and incessant roar. Rocket vapor trails and tracers crisscrossed the clear blue of the morning sky. Swarms of airplanes darted at the beaches, stinging them with bombs and bullets. Pillars of black smoke rose from the beachhead, beckoning to hordes of landing craft churning in to dump troops at "Red Beach" near the village of Pale and "White Beach" at San Jose.

MacArthur's initial vantage point was two miles from the beaches. Always the showman, he donned a fresh, starched uniform, pocketed a revolver as insurance against being captured alive, and boarded one of the landing craft with his staff, newsmen, and Philippine President Sergio Osmena. Light fighting was going on about a half-mile inland as the boat approached the beach. The general was aware of the *Crump! Crump!* of exploding naval shells and the peculiar gargling of a Jap machine gun no more than one hundred yards away in the jungle. Flames raced snapping and crackling through the tops of palms all along the beach. Acrid smoke stung his nostrils.

The landing craft's bottom scraped sand fifty yards from shore. The big nose ramp dropped, splashing. A harried beachmaster, too busy to worry about providing a boat for a bunch of sightseeing dignitaries, snarled, "Screw 'em! Let 'em walk ashore."

MacArthur expected nothing more. He dropped into surf up to his knees and, wading, led the entourage to dry land. He greeted his shore commanders, then stepped before a Signal Corps microphone. While gunfire and cannon rattled and thundered in the background, he broadcast a short, sermonlike speech that began: "People of the Philippines, *I have returned . . .*"

His hands shook and his voice quavered with emotion.

Weeks more would pass, however, before the much decimated survivors of Bataan in their miserable prison at Cabanatuan on the main island learned that "Dugout Doug" had kept his promise. For most of them, long dead and buried in their rags and misery, the return came years too late.

CHAPTER 14

October 21. Arrived at San Pedro Bay, Leyte. D + 1. Warships shelling enemy positions. No air raids.

October 22. Sitting in harbor. Warship *West Virginia* shelling shore positions.

October 23. Sitting in San Pedro Harbor on *Wachapreague*. Watched warships shell positions. Air raid—one Jap shot down.

October 24. Spent night on board, left *Wachapreague*, not knowing where. No enemy encountered.

October 25. Landed on Mindanao Island at 0545 by rubber boat. Escorted us to guerrilla headquarters. Welcomed by guerrillas carrying Philippine and American flags. People mad with joy. Called us their liberators. . . .

CHAPTER 15

It wasn't for a private in the U.S. "By God" Army, not even if he were an Alamo Scout, to know *why* higher headquarters required on-the-ground intel about Mindanao, the next island south of Leyte, which had been bypassed. All a private had to know was *what* needed to be done—then do it.

"In this man's army," exclaimed little Willie Wismer, "you do what you're told. That's how you get by."

Kittleson had been with 6th Army for nearly a year, operating in New Guinea and its coastal islands, and now, at last, in the Philippines. The little warrior had already won a Silver Star, the nation's third highest award for valor, and a Bronze Star underneath that for the Oransbari raid. But, as he wrote his new pen pal Darlene back in Toeterville, the medals were not so very important to him. A private was not vital to the war, not like generals and admirals who moved armies and fleets about on the globe, but a private could still fight well, help win the war—and then come home.

Patriotism ran deep in the little farmer's soul. He never questioned why the war had to be fought. He *knew* why without having to actually think about it. It had to do with good farmland, the right to worship God, pretty girls, and little kids safe at home because privates risked—and even sacrified—their lives. Ultimately, he thought, privates and corporals and sergeants and lieutenants like Nellist, Rounsaville, and Jack Dove were the ones who won wars. They won them one day at a time, following orders and smiting evil, usually while holding little inkling of their place in the greater scheme of things.

"We're to secure intel on landing beaches, water obstacles, dispersal areas, potable water, enemy strength, conditions, and locations," briefed Lieutenant Nellist prior to movement.

The landing on Mindanao was not much different from a dozen or so other landings Kit Kittleson had made either with the Scouts or, before that, with the 503d's Second Battalion. You see one idyllic, romantic South Sea island beach, as witty Willie Wismer put it, and you'd seen them all. A sandy beach, waving palms reaching for first morning light, a strip of jungle, and green hills and mountains rising beyond. That was it. The romance ended where the bugs and snakes and alligators and Japs started behind the beach.

Nellist Team scrambled ashore. The support team immediately returned to the PT boat with the rubber rafts. The PTs liked to do their dirty work in the dark and then scurry for cover when Zeroes started coming out to prowl the skies. A dark-skinned man, naked except for a pair of dirty khaki shorts, hurried out of jungle shadows—the team's contact ashore. He was grinning like at a family reunion. He ran up to the nearest man, who happened to be Gilbert Cox, and hugged him soundly while he jabbered in Pidgin English.

"Me, me so happy. You liberator. You 'Melican from 'Melica. Stars and stripes. So happy you liberator."

Cox blushed and extricated himself from the man's arms. He pointed at Lieutenant Nellist. "Hug him," he said. "He's the boss."

The Filipino embraced Nellist around the waist, as that was as far up the tall man as he could reach. He delivered his speech again, then pointed toward a high bluff overlooking the beach about a half-mile away.

"He says we have to hurry before the shadows lift," Nellist passed along. "The Japs have 75mm big guns on top of that bluff. They've probably seen us."

Kittleson took point with his Thompson and the native guide. His six team members spaced themselves into a Ranger file behind him. A footpath threaded its way through the jungle until it widened suddenly into a dirt street passing through a village of primitive nipa huts. As if on cue, throngs of happy villagers waving flags immediately surrounded the Scouts. Civilians in shorts and sarongs, naked children, dogs yapping, pigs and chickens running for cover jostled the Americans. The villagers struggled to touch them, everyone chatting and shouting, "Liberators! Liberators!" It was probably the only English word most of them knew.

Kittleson stood there in astonishment while kids tugged at his clothing and adults wrung his hand. Willie Wismer was grinning and trying to barter some rations for a jade bracelet. Andy Smith wondered just *how* grateful the pretty Filipino girls really were. Lieutenant Nellist cast uneasy looks in the direction of the bluff on the beach.

Cox, who had had one year of college in Oregon, could sometimes be cynical. "I wonder if they wave Jap flags when the Japs come through town?"

"Wouldn't you if you were them?" Kittleson asked.

A guide from the 114th Guerrilla Regiment met the team in the village. He was a skinny man carrying an '03 Springfield rifle. He smiled a lot and spoke little. Throughout the Philippines, guerrilla bands had formed after the Japanese invasion to harass enemy patrols and outposts and sabotage shipments and movements. They employed hit-and-run tactics designed to keep the Japs unsettled and uncomfortable.

The silent, smiling guide led Nellist Team out the back side of the village. They traveled hard for most of the morning through steaming forest, climbing into the guerrilla hills and penetrating deep into territory conquered but not always controlled by the Japanese.

At noon the Scouts came to guerrilla headquarters, which they were to use as a base of operations. There they accepted another jubilant reception. The camp consisted of a number of thatched-roof bamboo huts thrust deep into nearly impenetrable jungle at the end of a forest-clogged canyon. The forty or fifty Filipinos manning the camp were a ragged lot armed with an assortment of weapons ranging from captured Jap rifles and mortars to '03 Springfields and a Gatling gun somehow survived from the American Indian Wars. Siason, the team's radioman, set up in a hut assigned as the Americans' ops center and Morse-coded an arrival message back to headquarters while Cox hand-cranked the generator. Team Nellist was behind enemy lines and commencing operations.

Typically, an Alamo Scout team, being small in number, avoided enemy contact whenever possible. For the next three days, Scouts paired up with guerrillas to reconnoiter the entire northern tip of the island. They were up at first light and humping the boondocks until well after nightfall. On the second day, Kittleson, Cox, and two Filipinos scoured a valley north of the canyon from its narrows to a point about a half-mile from Ipal, the village that had first welcomed them to Mindanao. An excited runner from the village met them to pass on bad news. The Japanese knew the Scouts had come ashore and were patrolling for them. In retaliation for Ipal's cooperation with the intruders, Japanese *Kempeitai* with a twenty-seven-man detachment had seized the headman and four others, bound their hands with rope, and set out for Surigao with them.

"The guerrillas know their location and direction of travel," Kittleson explained in arguing for a rescue mission. "We could ambush them with the guerrillas."

The Scouts were in their darkened hut preparing to Morse-code recon findings back to Leyte. The various teams had, so far, pinpointed locations of enemy garrisons, gun emplacements, and land and sea mines and had concluded that the island was much more lightly defended than had been anticipated. It was valuable intelligence in planning for a possible invasion.

Nellist, who had not shaved, looked tired and even more gaunt than usual. He shook his head reluctantly.

"These are good people," Willie Wismer objected. "What happened to them is our fault. Sir, we *owe* it to them."

"We have our orders," the lieutenant responded softly but firmly. What happened to five villagers on an island paled in comparison to the global war effort. "Asis, you and Smith take a look at that Jap observation point tomorrow." Guerrillas had discovered an OP fortified with nearly forty Jap soldiers and a .50-caliber machine gun. "Kit, you and Gilbert take a look to see if there are any more supply barges in that cove." He jabbed at the map lighted by candles and flashlights. "Siason will stick to the radio. Willie and I will pull observation on the beach. Siason has already radioed for extraction. We're getting our asses out of here tomorrow night. Those are our orders," he added to cut off further argument.

Later, the lieutenant and Kittleson stood outside the hut in the darkness to smoke cigarettes. Nellist felt closer to the little Iowan than to any other member of the team.

"The guerrillas will rescue the villagers after we're gone," he said.

He looked away. Both Scouts knew the hostages would be dead by then.

"We can't save everybody, but maybe we can save the world," Nellist murmured.

They never spoke about it again. It was a part of the war better left buried.

Before dark the following night, the team skirted Ipal and burrowed into jungle on a rise overlooking the beach, three hundred yards south of where they had inserted. Approaching darkness spread across the sea like spilled ink. Kittleson settled in next to Wismer to await a signal from arriving PT boats. Three quick blinks from a light. If the Scouts answered it, rubber boats would be dispatched. If no response came from shore, the PT boats would scurry away and return to an alternate pickup spot the following night.

"See 'em?" Wismer whispered, excited, pointing.

"It's a glowworm glowing."

"You sure?"

"It's a glowworm."

"They're not coming. Something's happened."

Back before the Scouts *were* the Scouts, Lieutenant Beckworth and some Amphibious Force boys had been left ashore for eleven days after they were supposed to be picked up. Every Scout knew the story of how they almost starved while trying to elude capture. A Scout's greatest fear was that he would be forgotten and left to fend for himself among the enemy. "Save that last bullet," Andy Smith always counseled in a funereal voice.

Wismer squashed mosquitos without slapping them. Sounds carried distances at night. He opened a C-rat can with contents that smelled like chemicals flavored with ham.

"Watch my technique," he encouraged.

"I can't even see you," Kittleson said.

"I get a spoonful of pig guts," Wismer narrated, whispering. "I brush off the swarms of mosquitos and shove the meat in my mouth real quick. On a good run I can get it in without eating a single mosquito. I don't mind sharing chow with flies nearly as much as these big bastard mosquitos. A guy from the Air Corps told me a mosquito landed at Henderson Field one night and they filled it with a hundred gallons of fuel before they figured it wasn't no Flying Fortress."

"You're a funny man, Willie."

"It's a funny war." He paused. "Then how come we ain't laughing?"

"Can it, fellas," Nellist said. "Keep an eye peeled for the boats."

A misting rain slithered through the black jungle. Far to the north, a light show erupted in spectacular Technicolor. Lights flashed and squirmed and flickered in reflection off a low cloud bank. Cox said he had seen the Aurora Borealis once and that was what this reminded him of. Awed, Nellist Team hunkered in the damp rain forest for the rest of the night and watched in reflection the Battle of Surigao Strait. They were too far away to hear the thunder.

They waited, but PT boats did not come to extract them.

"Maybe tomorrow night," Nellist said.

CHAPTER 16

It was a long day hiding from Japanese patrols. The Scouts buried themselves in the thickest undergrowth they could find. They ate, dozed fitfully, pulled guard duty, and reinforced Willie Wismer in his personal war against flies and mosquitos.

That night, two PT boats flicked the light signal from offshore. Nellist and his men scrambled down to water's edge where Hollywood Jack Dove personally picked them up in rubber boats. As the team members paddled toward the PTs, Dove sprang it on them:

"Well," he said. "The good news is, you're not doing a Beckworth."

"You're not telling us something," Nellist accused.

"There's also bad news. Coming in, *Sea Bat* hit the coral reef and bent her screws. It's going to be a slow cattle boat trip back to Leyte."

Kittleson involuntarily glanced toward the east. It was already after midnight. The trip up the Surigao Strait and across Leyte Gulf to GI-occupied Tacloban was at least a four-hour run under the best conditions. Dove explained that last night's Battle of Surigao Strait had sunk two Japanese destroyers and two battleships, but the Gulf tonight remained alive with Jap warships and planes.

PT boats, faster than Japanese warships, scooted about with near immunity under cover of darkness. Daylight brought problems. Jap bombers and Zeros liked nothing better than to find one out of its nest after daybreak. They didn't even have to score a direct hit. Concussions from near misses ripped apart the plyboard hulls and spiked the air with deadly supersonic splinters.

Navy crews on *Sea Bat* and *Green Hornet* shoved food at the returning Scouts, but despite their hunger, almost no one ate. Out past the shallows and the offshore reef, swells of six feet and more smashed at the bows from squall lines moving rain out of Leyte and further slowed progress. *Sea Bat*'s screws sounded like they were rapidly banging themselves apart. *Green Hornet* cut her speed to half, then cut it again, in order to stay with the damaged craft. Crews and passengers alike sunk into tense silence, awaiting dawn with fear and misgiving.

"Did you ever do any duck hunting?" Wismer asked Kittleson. "That's what I feel like—a setting duck waiting to get the shit shot out of us as soon as the Nips can see."

Allied screens of destroyers and cruisers worked the waters of Surigao Strait, hunting Japs. The floundering PT boats were unaware of other company prowling nearby until an Australian cruiser radio-challenged them at 0200 hours. Ensign Jones, skipper of *Sea Bat*, cut power to idle and squinted into the night, seeing nothing but more night. Kittleson and Cox, lying together on the deck between the cockpit and the starboard torpedo tube, sat up to listen to the radio exchange. The injured boat caused their teeth to rattle.

"Sir, they're demanding the password," the boat's radioman said.

"I heard 'em, Folkes. I don't know what the fucking password is. The old one expired while we were out. Tell 'em that."

"Not good enough, mate," the cruiser responded. "Heave to and lay up until daylight."

Searchlight beams ran across the black water and played back and forth over the two dead-in-the-water boats. Ensign Jones grabbed the mike from his radioman.

"Look," he snapped into it. "We have a crippled boat. You hold us here until daylight, you're making targets of us. Can't you see we're Americans?"

"That *appears* so, mate. But it could be subterfuge."

Jones took a deep breath. "We're going through," he said.

"We'll blow you right out of the water if you don't stop."

"Hold your fire."

"Stand by, mate."

By the time an American ship, USS *Canberra*, was summoned and a boarding party organized to verify the nationality of the PTs, the cloud cover was starting to lift and push away from a growing paleness on the eastern horizon. The boats bobbed in the water. Ensign Jones paced the cockpit with an eye cocked on the lightening sky. Nellist squatted next to Kittleson and Cox.

"This bullshit is going to get us all creamed," Cox complained.

Nellist offered the Scouts cigarettes. They smoked quietly with their faces turned toward the east. Kittleson watched the outline of *Green Hornet* slowly materialize out of the dark next to them.

Once underway again, Jones gave *Sea Bat* all the power she would take and still hold together. She shuddered violently in the water, screws banging as though trying to break through the bottom of the hull. Jones eased off the throttle. *Green Hornet* ranged off to starboard as the boats staggered up the middle of Leyte Gulf toward Tacloban, and the rising sun burned off the clouds. Kittleson stood up and searched for land; he saw only water and more water, but the sea had calmed since the passage of the squall line. Everyone kept an anxious eye cocked for Jap airplanes.

"I feel plumb nekkid," complained Wismer.

Gilbert Cox gave him an appraising look. "That's not a pretty thought," he said.

The PT boats ploughed their way north with agonizing

slowness. It had been a sleepless night for everyone. Kittleson and Cox were bullshitting on deck when Cox's gaze
shifted over the shorter man's head and the expression froze
on his face. Jap bombers always poured on power just before
they released their bombs in order to have enough horses to
pull out of the dive. Kittleson heard that increased whine and
knew the plane was coming in.

It appeared out of nowhere, like the predator it was. Kittleson wheeled and caught the flash of the red morning sun
mirrored in red circles on the aircraft's fuselage. Something
long and bright separated itself and came screaming through
the air toward *Sea Bat*. The bomber was so low, Kittleson
saw the pilot's white *hachimaki* headband.

"*Incoming!*" Kittleson yelled, sounding the alarm. "Get
down!"

Where the hell could you get down *to* on a chip of floating wood?

If possible, Kittleson would have burrowed into the wood
like a termite. He and Cox dropped in a pile next to the torpedo tube.

The bomb thunked heavily into the sea aft of *Sea Bat*'s
port side. The whine of the enemy engine slapped against
the water. The bomb exploded as the plane howled pulling
out. A tremendous geyser of water blasted *Sea Bat* to the top
of its crest, then dropped it with a bone-jarring crunch.
Shrapnel ripped through the plywood hull. Somebody
screamed.

As in slow motion, Kittleson saw the sailor at the forward
machine gun mount clutch his chest and fly backwards. The
little Scout sprang to his feet. He leaped over the dead machine gunner and grabbed the .50-cal's twin trigger handles.
His only thought was to slap back at the bee that had stung
them. He pivoted the gun barrel. This action, along with lash-
ing spray from the passing plane's propwash and the turbu-
lence of the explosion, almost threw him overboard. He held
onto the gun and tried to ram its sights into the Jap's exhaust.

The enemy aircraft nosed toward the sun and climbed,
roaring into the distance and out of range before Kittleson

could pin it in his sights. He pivoted the gun forward again to catch the next dive bomber, but the sky was empty. It had been a one-run attack, a chance encounter in the great Pacific theater of war.

There was silence again, except for the lapping of the spent geyser against the hull. Except for the moaning of the wounded.

Lieutenant Dove had taken a sliver of steel through the calf of his leg. Asis, Andy Smith, and Lieutenant Nellist were all struck by flying splinters, but were not seriously wounded. Four or five of the sailors were peppered with splinters and two of them were dead: the forward machine gunner and a twenty-year-old engineman who had joined the crew a month before. Ensign Jones had a cut bleeding on his forehead.

Kittleson knelt to check the gunner slumped at his feet. People were now yelling and jumping about as they assessed and treated wounds. Kittleson's man had those sightless eyes of the empty soul. The little farmer warrior bowed his head and asked God to take care of that soul. He sat down on the deck and there was blood on it. Once again men had died around him while he hadn't even been scratched. Cox touched him on the shoulder.

"Are you a Methodist or Baptist?" he asked because he had to say something.

"Baptist," Kittleson said.

"I think maybe I oughta sign up with you Baptists."

CHAPTER 17

General MacArthur expected to take Leyte quickly, then move on to Mindoro, the next stepping-stone. Mindoro would provide airfields and ground-based air support for the final Philippine defeat of the Japanese on Luzon. He wanted to reach Manila as quickly as possible, not only to secure the city and its deep water port but also to free Allied prisoners held captive by the Japanese for over two years.

"I was deeply concerned about the thousands of prisoners who had been interned at the various camps on Luzon since the early days of the war," he wrote in his *Reminiscences*. "Shortly after the Japanese had taken over the islands, they gathered Americans, British, and other Allied nationals, including women and children, in concentration camps without regard to whether they were actual combatants or simply civilians. I had been receiving reports from my various underground sources long before the actual landing on Luzon, but the latest information was most alarming. With every step that our soldiers took toward Santo Tomas University, Bilibid, Cabanatuan, and Los Banos, where the prisoners were held, the Japanese soldiers guarding them had become more and more sadistic. I knew that many of those half-starved and ill-treated people would die unless we rescued them promptly. The thought of their destruction with deliverance so near was deeply repellent to me."

Unfortunately, the Leyte invasion fell during the rainy season. Typhoons and monsoons laced the island with thirty-five inches of rain. Trails and roads became quagmires that even carabao tried to avoid. Severe troop shortages, poor roads, rugged terrain, and lack of air support all hampered 6th Army's ability to gain a quick victory. Furthermore, the Japanese decided to fight the decisive battle for the Philippines on Leyte. They lost approximately 60,000 men in the long battle. The U.S. lost 3,500.

By Christmas 1944, both Leyte and Mindoro were in the hands of the Americans and Mindoro was fully operational in providing aerial support bases for the invasion of Luzon. On 9 January 1945, 6th Army landed at Lingayen Gulf on the west-central coast of Luzon and began to push rapidly toward Manila. The Japanese fought desperately in an attempt to at least delay the Allied march toward Tokyo.

News provided by the Alamo Scouts even before the Luzon invasion made MacArthur ever more anxious about the fate of POWs held on Luzon.

Dove Team, commanded by Lieutenant Woodrow Hobbs while Jack Dove recuperated from the wound he sustained during the air attack against *Sea Bat*, infiltrated Leyte to place surveillance on the northern half of Highway 2 from Valencia north to Cananga and then east to Carigara. During the two-week mission, Scouts found three thousand enemy troops concentrated in Cananga while another one thousand were dug in five miles to the east. Angered by their losses, Japanese were slaughtering entire villages in cold blood, including women and children.

During the latter stages of the New Guinea campaign, Alamo Scouts had begun rotating as bodyguards for both General MacArthur and General Kreuger. Lieutenant Nellist had assembled the team on a somber note. "The generals know too much to be captured," he said. "It's our job to make sure they're not captured. It's also our job to kill them.

If it's certain that the Japs are going to take either of them POW, we are to shoot him."

That order disturbed young Kittleson. Yet, he knew he could do it if necessary. During one of his team's MacArthur missions, he was bold enough to ask the stern-faced Supreme Commander when if ever they were going to rescue the Bataan Death March survivors. MacArthur had eyes like a hawk's. He rarely exchanged pleasantries with enlisted men. He fixed his sharp gaze on the little private.

"Were you on the Cape Oransbari raid, son?" he asked gruffly.

"Yes, sir."

"Well, son. Let me tell you this. You be ready when the time comes."

CHAPTER 18

During November and December 1944 while 6th Army and the U.S. Third Fleet battled to secure Leyte and Mindoro, Alamo Scouts conducted only five missions directly against the Japanese. None of these missions was assigned to Nellist Team. Lieutenant Nellist, Andy Smith, and Sabas Asis recovered from their close-call wounds aboard the PT *Sea Bat*. Then they waited, bodyguarded the generals, ran support for the other teams, and, through rumors and reports from buddies on the front line, attempted to keep up on the progress of the war. Their own unconventional war was going slowly, but not always without excitement.

Sumner Team smuggled boatloads of weapons onto Leyte for Filipino guerrillas encamped in the hills. Guerrilla security patrols, low on ammunition, made sharp contact with Japanese troops landing six miles south of the town of Puerto Bello where Scouts were establishing radio stations and an intelligence network. The Scouts retreated toward Ma-sin, only to discover themselves headed off by Jap combat patrols.

To make matters worse, the Scouts couldn't call for help or extraction; their radio was on the blink. Just when things looked hopeless, an enemy fighter bomber approached a hilltop where the team had holed up five miles west of the Japanese airfield of Valencia. A parachute popped from the aircraft. A wicker basket dangled from it. Inside the basket, which the Scouts retrieved, was a new radio. It was a miracle, however and for whatever reason it arrived. The Scouts cannibalized it to repair their own. Sumner then radioed 6th Army for an immediate airdrop of ammo to resupply the guerrillas.

Lieutenant Thompson and his five Scouts set up on Poro Island near Esperanza to observe Japanese barge traffic between Ceba and northwestern Leyte. They reported back to headquarters that civilians were being raped, tortured, and bayonetted all over the island. At 4:00 A.M. on 7 December, they were resting in a small two-story hut along the coast when six bargeloads of Japanese riflemen landed. Someone had apparently informed on them.

Enemy troops quickly surrounded the building. Thompson ordered his men to hold their fire; it would be suicide to shoot their way out. Instead, the lieutenant and three of his GIs dived out the window into the surf. Sergeant Leonard Scott and another Scout bumped squarely into Jap soldiers coming up the outside stairway. It was dark and the Japanese were too startled to react. The two Scouts threw themselves into bushes and crouched, motionless.

Nips thrashed the brush, blindly jabbing with bayonets. A bayonet point pricked Scott's belly. He felt a thin line of blood trickling into his waistband. He held his breath and didn't move. Soon the search moved on down the beach.

All six Scouts escaped.

Nellist Team sat out the time either in tents at the captured and newly repaired airstrips ashore on Leyte or in the Gulf aboard *Wachapreague*. Andy Smith bullshitted a lot, as he did when bored. Asis and Siason quarreled over cards. Kittleson found the waiting almost unbearable. Like the others, he was discovering how easy it was to get to like living on the edge. There was something addictive about it.

The weather was hot, humid to the point of dripping.

Food was barely edible. There was seldom anything fresh. Fare most often consisted of bully beef, dehydrated potatoes that cooks regenerated somehow into pebbles, dehydrated eggs that no hen would ever have claimed, and "jungle butter" that not only refused to melt in the tropics, but wouldn't melt in your stomach either.

Diversions assumed comical proportions.

"This steak is superb, Mr. Kittleson," Wismer would say over the bully beef in his best British accent. "However, it does require a dash of Tabasco sauce."

Kittleson played along. "I think I'll have the caviar—and please pass the martinis."

"You don't drink martinis with steak," Cox said.

"Cox oughta know," Andy Smith put in. "He's been to college and got etiquette. While Kittleson ain't nothing but a poor ol' shrunk-down country boy."

Anything to occupy the time. Sometimes they sat with their backs against trees in front row seats to watch the spectacle of air dogfights over Leyte. One afternoon a Zero broke loose and dived for the squad tent occupied by Cox, Smith, and Kittleson. All three were sitting on their cots inside, watching the fight through the tent opening. They heard the engine start to rev. Kittleson was nearest the foxhole dug just outside the tent. He made a leap for it—and landed on *top* of Cox and Smith. They laughed about it the rest of the day.

The war had to be winding down. Kittleson told the others that when he was detailed with a Jeep to escort a Japanese POW, an officer, from inland to 6th Army's G-2, the Jap's eyes actually bulged when he saw the tanks, trucks, aircraft, and mountains of other war materiel stockpiled at the airfield. Kittleson recognized by the guy's face that he knew the war was lost too; he let his chin fall on his chest and slowly shook his head, as if in resigned acceptance of the inevitable.

Strange, Kittleson thought, how all this could be considered *boring*. It revealed a remarkable human resiliency that the extraordinary could become the mundane. He actually longed for action.

November 2. Jap planes strafed airstrip, set gasoline drums afire. Huge fire, burned eight hours. Four Zeros downed by P38s and AA units.

November 10. Got off *Wachapreague*. Went to 6th Army HQ. Bombers over. Nice show.

November 15. Landed Thompson's Team on Poro Island, south of Ormoc Bay. PTs in enemy waters at night. Plane over, flashed on its lights. Scared as hell.

December 12. Team ordered to 6th Army to guard General Kreuger. Left camp 0830, arrived 6th Army 1130. Fixed Scout tent. Cleaned Tommy.

December 13. Idle. Cleaned tent. One Jap plane over.

On Christmas Day, all nine Alamo Scout teams currently in operation gathered for Christmas dinner at the A.S.T.C., which had moved to Abuyog on Leyte. It was the first time all the Scouts had been together in one place. They bowed their heads in the mess tent while a chaplain offered a prayer of thanks for their incredible good fortune. Eleven months and 49 behind-enemy-lines missions after the birth of General Kreuger's idea, and still they had lost not a single man to enemy action.

"How long can it last?" Cox solemnly wondered.

CHAPTER 19

On 9 January 1945, 6th Army invaded Luzon. Kittleson realized, even from his limited GI perspective, that he was living in historical times. Someday he would want to remember how it was.

January 1. Packed equipment. All set for invasion of Luzon. Extra ammo, heavily loaded 300 rounds Tommy gun ammo.

January 2. Loaded on LCI. Spent day in harbor. Part of 6th Ranger Battalion aboard.

January 3. Spent day in San Pedro Bay. Read book, played hearts.

January 4. Left San Pedro Bay. At 1045 convoy well out in bay. Joined another section of invasion force. Two flattops sending out planes.

January 5. Passed through Surigao Strait. Weather sunny and clear. Flattops still sending out patrol planes. Won five pesos on bet with Lt. Nellist.

January 7. Passed through Mindoro Strait. Enter S. China Sea.

January 8. Ready to leave ship (LCI-613). Seen nine aircraft carriers.

January 9. Jap planes overhead. Antiaircraft fire. D-Day on Luzon. Laid in Lingayen Gulf. Seen the bombardment troops capture airstrip in 20 minutes. Seen cruisers, battleships *California* and *W. Virginia.*

January 10. Went ashore 1500, spent night on beach. Seen one Jap plane shot down. Heavy arty firing.

January 15. Overseas one year today. Went swimming with Lt. Nellist, Cox, Wismer.

To Kittleson, it appeared Luzon would become more of Leyte: hanging around waiting for something to happen. General Kreuger moved 6th Army headquarters ashore in the Lingayen Gulf region while his assault troops fought their way into the interior toward Manila. Alamo Scouts erected their squad tents at the edge of the palms on the opposite end of the tent street from HQ.

Artillery continued booming steadily in the background and warplanes buzzed overhead. The beach was littered with the debris and materiel of invasion, while troop and transport ships kept busy vomiting even more ashore. Lieutenant Nellist came long-legging between the rows of tents. His men were settling in after morning mess. Cleaning weapons, conducting equipment maintenance. Routine, boring. Wismer always commented that an army really *didn't* travel on beans and bullets; it moved on chicken shit.

"Mission alert," Nellist called out. His team gathered around.

"It's about time," Wismer said, self-consciously rubbing the minute scars left on his skinny body when the Jap bomb had ripped into *Sea Bat.* "Where we going, sir?"

"General Kreuger will give the briefing in one hour."

"General Kreuger *himself?*" Kittleson asked.

The men looked at each other, suddenly grown tense.

"General Kreuger himself," Nellist confirmed. "Travel light. Be ready."

It must be one *hell* of an important mission if the general personally was to deliver the briefing. No one could ever remember it happening before.

When the seven silent men gathered on the sand in front of the command tent, they heard chatter from radio nets inside and the confusion of men occupied with controlling a war. General Kreuger walked out. He was at least sixty years old, but Kittleson thought he looked much older lately. Already lean and gray, he looked almost gaunt these days and the hollows in his cheeks were fuzzed with white hair. Rumor had it that MacArthur was on his ass for not moving fast enough toward Manila. MacArthur wanted to rush right up to Manila and through it, kicking Jap butt all the way, and free the POWs before the Japanese executed them. He figured he owed the POWs that much for the fight they had put up before Bataan fell.

"You men will be doing more this time than guarding a poor, old, tired general." Kreuger's attempt at humor fell flat. He got right to the briefing.

The Japanese, he said crisply, had formed a defensive line from San Jose south to Urdaneta. They had installed an extensive track-mounted artillery network in the mountain caves east of San Jose. The big guns were camouflaged by retractable doors painted to look like the mountainside. Doors opened, guns rolled out on rails, fired, then were jerked back inside before their locations could be pinpointed.

"Our troops can't get across the Rosario Road because of the Japs' big guns in the mountains," General Kreuger said. "It's your job to locate those guns so our planes and artillery can knock them out."

He paused to look around the silent half-circle of tanned young faces.

"I won't bullshit you fellas. You know that. There's a fifty-fifty chance you won't make it. And even if you do get in—only an act of God is going to get you out."

Part of the agreement between General Kreuger and his Alamo Scouts was that they could refuse any mission. They had to be, unquestionably, volunteers in the true sense of the word. Nellist looked at his men. They looked back at him. It wasn't their style to refuse.

"When do we leave, sir?" Nellist asked.

"Tonight."

CHAPTER 20

The LCM landing craft dropped its gate as soon as its flat keel ground on sands in the shallow offshore shoals. No rubber boats this trip.

"Into the water," Nellist hissed, his figure an indistinct shadow in the big boat's darkness. "We're wading in."

"That wasn't on my ticket," Wismer bitched. "I want a refund."

"Tell it to the War Department. Get in the water."

Cox was first in; the calm water reached above his knees. It swirled around Kittleson's and Siason's waists. The water felt warm in the night, and it was black. It stretched, fluid and undulating slightly, for nearly four hundred yards toward a blacker rise of land like a wide, darker ink mark inscribed on ink. There was not a pinprick of light anywhere except for the cold and distant stars above. A farmer's dog yapped somewhere. Yap! Yap! Yap!

When the team was in the water, the LCM's engines revved and it backed off and vanished into the night. There were no other sounds except those of the mutt barking and the riffling of water around the Scouts' legs as they plunged toward the beach. Seven GIs launched into the jungle teeming with enemy soldiers. Kittleson's imagination felt Jap eyes glaring at him from the approaching foliage. He turned it off and felt his other senses sharpening the way they always did when he slipped through enemy lines. At such times it was like he saw things, smelled things, heard and *felt* things that lay beyond his experiences.

It was not like the war ended merely because one small element required stealth. The war slowed down at night, but it seldom ceased. Suddenly, some navy gunner responding to a request from nervous troops on the island fired a flare high into the black sky. It burst almost directly above the Scouts and lit up a portion of Lingayen Gulf like a miniature sun. The Scouts stood out like tree stumps in its strange flickering glow. It brought out in static relief the outlines of distant ships riding in the Gulf.

Nellist slashed a hand. "*Down!*"

They sank into the surf up to their chins, holding their weapons at eye level to keep them dry. Kittleson braced himself for the expected barrage of gunfire. His heart thumped in the water hard enough to be picked up by sonar. Surely they had been seen.

An eternity seemed to pass before the little sun, hissing, arced toward the watery horizon and burned itself out. The world plunged back into darkness. It took another minute or so before the Scouts regained their equilibrium and night vision. Wismer later commented that he thought he had pissed his pants, but he couldn't be sure because he was wet anyhow.

The Jap guns lay in the mountains three or four miles inland. No Allied troops had yet penetrated this part of the island. Kittleson took point with his Tommy once they waded onto dry sand and entered the forest. Nellist intended moving fast for most of the night in order to have the daylight for maneuvering into position for observing the following night. *All* they had to do was avoid contact and wend their way through Jap patrols, observation points, and enemy strongholds.

Japs didn't move around much in the jungle at night. For that matter, neither did Americans.

After an hour or so of blindly going through forest that reached out to trip them with its many arms and stranglers, they came onto a wide footpath. After a moment's whispered discussion, Nellist decided to take it—to trade caution for time.

The path widened. Kittleson pointed out that weeds and grass grew up in it, indicating that it hadn't been used in a while. It led in the general direction of a village called Rawis, which the map showed to be on National Highway 3 at the foot of the mountains. The Jap guns on the tall ridges above had range and observation over most of the valley and shoreline of the Lingayen Gulf, including, seven or eight miles away, the vital Rosario Road required by 6th Army for rapid movement of troops toward Manila.

Kittleson almost blundered into the first nipa hut before he saw it. He immediately fell to one knee. He was close enough to the hut to reach out and touch it. Unable to see his danger signal, the others stumbled into each other like a line of falling dominos.

Jesus.

Nellist knelt next to his little pointman with his hand resting lightly on Kittleson's shoulder for nearly a half-hour, listening. Dogs would have been barking had the village been occupied; instead, there was not a sound, not a light or a voice to suggest it was inhabited. The residents must have all moved out—or been executed—when the Japs had come.

Kittleson led the way cautiously through the little ghost village. The team spaced itself out, then accordioned close once they reached the other side. Here, the pathway widened into an actual road. Weeds grew up through the gravel, affirming that it also hadn't been utilized much in recent weeks. The lieutenant pulled the team into the forest for a quick conference around the map. Although officers commanded, every Scout contributed to decisions made behind enemy lines. After all, each man's life was equally at stake.

From the map, it appeared the unused road they were on led toward a junction with Highway 3 at the little hamlet of Rawis. They had been climbing steadily since the beach. That and the fact that the forest was thinning and becoming more scrubby suggested they were gaining altitude. They couldn't yet see the mountains, but they probably would when day broke. Nellist consulted his watch.

"We have about three hours until dawn," he whispered. "Let's hole up here for the rest of the night. If those guns are up there, the Japs'll have patrols and outposts everywhere."

So far they had been lucky. Blundering into the abandoned village had been like a wakeup call. What if the Japs had had a machine gun nest set up in it?

First light found the team saddled up and moving stealthily up the road. Clouds were low and full and it looked like rain, but hadn't rained yet. There were puddles in the road from a day or so ago. Japs wore split-toed boots that were supposed to provide them better footing and did give them a distinctive track. None of their tracks were in the mud.

As the Scouts neared Rawis, they split into two elements. Nellist, Cox, and Kittleson took one side of the road, marching in the woods back from it, while Andy Smith, Siason, Asis, and Wismer humped the other side. It was still early; the sun had not yet burned the clouds off the rising mountains ahead. Smith flashed a hand warning. Everyone dropped and froze in place. It was called *dominoing*.

From across the road, lying in bushes, Sergeant Smith drew the edge of his palm slowly across his throat. *Enemy.* He pointed up the road where it bent to the right out of sight of Nellist's element. Nellist pulled a finger at his little pointman and then up the road. No further conversation was needed. Kittleson shucked his pack and disappeared into the woods ahead on the high side of the road.

Testing every step for the crack of a twig or the rustle of dry leaves, he proceeded through thick cover until he caught sight of a bridge, then went to all fours and crawled the rest of the way. The terrain rose to either side of the weeded road and then sloped off so that Kittleson found himself concealed in a patch of rhododendrons looking down upon the bridge.

It was a short concrete bridge with steel railings spanning a shallow streambed with only a trickle of water running in it. One hundred yards or so beyond rose the thatched or tinned roofs of Rawis. An occasional pastel wall—pink or blue or yellow—glimmered through the forest. The town this early remained in the shadows of the rugged escarpment that lifted out of the earth a mile or so farther on.

A truck or light tank rumbled past on the other side of Rawis: National Highway 3.

All this was caught by Kittleson's peripheral senses; his instincts converged upon the bridge itself and the Japanese sentries there. After watching for a few minutes, he counted three Japs. They had a small breakfast fire going in the stream bed. One stood near it fully uniformed with his rifle resting casually on one shoulder while he drank tea or something from a tin cup. The other two, chatting, walked up onto the bridge and leaned their weapons against the railing while they shared a morning cigarette. They giggled and goosed each other and kept leering down the road toward the town, undoubtedly talking about girls—just like GIs.

There was a new thatched hut on the other side of the draw, probably quarters for the sentries. Kittleson studied it until he was reasonably certain there was no one else. From previous experience, he assumed these particular Nips were probably alone in the area. Japanese rarely quartered in the villages; they found it too hard to maintain security and they trusted Filipinos less than Filipinos trusted them. However, they routinely left sentries to guard bridges, roadblocks, and other key features.

The Scout made his way back to report to the lieutenant.

"Maybe we can take a prisoner," Nellist decided. "They'll know about the guns."

The two elements closed on the sentries. Smith and his band were to take care of the two jokesters on the bridge while Nellist, Kittleson, and Cox attempted to sneak up on the tea drinker and snatch him alive. They crept up to the rhododendron bushes and looked down. The guy was only about thirty yards away and his entire attention seemed focused on his tin cup. He had a broad, yellow face. He was young, but he looked old. Kittleson almost felt sorry for him.

The two clowns on the bridge were still goosing and giggling.

Their day was about to blow up in their faces.

The three Scouts took aim on their expected prisoner.

"*Surrender!*" Nellist shouted in Japanese. It was one of the few Japanese words he knew.

At that same moment, Smith and his bunch opened up on their targets. Carbines cracked sharply in unison. One of the Japs crumpled where he stood. The other toppled over the railing and landed hard and still on the washed stones below.

The tea drinker made the mistake of thinking he had a chance. Japs were a suicidal lot, especially as the war turned against them. He barely had time to flip his rifle off his shoulder before Nellist's deep-throated Garand spat once. The .30-caliber slug knocked him back three steps before he sat down with his legs straight out in front. He dropped his weapon, lay slowly down next to it, coughing blood, and died.

"Shit," Nellist said. "Kit, take security on the other side of the bridge. We'll take care of the bodies."

Enough adrenaline was pumping through his veins to run a fire hose. Kittleson darted out onto the road and across the bridge, casting a quick look at the dead man. Smith and Asis ran out from their positions. Siason was hauling ass across the streambed to post security on his side of the road. Wismer stumbled on the hill and ploughed down it on his face the rest of the way to the road.

"Grab the stiffs and drag them up in the woods," Nellist shouted. "Hide them."

The Japs would think their sentries had deserted or were off somewhere with native girls. It would buy time if their absence was discovered but their bodies were not.

Kittleson threw himself into a shallow ditch to block the

bridge from any troops in the town. To his amazement, the first life he saw wasn't a Jap. It was a carabao, a black water buffalo, and ahead of it an old guy in ragged shorts pedaling a rust-red bicycle as fast as it would go. The carabao seemed to be chasing the bicyclist until the Scout, to his further astonishment, saw that *chasing the carabao* were all or most of the villagers in town.

"*Americans! Americans!*" they chorused in English gone frantic. "*Americans come! Liberators!*"

How the hell did they know that so fast?

Celebrating Filipinos mobbed the GIs and swamped the bridge to help drag off the Jap corpses. It was their idea to toss the cadavers into an old water well where they likely would go unnoticed for years. Kittleson felt like the Pied Piper. Women and girls crowded around to hug or at least touch them. Somebody passed out flower garlands. Most Filipinos had grown an intense hatred for the Japanese during the occupation.

"We've got to get out of here," Lieutenant Nellist said, worried, hurriedly leading his men through Rawis at the head of a growing entourage of festive natives looking for a reason to party.

"Ain't it great being like a movie star?" quipped witty Willie Wismer with a big grin flashed in the direction of one of the cuter girls with a colorful sarong and a gardenia behind one ear.

"She was probably sleeping with them Japs last night," Smith said.

"Let bygones be bygones, I always say. Right, honey?"

By making shooing motions and frowning, Nellist finally convinced the townspeople that their noisy reception endangered the Scouts' lives. The old man on the rusty bicycle parked it across the road and stood in front of it with his palms out. When the people were quiet, Asis the Filipino told them to return to their homes, *please?*, and not to speak of what they had witnessed.

"MacArthur returns?" asked a woman.

"He's not far away," Asis assured her.

"*MacArthur returns!*" the woman shouted, dancing around and around. Then everyone cheered and shouted, "*MacArthur returns!*" While they were thus occupied, Nellist Team slipped away into the jungle.

CHAPTER 21

The twilight of dusk arrived quickly, as it always did near the equator. Kittleson and Cox fell back periodically during the march to brush out their backtrail and scout for trackers. As they climbed into the foothills, it became easier to find vantage points from which to glass the lowlands between the mountains and Leyte Gulf. The mountains rose in craggy steps. Thick jungle with bare gray stone containing dark places that were probably limestone caves. A dirt road hogbacked up from Highway 3. Several times the Scouts watched enemy convoys on the road and on the highway—Howitzers, troops on trucks, and tanks rumbling along behind. None of them turned off into Rawis, which meant the Japs still didn't know about their dead sentries and the GI patrol in their midst.

Kittleson scouted out a thickly wooded ridge that offered both a view of Rawis now far below in the valley and a long expanse of mountain frontage. Somewhere up there hid the monstrous 240mm Jap guns that had clotted 6th Army's advance along Rosario Road. They had to be found and destroyed. Using the village as one point, the Scouts could compass-triangulate the guns' location, once they fired, to within a few yards—close enough for air strikes or naval guns to collapse the mountain on the Jap gunners' heads.

They burrowed in to wait. Each man secretly hoped the guns fired tonight. It meant death for GIs somewhere, but the guns had to fire before they could be pinpointed. The longer the Scouts stayed behind Japanese lines, the greater their chances of being discovered.

"Have you prayed?" Cox asked Kittleson.

"Yes," replied the devout little farmer.

"Good."

They hadn't long to wait. Shortly after full nightfall, a stabbing flash of light streaked from the mountain about three-quarters of a mile away but up high, near the crest. Seconds later, thunder from the discharge reverberated down the valley, rattling dry leaves and stirring up a hot little wind. It was one hell of a gun. The big shell passed over with the sound of a Jeep being thrown at supersonic speed. It kept shrieking until it went out of earshot.

"Christ, have mercy!" Cox breathed in hushed awe.

Willie Wismer grasped his head with both hands. "Them poor bastards down range."

Kittleson crawled over to the lieutenant. "Did you get it?"

"I don't know. You?"

"See that little jut there, over to the right of that light spot? I think it came from there."

"Everybody," Nellist requested, "keep watching."

An hour later, the gun fired once more. One shot. That made it difficult to find and target. Nellist triangulated a grid location. They waited again to confirm his figures.

The gun fired about once every hour or so. Lightning, thunder, and the lightning bolt howling across the sky.

"One gun," Nellist declared. "*One* goddamned gun is holding up the whole United States Army."

It stopped firing about midnight. Nellist made everyone memorize its grid location. If only one of them made it back, it would be enough. They hadn't brought a radio; too heavy and awkward for the humping they had to do.

"I think we got all we need," the lieutenant said. "Saddle up. I bought us round-trip tickets. Let's use them."

"Sir! I got some Scouts coming through the north line. They've been out with the Japs three days. They don't know today's password. They say they have urgent information."

The speaker in his battalion's command post was a company commander from the 158th Regimental Combat Team, which manned revetments to the north. It was his position Nellist Team approached after humping out of the mountains, crossing Lingayen Gulf in native dugout canoes and skirting through the jungle until they found friendlies.

Sometimes the most hazardous part of long-range patrolling behind enemy lines was reentering friendly lines. GIs had a tendency, with good cause, to be loose on their triggers. Lieutenant Nellist halted his Scouts out of range while they mulled over the best way to come home. Simply shouting in English didn't always work; Japs did that all the time as a ruse or diversion.

Nellist studied Cox for a moment. He had an idea. The guy had blond hair bleached even lighter by the tropical sun and was at least a foot taller than the average Jap.

"Take off your shirt, Cox."

Cox looked bewildered, but he stripped. While his face, neck, and hands up to the elbows were burned and darkened by the relentless sun, his broad chest and flat belly were so pale they might have glowed in moonlight. The lieutenant grinned.

"No," Cox protested, catching on.

"Who else?" Nellist asked. "No one would ever mistake *you* for a Jap unless he was blind."

That was how the company commander from the 158th encountered the returning Scouts: Cox walking along in full view, naked and pale from waist to neck, waving his shirt over his head and calling out, "I'm an American! I'm an American!"

No shots were fired.

It didn't take reports of the Scouts' return long to reach

6th Army HQ and General Kreuger. The lean old man nodded his head and looked pleased. "My Alamo Scouts always come back," he boasted. "I can send them anywhere—any *damned* where—and know they'll accomplish their mission."

The next day, 43d Division artillery permanently silenced the death thunder in the mountains, opening up Rosario Road and clearing another obstacle in MacArthur's race to retake the Philippines and liberate the few survivors of those brave men left behind to fight on Bataan in the early months of the war.

CHAPTER 22

A thin GI major in a worn uniform, riding an even thinner and more travel-weary bay horse, halted his mount at the edge of 6th Army HQ near Calasio south of Lingayen Gulf on the afternoon of 26 January 1945.

"Which way to HQ?" he asked.

Corporal Willie Wismer, on stand down with his team after the Big Japanese Gun mission, pointed him in the right direction, then stood with Kittleson and Cox and watched him walk his horse through the middle of the tent city blistering amidst rocks, tall grass, and dust. General Kreuger's headquarters tents were located on the far side.

"I wonder who that is?" Kittleson mused.

"Don't you know nothing, private?" Wismer joked. "Don't you recognize the most famous American guerrilla chief in the South Pacific?"

"*That's* Major Lapham?" Cox said, his eyes widening.

Wismer always seemed to know such things.

Major Bob Lapham had urged his spent horse through thirty miles of Jap-infested terrain to bring crucial information about the Bataan Death March survivors at Cabanatuan.

He tethered his horse to a palm and declined food and water. He was in a hurry.

"Take care of my pony," he requested, and was then escorted to the tent of Colonel Horton White, General Kreuger's intelligence chief.

"Sir," he began intensely without preliminaries, "there is real danger, *imminent* danger, that the prisoners at Cabanatuan will be massacred out of vengeance when our units start approaching the camp."

Lapham, now twenty-four years old, was an Iowan of the same sturdy northern stock that had produced Galen "Kit" Kittleson. His reputation had built a legend that transcended the Philippines and reached all the way back to Washington.

During early 1942 when the Battling Bastards of Bataan were being systematically pounded and starved into submission, Lieutenant Robert W. Lapham and thirty-five other American GIs volunteered to infiltrate Jap lines, make their way north through fifty miles of enemy country, and blow up as many Japanese aircraft as possible at Clark Field. Bataan surrendered when they were only ten miles from their target. The small combat force split up to escape and evade and headed for the hills.

Lapham made his way to Nueva Ecija Province where the Cabanatuan POW camp was soon to be located. He began recruiting guerrillas from the Filipino natives. Promoted to major by the U.S. War Department, he eventually commanded a guerrilla force numbering more than two thousand. His guerrillas and other guerrilla bands, many of which were also led by Americans, continued to fight against the occupying Japanese army while awaiting MacArthur's return.

The fight was largely psychological warfare at first. The Philippine Guerrilla Postal Service printed thousands of *I Shall Return* stamps used by partisans in rural regions as letter postage. The same slogan—*I Shall Return*—mysteriously appeared painted on walls and billboards and even on Japanese trucks and troop trains. Sheets of paper bearing nothing but the slogan turned up stuck in Japanese military files.

The underground war on Luzon gradually moved into bloody conflict as Allied submarines began slipping in weapons and ammunition. Throughout the nearly three years of his fight, Major Lapham possessed a burning passion to liberate the American POWs at Cabanatuan. He had a number of friends and acquaintances inside the camp; many had already died and now resided in the makeshift cemetery outside the wire.

He and his guerrillas kept the camp under constant surveillance, looking for an opportunity. They set up elaborate underground systems by which to communicate with the prisoners. They smuggled in small amounts of food, along with a weapon now and then to add to the POWs' stockpile for an eventual prison break.

But mostly they waited, growing increasingly frustrated at missed opportunities.

During the spring of 1944, months before MacArthur's return, Lapham and some of his partisans met the U.S. submarine *Nautilus* to offload smuggled munitions at Debut Bay, halfway up the Luzon coast and about fifty miles east of Cabanatuan. It occurred to him that if *Nautilus* could navigate into Debut Bay, why couldn't a small fleet of submarines slip in under nightfall to carry away any American POWs freed from Cabanatuan? He drew up a preliminary plan for a raid to free the POWs, then estimated to number about three thousand, and sent it to General MacArthur.

MacArthur's headquarters gave it a thumbs down. Granted that a raid succeeded, MacArthur pointed out, how would the ill, feeble, and emaciated POWs be able to cross fifty miles of towering Sierra Madre Mountains on foot to reach Debut Bay?

"The Japs would easily catch up and massacre the lot of them," the general said. "I can't let that happen."

"If we wait much longer," Lapham argued, "we'll be able to rescue what's left in one carabao cart."

Lapham called for rescue again and again. Each time his plan was turned down as too risky for the POWs.

He thought an ideal time for attacking the camp would be

when MacArthur landed on Luzon. The Japs would be too busy fighting off the invasion to worry about a few hundred half-skeletons about to dry up and blow away over the grasslands of central Luzon. Living skeletons were all that remained by that time; as soon as it looked like the Americans were about to land on Luzon, the Tokyo high command ordered all American prisoners in the Philippines be shipped to Japan as rapidly as possible. Only those who could not walk or work were left behind.

Now, two weeks and four days after the invasion of Lingayen Gulf, Colonel Horton White stood up and looked at his visitor who had ridden so hard on horseback to enter another plea for the American POWs' rescue. He walked to a map on the wall and located with his finger the town of Guimba, 6th Army's most forward position. It was twenty-five miles northwest of the prison camp. U.S. mechanized reconnaissance units had rolled into the town only that morning shortly after daybreak. Barrios housing Japanese soldiers in the town of Cabanatuan four miles away from the POW stockade were being dive-bombed.

Guimba wasn't much, but it *was* a toehold. American 6th Army troops were still advancing toward it as part of their lightning bolt strike for Manila. They were snaking fitfully along a few dirt roads and paths edged by thick jungle. A standard GI joke went: "The front is thirty feet wide and thirty miles long."

"What's the enemy situation around the camp?" White asked.

Lapham went to the map and pointed out locations as he spoke. "There are approximately nine thousand Japs in the area either withdrawing toward the mountains or establishing defensive positions. The road in front of the prison camp is heavily traveled by tanks and vehicles. There are five thousand Japs in and around the town of Cabanatuan and a strong enemy force bivouacked here along the Cabu River less than a mile northeast of camp. They use the camp as a stopover, a way station. At any given time there may be between one hundred and three hundred Japs inside the compound."

Colonel White sighed deeply. He let out an explosive breath.

"I understand," Major Lapham agreed. "It looks impossible. But it's not. They *must* be rescued. We owe it to them to at least make the effort."

As usual, Willie Wismer picked up the news first from somewhere. He burst into Kittleson's squad tent.

"I know where we're going next," he blurted out. "You boys remember the Bataan Death March? Kit, you weren't even out of high school then."

CHAPTER 23

Morale inside the Cabanatuan hellhole rose and fell according to how the fortunes of war were perceived through snatches of news infiltrated into the camp. Signs appeared as early as September 1944 that MacArthur and the Allies were coming. Sergeant Bill Seckinger and several other prisoners were in the courtyard getting water from the one trickling spigot when the roar of aircraft engines startled them. Seckinger looked up. He saw two airplanes in a fierce dogfight. One was a Jap Zero. He didn't recognize the other one. It was an American Hellcat fighter, but America hadn't had Hellcats at the time of Seckinger's capture.

The Hellcat dived and got hot on the Jap's ass. Puffs of smoke trailed the U.S. Navy plane as it opened up with its machine guns. The Zero wavered. One wing broke up and disintegrated in the sky. The plane corkscrewed into the side of a mountain, exploding.

Every POW in the camp shambled outdoors and cheered. That one episode was enough to shoot hope through the top of the morale thermometer. Inmates speculated endlessly over how long it would be before Americans came roaring across the plains. Right in the nick of time, just like the cavalry of the Old West.

After that, waves of Hellcats filled the skies on their way to raid inland enemy targets. Jap guards warned the prisoners to remain inside. But even beatings with rifle butts and sticks failed to prevent the ecstatic POWs from rushing outside to wave pieces of clothing.

A happy slogan raced through camp: *Thanksgiving Turkey in Albuquerque!*

Using a patchwork radio built from pieces smuggled in by Major Lapham's guerrillas and underground, POWs heard through its static about MacArthur's landing on Leyte, then on Mindoro. He was coming. *He was coming.*

But he had better hurry: Only about 530 prisoners celebrated Christmas behind the wire, and the number dwindled daily. Their elation also faded as fear increased that their nervous guards would kill them rather than permit the Americans to free them. They secretly devised knives and clubs to defend themselves. Sergeant Seckinger had 20 rounds of .45-caliber ammunition buried—but no pistol with which to fire it.

"We'll at least take *some* of the bastards with us when we go," POWs vowed.

Major Lapham received a desperate message sent out of the prison through underground contacts: *The Japs fear we will attempt a mass breakout. They may kill us.*

On 6 January 1945, the POWs didn't know what to think when the camp commander came out at morning prisoner formation and roll call to announce that henceforth the camp was no longer considered an internment facility. It was a *hospital.* Then, even more astonishing, most of the Jap guards formed up and marched out the front gate and down the road.

None of this meant the POWs were free to go. To begin with, over half the men were so feeble they couldn't walk across the courtyard without help. The rest suffered from gangrene and an entire array of tropical diseases. Many am-

putees were missing one or more limbs. Ironically, with
their keepers gone, these Bataan survivors discovered disease, malnutrition, and physical feebleness to be even more
effective jailers. Besides, they were still in enemy-occupied
Luzon. Outside the fences, they were ready prey for venge-
ful Japanese troops.

Also, just because the guards fled did not mean the camp
was unoccupied. Thousands of Japanese soldiers withdrawing northwest toward the mountains around Bagnio passed
by on the road outside the front gate. Dust stirred up by
marching Jap feet, tank tracks, and vehicle tires rose in
choking clouds. Troops stayed nights in the camp. There
were always sentries to protect the troops and prevent the
American "patients" from leaving. POWs lived in constant
fear that the Japanese would go into a rage, turn on them,
and massacre everyone.

Still, in many ways, the Americans were better off than
they had been previously. The guards had departed in such
haste that they left behind cases of rice, sugar, beans, corn,
and even milk. POWs walked, hobbled, and crawled to the
abandoned Jap side of the compound to steal the food and
supplies left behind.

Even more surprising, most of the Jap troops who subse-
quently passed through avoided the prisoners as though they
were afflicted with plague. A dirt road running through the
camp from the front gate to the back divided it into two sections. Japs used facilities on one side of the road; the POWs
isolated themselves on the other side.

"It's fantastic," exclaimed Sergeant Seckinger in disbe-
lief. "The same kind of Japs who have starved and beaten
and murdered us through two years and nine months of hell
are now ignoring us."

Prisoners grew bolder in light of the Japanese disinterest
in them. Three days after the Lingayen landings, they spotted carabao in a dust wallow on the other side of the road.
Several of the less-debilitated GIs organized a midnight raid
to butcher them. Although jittery that they might be shot for
attempting to escape, they nonetheless marched boldly out

the gate carrying empty litters upon which to bring back the meat. With the guards gone, what little food provided by the Japs had been discontinued.

The Jap sentries merely stared, unsure how to react. The GIs snapped them a sharp salute and kept moving. They butchered two carabao using improvised knives, loaded the fresh meat on litters, and returned through the gate.

"Halt!" one of the Japs shouted.

The men froze.

The sentry walked up and, in English, said, "I am starving please. May I have please a little of the meat?"

He was given a large portion. When the GIs reached the POW kitchen, they dropped to their knees and said a prayer. All knew, deep down, that it was only a matter of time before the Japanese grew weary of their presence.

CHAPTER 24

It seemed the entire Allied army was advancing down the one single narrow road that led to Guimba and Manila beyond. The invasion of Leyte began in the rainy season; the weather cleared by the time of the Luzon invasion. Now in that January of 1945 the dry months were beginning and tanks, trucks, and marching feet kicked up gigantic clouds of dust that hung in the air like storm clouds and threatened to suffocate the men of Nellist and Rounsaville Teams. The thirteen Scouts—a baker's dozen, Wismer quipped—held onto the slatted sides of the two-and-a-half-ton troop truck and coughed and hacked at the dust swirling underneath the tarp with them. The truck weaved and rattled violently as the driver threaded his way through traffic toward Guimba. Lieutenant Jack Dove sat up in the cab with him.

Hellcats zoomed overhead and the crumping sound of bombs exploding in the distance told of air strikes against retreating enemy forces.

"Give 'em hell, boys," Wismer cheered, looking up.

The comment failed to elicit the usual response. Each silent Scout was acutely aware that he was embarking upon one of the war's most perilous and spectacular operations.

They were heavily armed for it. Aside from his personal combat weapon, each soldier carried a .45 pistol and spare clips, three hand grenades, extra bandoleers of cartridges, and a trench knife. PFC Kittleson had his Tommy gun. Action from New Guinea to the Philippines had revealed to him Tommy's particular effectiveness for close-in jungle fighting.

Wismer, as usual, had been right about the team's next mission. No one thought it a coincidence that Lieutenants Nellist, Dove, and Rounsaville were summoned to Colonel Horton White's tent the day after Major Lapham's visit. The longer the officers stayed gone, the greater tension built in the Scout section of the bivouac area. Pontiac Vaquilar, the ex-con from Rounsaville Team, eased down the way and casually squatted between Wismer and Tom Siason. Subdued as always, Vaquilar drew geometric figures on the ground with a stick.

Alfonso and Frank Fox ambled down. Soon, both teams hunkered in the dust in Nellist's area. They kept glancing toward the long headquarters tents at the other end of the street.

"Consider this a mission alert," Nellist had barked before leaving, and that was all any of them knew so far.

Kittleson got his gear ready, laying it out on his cot. Then he came outside the tent to write a letter to Darlene. Correspondence between him and his hometown pen pal had gradually and perhaps inevitably grown more personal with time. They were now exchanging expectations about the things they would do *together* after the war.

Beyond the row of tents at the edge of the forest, latrine orderlies were dumping used engine oil into the waste pits and burning them out. Black smoke oozed disgusting odors.

"Smells like *shit*," Wismer complained, making a face.

Gilbert Cox looked up. "It *is* shit."

"Doesn't any of this ever bother you?" Wismer demanded of Kittleson, not referring to the stench from the burning latrines.

"You do what you have to do," Kit said.

Willie chuckled. "The unflappable PFC Kittleson." It was a compliment.

Kittleson finished his letter. He experienced a pang of homesickness as he slipped it into an envelope left unsealed for the censor.

"It's chow time," he said presently, and stood up.

They walked in a dusty group to the chow tent. They ate and speculated some more, and when they returned the officers were back.

Nellist's lean face looked somber through the sweat-caked mud. His expression was grim, but it also showed a trace of pride. They were tasked with an important mission, he said.

"We're going twenty-five miles inside Jap lines to rescue five hundred GIs being held at the Cabanatuan POW camp. Lieutenant Rounsaville's Team and ours, along with Charley Company from the 6th Ranger Battalion and two companies of Major Lapham's guerrillas, are going to conduct the raid. Oransbari was a cakewalk compared to this. There are probably three thousand Japs in the immediate area. Headquarters figures the goddamned Japs may murder all the prisoners unless we can get 'em out. Be ready to move out at 1630 hours this afternoon to our forward positions in Guimba."

Even Willie Wismer, who almost always had something to say, fell quiet at the enormity of it. Never before in American history had U.S. soldiers been called upon to rescue such a large number of POWs from so deep inside enemy territory. Everyone had to be in position to kick off the raid at 1930 hours—7:30 P.M.—day after tomorrow, 29 January. Exactly 53 hours away.

"Guerrillas tell us there'll be about 250 Japs inside the camp," Nellist went on. "We have to break inside quick. We're bringing out every GI, even if we have to carry them on our backs. Colonel Henry Mucci, commander of 6th Ranger Battalion, is overall commander of the operation. He told me and I'll tell you: This is another strictly volunteer mission. You can decline to go and no one is going to question your guts and dedication. So speak up now."

No one stirred. Put that way, how could anyone refuse? Kittleson stood up and stretched himself to his full five-four. He slowly lighted a cigarette. His heart was pounding when he spoke for the team.

"If I was in that camp, I'd sure hope there'd be volunteers to come get me."

Dusk had not yet come when the truck hauling Nellist and Rounsaville Teams halted in a grove of trees outside Guimba. Guimba was little more than a cluster of nipa huts and tin-roofed buildings clotted at a bend of the road. Some of the buildings were painted in Spanish pastels, but it had been a long war and the pastels were fading. Rice paddies and other agriculture lay beyond in a valley. An American cavalry outfit was spread out among the huts, taking a breather and waiting for further orders. Everything beyond this point was Indian country.

Major Lapham and one of his guerrilla chiefs who spoke English greeted the Scout officers. Nellist, Rounsaville, and Dove accompanied them to one of the huts surrounded by guerrillas napping or eating. There was a big iron pot on a fire outside. While the officers conferred inside, the teams ate a meal of black beans and rice. Enlisted men, especially privates, seldom shared in mission planning. As Wismer always joked, privates were legs and balls, officers were brains.

Nellist came out of the hut. "Boys, get some sleep if you can. It's gonna be a long night."

Cox and Kittleson picked out a building to hold up with their backs. Why walk when you could stand, stand when you could sit, sit when you could sleep? It was the infantryman's credo. Kittleson pulled his patrol cap low over his eyes.

"I'm too nervous to sleep," Cox said.

Kittleson inhaled deeply and was soon snoring lightly, the Tommy gun across his thighs.

CHAPTER 25

It was 9:00 P.M. and a half-moon drove black shadows across the stubble of dry rice fields as thirteen Scouts and about fifty of Major Lapham's guerrillas set out from Guimba. Lieutenant Dove stayed behind with Lapham to help coordinate the different elements of the raid's movements. Colonel Mucci and his Rangers were exactly twenty-four hours behind the Scouts. The Scouts and guerrillas would lead the way to establish advance surveillance on the prison camp.

"I'll see you fellas tomorrow," Dove said with his cavalier Hollywood grin.

As the Scouts' most-trusted pointman, Kittleson took the lead along with two of the Filipino guerrillas who knew the way to the village of Balincarin, a twenty-four-mile forced march away. Most of the distance, Kittleson had been told, lay over harvested rice fields, now dry, or through prairies of tall Kunai and cogon grasses. They had to cross several streams and ravines and two main highways. Any sighting by the enemy might compromise the mission. It also might mean quick and brutal deaths for the small band.

Kittleson's senses sharpened as they did whenever he entered hostile territory. Night magnified strange sounds in the rice paddies and bamboo thickets. Birds startled at their advance. They wide-skirted villages, but the town dogs yapped anyhow. Carabao tracks tramped in the rice fields during the rains had hardened and made walking difficult. Nonetheless, Lieutenant Nellist ordered the pointman to set a fast pace in order to reach Balincarin by daybreak. They had to trust the guerrilla guides to know where Jap strongpoints were located, and to avoid them. Right now, the enemy was so concentrated on retreat that he stuck mainly to the roads and main trails.

They marched in a Ranger file and played dominos. If one man thought he saw or heard something, he dropped. All the others then fell like dominos.

About nine miles into the march, they approached the National Highway that ran from Manila through Cabanatuan town and on to San Jose. Nellist and Rounsaville called a halt and crawled underneath a poncho to check the map with a red-lensed flashlight. Kittleson and the two Filipino guards scouted ahead, following a dry east-west ravine as it deepened and widened. Razor-sharp Kunai grass grew head-high on either side.

Japanese truck convoys and tank units were using the National Highway in pulling back to defensive positions in the mountains. As Kittleson approached the thoroughfare, he caught the unmistakable clanking sound of tanks. He went to all fours and crawled up to the lip of the ravine for a look. The roadbed lay just ahead. The pale moon obligingly broke out from behind a drifting cloud long enough to reveal three tank silhouettes stopped on the road. They were smaller and more squatty than American tanks. Their tiny vehicle running lights glowed like cats' eyes.

They were obviously guarding a small bridge about thirty feet long. One tank squatted alone on the north end of it while the other two huddled together at the sound end.

Kittleson took one of the Filipinos back with him to the main element while the other continued observation of the bridge.

"How tall is the bridge?" Nellist asked.

"It's like a big culvert grown up with weeds and grasses. It looks tall enough to walk underneath."

"Do we have another option?" Rounsaville asked rhetorically. The road had to be crossed.

Scouts and guerrillas snaked down the ravine to where the other guide waited. They observed the road to get an idea of the action. It was about fifty yards away. A convoy of Jap trucks rumbled by, their cats' eyes winking. The three tanks remained at the bridge.

Lieutenant Nellist tapped Kittleson. "We'll cross a few at a time," he whispered. "Check it out with one of the Flips. Wait for us about a hundred yards on the other side. If nothing happens, we'll be coming right along."

Kittleson merely nodded. He and the guide slithered into the bottom of the ravine and made their way toward the bridge. The grass shortened in places and they fell to all fours. The tanks grew larger and more clearly outlined. Footfalls crunched in the gravel at the side of the road. One of the Japs was smoking a cigarette. He laughed.

Kittleson's heart seemed to echo underneath the concrete bridge. The bridge was about ten feet high. He thought the Jap tankers must be deaf not to hear the pounding.

Another Jap convoy approached. It was almost upon the bridge before the two anxious men underneath heard it. They cowered in the darkness as trucks rumbling by overhead jarred loose dust and gravel. Silence followed. The Scout and the Filipino slipped out the other side of the bridge, expecting at any moment to hear shouts and gunshots when the tanks discovered the raiders.

Apparently, fortunately, the Japs were too busy smoking and joking to pay attention to the mice stealing the house from around them. In less than fifteen minutes, everyone was under the bridge and across. They continued through the night.

The Rizal Road proved less of a barrier when they came to it. Traffic was light. Raiders crawled through the grass to the road, leapfrogged across the danger area, then doubletimed for a mile before halting for a rest.

The ex-con Vaquilar was a stern man prone to silence and brooding. Like Kittleson, he remained standing during rest halts. Twelve hours of running, marching, and playing dominos and hide-and-seek had left him exhausted. Most of the men immediately fell asleep when they sat down. Vaquilar stood looking in the direction of Cabanatuan.

"I have been in prison," he said in a solemn voice.

Kittleson nodded. "Yes."

They arrived like nomads in Balincarin at daybreak. The village was typical: huts; poor natives; naked dusty kids playing amidst chickens, pigs, donkeys, and carabao. More partisans were waiting there, along with the guerrilla leader Pajota.

"My men observed a Japanese unit of division strength this morning going north on Highway 5 in front of the prison," Kittleson overheard him telling the Scout lieutenants. "Another one thousand are bivouacked near the Cabu Bridge."

"My mama told me I should have been a mess cook in a nice safe kitchen," Wismer wisecracked, adding in a dramatic voice as though later relating the adventure to GIs who *were* cooks. "No shit, there we was—up to our asses in alligators and Japs . . ."

After a brief rest and bowls of rice and beans, the Scout teams saddled up and a guerrilla guide took them for their initial appraisal of the POW camp. They climbed a jungle rise a few hundred yards out of Balincarin, then descended into the lowlands along the Pampanga River. Kunai grass grew more than head tall, providing excellent cover. The river itself was two hundred yards wide in places, but it was lazy and shallow. Only an unexpected rainfall, rare for the season, could bring flooding and make it unfordable.

They waded across at a narrow point. Beyond rose a low knoll covered with more tall grasses. Cautioned by the guide, they crawled to the top of the knoll, parted the grass, and peered out. Vaquilar looked first, then passed his binoculars to Kittleson. The little Scout took a long look through the lenses. His heart sank.

The camp sat by itself in the open about seven hundred yards away. All Kittleson saw from this distance were the tops of high fence poles and roofs of thatched palm fronds or tin. There was a guard tower to the left corner of the front gate. Some Jap troop trucks dusted by on the road that passed in front of the camp.

What unsettled the Scout was not the stockade itself, but the *openness* around it. It was surrounded by farmland—flat, cultivated fields of turnips, sweet potatoes, or something. There were patches of Kunai here and there, but otherwise even a lizard would have had a tough time running from the river to the camp's front gate unseen.

Filipinos labored in the fields in the bright, morning sunlight. There was a single nipa hut isolated in the field a short distance outside the prison gates, on this side of Highway 5. A little farther on and off to the right were several more huts. None of them appeared occupied.

Kittleson panned the binoculars across the disconcerting scene. Cabanatuan town lay out of sight along Highway 5 to the southwest, four miles away. Cabu Creek where the large contingent of Japanese troops had dug in was less than a half-mile from the prison to the northeast. The bridge rested in a low area, so Kittleson was unable to see any activity.

As he returned Vaquilar's binoculars, he happened to catch the look in Lieutenant Nellist's eye. In that instant of contact he saw all he needed. Nellist unintentionally confirmed Kittleson's own assessment: It was going to be one touchy operation.

CHAPTER 26

Utilizing a slightly different march route, Colonel Henry Mucci, overall raid commander, led his 6th Rangers out of Guimba at 2:00 P.M., 28 January, not quite twenty-four hours behind the lead Scout element. His force consisted of Charley Company reinforced with a platoon from Fox Company, 121 soldiers in all. It was a large number of men to move through enemy country, but luck held. The Rangers linked up in the predawn of 29 January with Filipino guerrilla chief Captain Eduardo Joson and about eighty of his fighters in the barrio of Lobong, some miles to the west of Balincarin. From there, now numbering more than two hundred, they continued to their staging area at Platero about a half-mile to the Scouts' rear and a mile-and-a-half from the POW stockade.

Colonel Mucci discovered the bamboo telegraph had been at work. It was a bit unsettling. The teenaged girls and young women of Platero ambushed the dust-caked Rangers as soon as they came within sight of town. They wore white dresses and draped fresh flower garlands around the embarrassed GIs' necks. It was the first time many of the townspeople had ever seen Americans. A cow had already been butchered for the occasion. Everyone gathered in the village square and asked Colonel Mucci for permission to sing a song. The colonel glanced uneasily in the direction of the prison camp.

"Softly," he urged. "The Japs will hear."

The village *alcalde*, the mayor, lifted one finger. He waved it in the air. The Filipinos began to sing:

> God bless America,
> Land that I love . . .

In the meantime, a half-mile forward of the Rangers, Nellist and Rounsaville Teams continued surveillance on the target. The Scouts had spent the night in the tall grass along the Pampanga River, sharing watches while those off-duty curled up in the Kunai grass like field mice to sleep. Bill Nellist and Stud Rounsaville left their men watching the prison compound while they hiked to Platero to meet with Colonel Mucci and Captain Pajota. Major Bob Lapham would not be there. His knowledge of Japanese troop positions and installations in Nueva Ecija Province made him far too valuable an asset to risk losing. Lapham was both frustrated and disheartened.

Although Colonel Mucci had not slept since before leaving Guimba, the Scout leader found him animated and anxious for the raid to come off. Planning for it was still in flux pending last-minute information, but everyone focused on tonight. The longer they remained behind enemy lines, the greater was the chance of discovery. Even the Japs were bound to tap into the bamboo telegraph somewhere along the way.

Nellist and Rounsaville disclosed crucial intelligence gleaned from the camp overnight.

"A Jap division was moving past all night and was still moving until it shut down at dawn to hide out from planes during the day," Nellist explained. "It'll probably finish moving past the camp tonight. Our bacon will be out for frying if we collide with those bastards."

"What does it look like otherwise?" Mucci wanted to know. He was a hawk-faced man wearing his trademark shoulder holster. He tapped tobacco ashes from his ever-present pipe.

"The terrain around the camp is mostly open farmland," Rounsaville said. "There are some patches of tall grass for cover here and there, but we haven't been able to personally get close enough to look inside the camp. We've seen no movement inside from where we are at the river."

"Could the prisoners have been moved?" Mucci fretted.

Captain Pajota reassured him. Local farmers and villagers kept him informed of activities at the camp. The prisoners, they said, no longer labored growing crops for Japanese food. Most were too ill and dissipated to work anyhow. These days they simply cowered inside the stockade, waiting either to die or be rescued, largely ignored by the Japanese—at least so far.

Colonel Mucci straightened and arched his back. "We'll postpone the raid from tonight to tomorrow night to let that Jap division clear out of the area."

He tapped tobacco into his pipe and lit it. His hawk's gaze fixed on the two Scout leaders.

"In the meantime, we've got to get someone close to the front gate," he said. "We're going to bolt through that entrance, so the gate is the key to the entire operation. Which way does it open—in or out? How is it secured? Where are the exaction locations of the watch towers? How are they manned? How many Jap sentries are there? How is the fence constructed . . . ?"

Part of the intelligence might be supplied by Pajota's contacts. But how reliable were these simple villagers? Someone with a military background had to take a closer, personal look.

"I don't care how you get the dope," Mucci stressed. "Just get it."

* * *

The sun burned straight overhead—a hard, mean sun. Filipino laborers toiled in the fields that surrounded the camp. Lieutenant Nellist and Pontiac Vaquilar, who was shorter and dark and could easily pass for a native, shucked their green uniforms in exchange for the loose off-white garb of the local peasants. They stuck .45 pistols underneath their garments and pulled on wide-brimmed straw *buri* hats to conceal their faces.

"None of the Filipinos are as tall as you fellas," Cox objected. "There's no doubt the Japs'll be watching. If they get suspicious . . ." He left it hanging. If caught, they would be tortured as spies.

"I'm small like the Filipinos," Kittleson volunteered. "I should go."

"I *am* a Filipino," Asis interjected.

"Lord, fellas, I appreciate it," Nellist said, touched by the concern of his men. "But this is a leader's recon. I need to do it. The Japs can't tell from a distance how tall we are as long as we don't mingle with the locals. Besides, Pontiac speaks the lingo, right?"

Pajota gave his word that none of the farmers in the field dared betray the Americans. Although they were forced to rub elbows with their conquerors and to labor for them, they remained loyal to their country and inwardly hostile toward the Japanese.

"Besides," Pajota added simply, "traitors to our country have more to fear from us than from the Japanese."

Stands of bamboo skirted between the river and the fields for some distance. Two "farmers" ambled from the thickets into an open plot of young sweet potato plants. Several other peasants worked nearby, but they had already been cautioned to pay no attention to whatever happened or whoever appeared. They kept their heads down and their backs bent. Jap sentries, if they were alert, could see anyone approaching for at least a half-mile in any direction.

Nellist appeared uncommonly tall and lanky as he and Vaquilar strolled across the field, pointing and occasionally squatting as though to inspect the crop. In this manner they made their way toward the hut that sat not two hundred yards from the compound's front gate. Farmers used it as storage for their implements and other supplies. It was set isolated and exposed to the compound and the road that ran in front. Kittleson and the other Scouts watched breathlessly from hiding as the lieutenant and Vaquilar reached the hut, fooled around outside for a moment to allay suspicion, then stepped inside.

Nellist found it unsettling to be so near the enemy while virtually unarmed and doomed to die were the ruse discovered. But he had little time for his fears. He located a crack in the bamboo walls that provided an unobstructed view of the gate. He took out his notebook and began plotting and drawing and making notes.

The front gate, he observed, was about nine feet high and made of saw lumber. Strands of barbed wire ran from its supporting posts in double eight-foot-high fences around the entire stockade, which was about twenty or thirty acres in size. He marked on a sketch the locations of sentry towers and noted that neither of the two he saw in front was manned—at least not in the daytime. He couldn't make out much about the construction inside, except that many of the buildings were of one- and two-story bamboo with thatched palm roofs, while the others were mortar or concrete with corrugated tin roofs.

"I have to get closer," he decided.

Vaquilar was a man of few words. "Impossible," he said. He had an alternate suggestion. Since he could pass as a native, why didn't he circulate among the field hands and escort to the hut those individuals who worked in and around the camp? They might be able to answer the lieutenant's questions while actually pointing out features to him. It was dangerous, but not nearly as risky as their moving any nearer the prison. Neither of them relished joining the inmate population, granted that they survived capture.

It worked superbly. It seemed whatever Nellist needed to know, Vaquilar could sift out a local who knew the answer. The Scout leader filled up a notebook as the hot afternoon wore on.

The front gate opened in the middle and swung either inward or outward. A huge padlock kept it chained together. The road inside the compound that beelined from the front gate to the back marked the boundary between the prisoners and their now-informal keepers. POWs stayed in filth-ridden billets on the left side of the road near the northeast corner of the enclosure. Across the road from them were enemy officer and enlisted quarters. Beyond, also on the right side of the road, were a tin shed housing at least one tank and several troop trucks and some Japanese administration offices. Near the back gate were enemy transient quarters, billets for guards, and a third sentry tower. The road tying Cabu to Cabanatuan town ran close alongside the front length of the stockade.

The compound supported two pillbox bunkers—one beneath the northeast guard tower near the road, and the second along the south fence. These could prove to be formidable defensive positions, except Filipinos who were admitted inside to trade produce with the Japanese had never seen either of them manned. These same traders estimated 225 to 250 Japanese presently occupied the compound. That number included 75 permanent party; the others were transients retreating from advancing Americans.

Nellist folded his notepad and stuffed it into his trouser pocket. "Let's get the hell out of here."

"Wait." Vaquilar gripped his arm.

A young and pretty Filipina, shiny black hair flowing down her back, sauntered up the road and stopped to talk to the guards at the gate. Had she seen the Yanks in the field? Was she tipping off the Japs? Anxiety all but crushed the Americans' breath in their lungs as they watched her flirt with the enemy soldiers for what seemed hours, but in reality consumed only a few minutes.

Finally, she left and walked on down the road and out of sight, without even a glance toward the nearby hut where Nellist and Vaquilar hid. The Jap guards returned to their posts, likewise showing no interest in the hut. Apparently, like most men, they had merely been distracted by a pretty face and figure.

"Now," Nellist said, letting out a sigh, "let's go."

That night in Captain Pajota's hut in Platero, Colonel Mucci called together his element leaders to finalize the attack operations order. Ranger platoon leaders, guerrilla chiefs, and Scout lieutenants crowded into the bamboo hut, on the table in the center of which burned an oil lantern illuminating spread-out maps. Information obtained by Nellist and Vaquilar contributed to a better grasp of the camp layout and what was required to penetrate it.

"As I see it," Mucci began, talking around the pipe in his mouth, "our main threat after the last of the Jap division moves on through tonight is posed by the two thousand Japs bivouacked at the Cabu Bridge. They could rush over us within ten minutes after the assault begins."

"They won't," promised grim-faced Captain Pajota.

Major Lapham's partisans—two companies totaling 280 fighters commanded by Captains Pajota and Joson—were to provide security and a blocking force around the camp while U.S. Rangers and Scouts conducted the actual raid. Pajota's men would establish a roadblock at the Cabu Creek Bridge to stop the Japs from crossing the creek and charging the prison compound once action commenced.

Joson's guerrillas, along with a Ranger bazooka team, would set up a similar blocking force on the road eight hundred yards southwest of the camp to catch Jap elements that might attempt to break through from Cabanatuan town. Each guerrilla band was armed with bazookas and twenty-five land mines.

"We need a half-hour to shoot our way into the camp and herd out the prisoners," Colonel Mucci said, looking pointedly at first Pajota and then Joson.

One unspoken question preyed on each American's mind: Although the guerrillas proved themselves deadly in hit-and-run tactics, would they stand their ground against an organized assault supported by tanks hell-bent on reaching the prison camp?

"You will have your half-hour," Captain Pajota said, his jaw set. "I and Captain Joson promise you a half-hour."

The rest of the raid would work this way: From the assembly point at the Pampanga River, the guerrillas would proceed to their positions. The Rangers and Scouts would cross the seven hundred yards of open fields under the cover of darkness to reach the prison's main gate before 1930 hours. Rangers Lieutenant William J. O'Connell and Lieutenant Melville H. Schmidt received the main task of breaching the front gate with their two respective platoons and the Alamo Scouts. Lieutenant John F. Murphy would lead his platoon crawling all the way around the left of the prison camp to the rear gate.

"Lieutenant Murphy initiates the attack by opening fire on the guards at the back gate," Colonel Mucci directed. "That should provide a momentary distraction to allow one squad to take out the Jap guards at the main gate and bust through into the compound.

"Lieutenant O'Connell's platoon sweeps the Jap side of the compound on the right of the road. Lieutenant Schmidt and his platoon take the left side, the POW side. Murphy breaks through the rear gate and covers Schmidt with a crossfire while one of Schmidt's squads under Captain Bob Prince rounds up the prisoners and gets them out the front gate pronto. Alamo Scouts and a squad of Rangers have secured the front gate and will start the prisoners in batches of fifty toward the river where we have 150 Filipino irregulars waiting for them with all the carabao carts we can round up by tomorrow night. Remember, these boys have been in that shit hole beaten and starved for nearly three years. If they can't walk to the river, carry them. We don't leave one of them behind. *Not a single one.*

"I will fire two red flares from my Very pistol as a signal that all the prisoners are out and at the river."

That was also the signal for Pajota to withdraw to the northwest and Joson to the southwest to lure Japanese forces after them and widen the gap through which raiders would make their return march to Guimba with the rescued POWs.

"Any questions?" Colonel Mucci finished, standing up and looking at his officers, hands on his hips and pipe jutting from his jaw. "Good. You all have Lieutenant Nellist's sketch of the POW camp. I want to see you back here at 0800 with your platoon and squad operation plans. We attack tomorrow night. I think that the date of 30 January 1945 will be long remembered. Go with God—and bring our boys home. They have not been forgotten."

CHAPTER 27

There had been fierce fighting near the village of Baloc fifteen miles northwest of the POW camp. Heavier sounds such as artillery and tank round explosions drifted into the compound. The sounds were dim and distant, but nearer than ever before. Sergeant Bill Seckinger hobbled out of his billet where he had tried to sleep in spite of the heat and flies. With a combination of hope, elation, and apprehension he tilted his head to listen.

A pair of Japanese soldiers on the other side of the dirt road also paused to take in the battle sounds. Their baleful glares soon fell on the emaciated POW. They stared at him as though they personally held him responsible, like they contemplated lowering their rifles and opening fire.

Anger flashed through the inmate, the first he had dared exhibit for years, because to let the Japanese see it was to die cruelly and immediately. *Screw 'em, the bastards would all soon be dead meat*. But he lowered his head to avoid a direct confrontation; his continuing to stand there under the Japs' gazes was an act of defiance itself.

For the past several days Allied warplanes had been omnipresent in the skies above Cabanatuan, repeatedly strafing forest and bamboo thickets on the distant hillsides where Japs hid and making runs at traffic on the road. Such close action made Japanese staying in the camp edgier and more hostile than normal. Tension increased among the prisoners, both out of anticipation of being freed at long last and out of fear at how the Japanese might react. With little else for the captives to do now but survive, they consumed endless hours speculating on such topics.

"They'll shoot us down like dogs as soon as the first GIs come down that road," went the argument.

"Our buddies are almost here. Why else all the air activity?"

"What are we going to do if the Japs start massacring us?"

"Keep a low profile," cooler heads counseled. "Don't provoke them. Don't even look at them. All we have to do is hang on for a few more days, a few weeks at most."

"They'll kill us first. Or they'll move us. They can't let the world see how they've treated us."

"We'll fight. We'll take all of them with us that we can."

"We'll *fight*? Look at us. Most of us can hardly *walk*."

Private George Steiner limped into the courtyard and stood next to Sergeant Seckinger. At that moment, two American P-38s buzzed the camp. Sun glinted dully off stubby wings as the planes came in low and fast, then lifted in a near vertical climb, leaving the throbbing of their engines settling over the compound. The two Japanese across the road panicked. They ran and tumbled into a foxhole. A rain shower the day before had left a puddle of muddy water in the hole. The Japanese sprang back out of the hole, ran inside a building and came out again tugging on wet weather gear. Ignoring the POWs, they again jumped into the hole and crouched there, rifles pointed at the sky.

Seckinger and Steiner concealed wry smiles by turning away.

Inside the barracks, where many men were too sick to get out of their makeshift bunks, where arms and legs and spirits were missing, Private Robert J. Body and two other prisoners huddled together conspiratorially, whispering. They were planning an escape, even though a failed attempt meant automatic execution. Their guards might have packed up their shit and left, but that had not changed the inmates' prisoner status.

"Anything's better than just waiting here until the damned Japs decide to blow us away," Body argued. "I figger American lines can't be more than thirty miles away. Way I look at it, we got a fifty-fifty chance of making it. We don't have that much chance if we do nothing."

Tonight was the night. At 8:00 tonight, they would wriggle through the wire. It was 30 January 1945. Body, Seckinger, Steiner and the others had been held prisoner since the fall of Bataan two years, eight months, and three weeks ago. They had no way of knowing that Alamo Scouts hid less than a mile away watching the stockade, nor that U.S. Rangers at Platero were making final plans to break them free that very night.

CHAPTER 28

The day Colonel Mucci declared a day to remember, 30 January, started in Platero with the villagers treating the Rangers to a breakfast of coffee, eggs, and fruit. A half-mile forward, PFC Kit Kittleson opened an OD can of ham and lima beans and stared at the greasy scum on top for a full minute before he made himself eat. He washed it all down with an iodine-treated canteen of river water. Then he got up and, crouching in the weeds that waved above his head, made his way carefully to the observation knoll. During the early night the rear elements of the Jap division had passed through. There had been little further traffic on the road. An Allied P-38 buzzed the camp in the morning, but the camp now lay smoldering quietly in the sunlight.

The day dragged more than any Kittleson could ever recall. Lieutenants Nellist and Rounsaville returned from Platero and briefed the teams on their jobs that night. They were to help secure the main gate and escort prisoners to the river. They didn't need to know job details of the other elements.

After the briefing, Scouts alternated the duties of observing the camp or performing picket watch. And they waited.

And because talking had to be kept to a minimum, they mostly waited in silence with the waiting eating into their insides.

"I hate this most of all," Cox whispered.

Kittleson lay sweating, trying to blank out his mind and make it ready for the night. Trying not to think about all the things that could go wrong. Although all seemed normal out front, a single thought had plagued him ever since they passed through Jap lines. He dismissed it as the pre-combat jitters, but it kept returning when he was quiet and had time to explore his inners.

What if they had been betrayed? What if the Japs were lying in ambush tonight to unleash all hell upon them as they came sneaking across the open fields toward the compound?

Skinny Willie Wismer with the big ears murmured, "Do you think the Japs know we're coming?"

Kittleson wasn't the only one with the jitters. Others were apparently thinking the same thing.

"We'll find out tonight," Kittleson said. He seldom permitted emotion to show on his young face.

He shifted his position to a more comfortable one. The Thompson's barrel rested on one outstretched arm to keep it out of the dust. He treated the weapon with the care of a father for his infant child. He checked Tommy's function now, for the tenth time that morning. He eased open the bolt to make sure it slid smoothly on its light film of oil. He closed the bolt again and rolled over onto his back and looked up into the tropical blue of the sky. A few clouds drifted by. He hoped it was cloudy tonight and that the moon would not shine on them, but that God's grace would.

He strived to displace his sense of uneasiness with thoughts of home. It was a thing men often did in the face of danger. There was a special place he had on the farm where oak trees one hundred years old grew in lush grass next to a stream, an oasis of sorts in a land of crops and pastures. He often lay on his back among the ancient trees on a late sunny afternoon and daydreamed away the last hours of light. When the crickets and tree frogs started chirruping, he got up and drove the milking cows to the barn. He stood up right out there in the open, bold as could be, and drove them across the wide fields. Anyone who looked from the road could have seen him. From the pasture gate to the barn was about seven hundred yards, roughly the same distance as now between the knoll and the POW stockade.

What a difference time made in a man's judgment of distance.

He thought about Darlene—the Darlene he knew from her letters, for he had never really known her at home. She was a pretty face from around, a few casual dates, because somehow it was convenient for both of them. That was about all. He had never held her in his arms, never kissed her. They had grown close only through correspondence transcending five thousand miles or so of war-ravaged globe.

Today, he felt far older than his twenty years.

Would he never lie on his back again, *anywhere*, and watch clouds in the sky?

Rangers moved up from Platero in the afternoon. They hid in the grass and got ready for the night.

The blazing sun inched lower toward the western horizon. At long last it kissed the earth, turned red, and started to die. Insects buzzed in annoying swarms. Then the sun went away suddenly and it was dark in that way peculiar to the tropics. Scattered summer clouds moved in to play tag with a waning moon. Light breezes ruffled the tall grass—or was it the word quietly passed from man to man that ruffled it?

Get ready to move out.

CHAPTER 29

PFC Kittleson cradled his Thompson in the crook of his arms and used his elbows and knees to draw himself across the uneven fields like a lizard with its front feet removed. He heard other indistinct scraping sounds—bellies on earth—around him in the dry rice beds and sweet potato fields. What he saw, even more indistinctly than he heard the sounds of moving men, were Gilbert Cox's large shadow and big feet not twelve inches in front of Kit's nose. He followed Cox's boots with the same near-blind trust that Cox followed Siason's in front of him and Andy Smith behind adhered to Kittleson's soles.

They moved on their bellies like giant reptiles—121 Rangers and thirteen Alamo Scouts. Partisans had already split off to reach their sites. It was torturous progress. Sweat soaked Kittleson's fatigues. It was a warm night, but not all the sweat came from physical exertion and climate.

Lieutenant Murphy's platoon separated to worm its way around to the back gate. Kittleson failed to notice, for all he saw were Cox's boots. And he saw the U.S. P-61 Black Widow warplane when it buzzed the camp at treetop level. It swept low like a night hawk over prey and screamed over the prison camp. A planned diversion to force Japs inside the compound to focus on the sky instead of on the ground.

Kittleson prayed it worked.

He prayed that they had not been betrayed.

Eerie silence hung over the field like the fall of an early summer's dew. The southerly breeze tasted of distant saltwater. It failed to cool sweaty faces. Giant crawling reptile sounds were surprisingly muted, but they magnified themselves against Kittleson's eardrums. He rationalized that no other body of armed men could have advanced more silently, but still what noise they made beat inside his ears like a marching percussion band.

They would be heard.

They would be heard.

He kept following Cox's boots.

Suddenly, the night silence shattered into shards of black crystal. The clear gonging of a bell reverberated out of the prison camp. Kittleson's heart vaulted from his chest and it was like it needed to be manually replaced before it continued beating. His mouth dried instantly and when he tried to swallow he discovered sandpaper inside his throat. Cox ahead of him froze in place, as did every other raider on the field.

An alarm?

Had they been detected?

Kittleson expected search lights to flood the field with hostile light. He would never see Iowa again.

The gonging continued. Slowly, methodically. Not frenzied like a burglar alarm. More like a grandfather clock or the sounding of a ship's bell.

And nothing happened: No flood lights, no enemy troops pouring out the gate.

The gong sounded, then it stopped and there was the sound of summer's dewfall again. Only later did Kittleson learn that the gonging came from a ship's bell improvised by a U.S. Navy POW who sounded the watch at periodic intervals.

After an eternity condensed into an hour, raiders slipped

into the drainage ditch that paralleled the road in front of the stockade. Cigarettes glowed where Jap guards twenty yards away were smoking at the gate on the other side of the road. From his vantage point, Kittleson peered through the barbed wire directly into the compound. Like a Peeping Tom, he discerned Japs in their underwear lounging in the open doorways of lighted barracks. Oriental music with its peculiar counterpointing flavor lilted out of the wire and drifted with the breeze across the raiders' heads. Apparently, the Japs felt secure here twenty-five miles behind the front.

Glancing a bit higher, the little Scout spotted sentries silhouetted in their watch towers against the lighter sky.

"Please, God," he silently prayed. "Don't let them look this way and see us."

The earth felt like it was hurtling at runaway speed and that he would have to dig his fists into the soil to keep from being thrown into space. Crickets and frogs serenading each other blasted him with their strident orchestrations. The moon slipped out from behind a cloud and bathed the raiders in soft light that made shadows. Kittleson looked into Cox's broad, startled face. It was camouflaged black, out of which his eyes glowed wide and white. Simultaneously, the two Scouts buried their faces into the dust to prevent their eyes from giving them away.

They waited for the attack signal.

As they waited, Lieutenant John Murphy and his Ranger platoon slithered along a filthy sewage ditch to within fifteen yards of the back gate. It was 1920 hours by Murphy's watch, ten minutes away from H-hour. Rangers crawled up, rested their rifles on the outer strands of barbed wire and began selecting targets among the unsuspecting Japanese inside.

Murphy sent three of his men creeping to the other side of the gate to be ready to neutralize the sentry in the guard tower. Either the sentry possessed some acute sixth sense or the moon playing peek-a-boo with the clouds revealed something suspicious to him among the night shadows—for he shouted a ringing challenge that could only be translated as: "*Halt!*"

CHAPTER 30

"*Halt!*"

"*Halt?*"

Obviously, the sentry was none too certain about what he had seen, only that it must have been *something*. He shouted back into the camp, apparently summoning help. No one paid him the slightest attention. It was like he was a green troop fresh to the war yelling *Wolf!* Near-naked Japanese continued their leisurely comings and goings among their lighted quarters.

Lieutenant Murphy took bead on a Jap sitting with two others on a back stoop. It was close enough to H-hour. A few more minutes and some gung ho Jap officer just *might* heed the overwrought sentry's excited calls for help. Murphy squeezed his trigger. His carbine barked and spat flame. His target jumped like an electric bolt had shot through his body. He fell off the stoop.

At the same instant, the rest of the platoon opened up with a murderous crescendo of rifle fire. The three GIs underneath the guard tower ended the guard's "*Halt!*" for eternity. Searing gunfire splintered the tower. Poor sonofabitch must have thought the world exploded in his face. His body somersaulted out of the tower and crashed onto the stoop of the Jap transient quarters below.

It was a go!

At the front gate, Kittleson scrambled out of the ditch a few paces behind Ranger Sergeant Ted Richardson. Everyone charged the front gate. It was Richardson's job to smash the oversized padlock on the gates to allow troops to throw them wide and surge inside.

He struck at the lock with the butt of his Tommy gun. It refused to yield. He backed off a step, whipped out his .45 pistol and took aim. Before he could fire, a Jap on the other side of the gate shot at him through a crack. The bullet struck the sergeant's pistol. The weapon spun from his numbed hand.

Kittleson spotted the movement. A Ranger's BAR— Browning Automatic Rifle—flickered a tongue of flame two feet long from the Scout's right flank. It flashed open the darkness and roared with the much-amplified sound of parachute cloth being torn.

Kittleson added the more accented guttural song of his Tommy gun to the racket of a half-dozen automatic weapons busting loose at the same time. Lead scythed through the gate, exploding splinters. A Jap screamed as he died. There was no further fire from inside.

Richardson shook his stinging hand. He picked up his pistol. It still worked. He fired bullets into the lock, busting it. Kittleson and several others heaved at the gate. It caught on something. A corpse.

"Pull it toward us!" Kittleson shouted.

Rangers stormed through the opening, bounding over the dark clumps of three Jap guards lying dead in the entranceway. They disappeared down the road beyond, scattering into the maelstrom of their own creation. Kittleson helped throw the gate wide. He knelt in the road with Willie Wismer as the raucous din of sharp battle erupted inside the compound.

Grenades flash-banging. Tracers weaving a ceiling of iridescent geometric patterns. Rifles cracking. Machine guns rattling. Screams. Orders shouted in English and in Japanese. Dim figures darting like the shadows of ghosts. It all echoed across the flatlands, splintering the night.

Only the fact that raiders knew their assignments and missions to precision prevented total confusion from reigning. Squads and teams broke off to conduct their assignments. They worked swiftly and mostly in silence.

As Murphy's platoon crashed through the rear gate, a Japanese mortar squad began lobbing rounds. Murphy spotted the tube flames. His Rangers opened fire on the mortar, silencing it, but not before three high explosive shells detonated in the roadway and in the ditch among the Scouts and Rangers at the front gate waiting to guide POWs to safety.

"Incoming!"

Kittleson hit the dirt face down. Explosions hopped around the front gate in succession, with roars and blinding flashes of light. The ground shook violently. Shrapnel shrieked overhead and pelted the road with hot metal.

"I'm hit!"

Lieutenant Stud Rounsaville.

"I'm with him," Nellist called out. "Everybody hold where you are."

The first mortar shell had exploded directly behind the two Scout leaders. The concussion knocked them down. Nellist's ears rang and he could hardly hear, but he had escaped injury. Shaken, he crawled to his friend's side. Rounsaville groaned.

"You're wounded, Stud?"

"I guess. I'm bleeding."

"Where're you hit?"

Rounsaville paused. "In the ass."

"The ass?"

"Bill, I may need you to look at my ass."

"I've seen your ass."

The two officers had been close friends since A.S.T.C. This was their second POW rescue mission together. Nellist drew his trench knife and cut open the bloody seat of Stud's trousers.

"I can see a piece of metal sticking out. Hold on. I'm going to pull it out."

He tugged gently. Rounsaville emitted a cry of pain.

"I'm sending you back to the river," Nellist decided.

"Bill . . . ?" the wounded Scout started to protest.

"You're going back."

"Bill?" Rounsaville managed through gritted teeth, in that rough banter common to comrades in arms. "Thanks for caring about my ass."

The mortars had scored other casualties. Scout Alfred Alfonso took a full load of shrapnel in the gut. He lay on the ground writhing in agony. The guy was in bad shape. One of Captain Jimmy Fisher's two medics injected him with morphine. Ranger litter bearers started to the river with Rounsaville, Alfonso, and a Ranger whose inner thighs had been ripped open by shrapnel.

The battle continued inside the compound; no further shells fell at the gate.

"Captain Jimmy? Where's Captain Jimmy?" someone shouted.

Fisher, the Ranger surgeon, had become separated from his medics during the mad scramble at the gate and the confusion of the mortar shelling.

"Man down up ahead!" came another cry.

A Ranger sergeant named Nelson dashed to the side of a crumpled figure lying on the road. It was too dark to make out the GI's identity.

"Where are you hit?" Nelson asked.

"Stomach," came a weak reply. "My belly."

Ranger First Sergeant Bosard came up. "This fella looks to be hit pretty hard," he said. "Better go find Captain Jimmy."

The man on the ground coughed. He whispered hoarsely. "I *am* Captain Fisher."

By this time the fight for the Cabu Bridge a short distance down the road was joined. The earth tremored as Captain Pajota detonated mines that chewed a big chunk out of the bridge. The partial destruction prevented attacks by tanks, but girders remained to provide footpaths for determined infantry. Pajota's machine guns opened a deadly cackle. Jap officers urged their first suicide platoons at the partisans on the other side of the creek. *Banzai! Banzai!* That seemed the only battle doctrine the Japs knew.

Waiting at the front gate for the first POWs to appear, Kittleson cast an anxious eye up the road. The horizon was now ablaze with tracers and explosions; two battles were being fought simultaneously.

The only thing between the freedom of five hundred American POWs and two thousand pissed-off Japanese were approximately one hundred Filipino guerrilla irregulars at the Cabu Bridge.

Would they hold? *Could* they hold?

CHAPTER 31

PFC Kittleson need not have worried about betrayal. The Japanese were caught totally by surprise. Panicked enemy darted about the compound as frantically as defenseless chickens caught by foxes on a hen house raid. Here and there individuals resisted, but, demoralized and caught off guard, few of the 250 Japanese troops inside the camp managed to rally anything like an effective defense. Lieutenant O'Connell's men on the Jap side of the road were stacking up bodies against the anvil provided by Murphy's Rangers pouring through the back gate.

Sergeant Richardson, hand still half-numb from having had his pistol shot from it, led two fighters running through the front door of a Japanese officers' quarters. Two officers caught in their underwear in a common area, a kind of day room, stared in shock at the blackened-faced combat GIs, who took advantage of their hesitation to stitch them with bullets.

There was a long hallway down the middle of the building with doors on either side. Shouting and roaring with adrenaline and excitement, the Rangers kicked in doors and sprayed the tiny rooms with lead. Japs screamed. Windows shattered. Tracers punched through thin walls and blazed through the night like souped-up fireflies gone berserk.

In the front door, shoot up the place, then out the back door and toward the next barracks.

A darkened figure leaped to its feet and thrust arms in the air. PFC Provencher swung his Tommy gun and was already on a trigger squeeze.

"Don't shoot! I'm an American."

This wasn't the POW area. Japs often spoke English in combat to confuse the Americans. Provencher hesitated.

"Hold it!" Sergeant Richardson shouted.

"Look! Look at me! I'm an American!" the ragged figure shrieked.

He really was a Bataan Death March survivor. He was in the Jap area tending a generator providing electricity to the officers' quarters.

"Get to the front gate as fast as you can," Richardson instructed.

The scarecrow shambled off toward the gate. "God bless you. God bless you. Thank God you've come."

In another part of the Jap side of the camp, bazooka man Sergeant Stewart and his ammo bearer/loader trotted toward the corrugated tin shed that housed tanks and trucks. He dropped to one knee and hoisted the tube to his shoulder. His loader slapped a rocket into the rear of the tube and tapped Stewart on the head. Ready to fire. He aimed at the shed to take it out.

At that moment, two trucks packed with Jap infantrymen roared into sight on a feeder road beyond the tank shed, apparently headed for the main gate in an escape attempt. Stewart shifted his aim. The rocket streaked through the night. The lead truck exploded in a bright orange blast of flame.

The loader quickly slapped a fresh rocket into the tube. Stewart destroyed the second truck as it skewed sideways to avoid colliding with the first. Streaks of burning gasoline tentacled from the explosions, setting nearby buildings on fire. Amid screams of terror and anguish, minibonfires tumbled from the blazing trucks—human torches. It was a Danteesque scene of horror. Some of the torches mindlessly stampeded in all directions, shrieking and fanning their flames. Others staggered around screaming until they collapsed to burn on the ground.

Stewart blew up the tank building. Then he and his loader threw carbines to their shoulders and started picking off the torches, blasting them out of their panicked misery.

On the left side of the road in the POW section, Lieutenant Mel Schmidt and his men veered toward the prisoner quarters. Tommy gunfire silenced a terrified enemy soldier cowering on a rooftop and screaming uncontrollably. He tumbled to the ground. Rangers filled him with bullets as he spasmed.

A Jap roared "*Banzai!*" from the shadows and charged. A wall of Thompson .45 slugs cut him nearly in half.

The attack caught Allied POWs as much by surprise as it did their Japanese keepers. Thinking the Japanese were starting to execute them, the prisoners were either too petrified from fear or too physically weakened to resist. A few, like Sergeant Seckinger, attempted to either hide or recover hidden weapons for a last-ditch fight, but the majority, clad in their underwear, pressed themselves against split bamboo floors and waited in mute stupor for the end of their long torture.

POW Lieutenant Merle Musselman, a company surgeon captured when Japs overran his field hospital during the final days of Bataan, was sitting on the steps of the camp dispensary when violent gunfire erupted. He feared the Japs were slaughtering inmates. Thinking he might save some of them, disregarding his own safety, he ran on weakened legs toward the camp surgical ward that housed one hundred patients. To his consternation, he discovered all the beds empty. He staggered outside, bewildered, where a huge man in green with a blackened face startled him.

"Get the hell to the front gate," the invader ordered. "You're being rescued."

Airman George Steiner fled his barracks to hide just as an attacker demolished a guard tower with a long pipe that shot flame. Steiner had never seen a bazooka before. His bladder let loose. He tumbled into a drainage ditch from the latrine and began crawling in the muck toward the fence. He didn't see the man until a strong hand grabbed him and jerked him up. To his surprise, the apparition spoke English with a deep Southern drawl.

"Y'all get to the front gate," the voice commanded. "It's a prison break. We come to get y'all out."

Steiner needed no further encouragement. Although gangrene had nearly crippled him, he was one of the first to reach freedom.

Sergeant Bill Seckinger hit the floor as bullets shrieked and punched holes through the walls of his billets. Thoughts of how he could fire the .45 bullets he had hoarded raced through his mind. How could he resist?

"It looks like they're killing us all!" someone yelled.

"Tear the legs off your bunks," Seckinger snapped. "Get anything you can. Some of them are going to die when they come in."

The man was so debilitated he could hardly walk, but he wasn't going down without a fight.

Then came a drawling, "Y'all are free. Head for the front gate."

POW Robert Body was less than a half-hour away from making his escape attempt when the attack started. He collided with a GI as he ran out the door of his barracks. He thought the intruder was a Jap. He jumped back, ready to fight.

"Go to the front gate!" the Ranger commanded.

"You don't have to tell me again. I want *outta* here."

Such was Body's haste to escape that he didn't bother with the gate. He barged completely through two rows of barbed wire fence, ripping off what remained of his clothing and cutting a deep gash in his nose.

A POW named Jackson didn't let the inconvenience of

having only one leg slow him down. He jumped into a drainage ditch and actually reached the front gate on one leg and the stub of the other.

A number of prisoners were too weak and debilitated to get out of their beds. They struggled feebly as GIs stormed in to rescue them. One Ranger gently lifted a man in his arms and started toward the door. The skeleton thrashed about and attempted to stand on his feet.

"I gotta go back inside," he protested.

"We have to keep moving," the Ranger said.

"No. I have to get some documents I hid."

The man seemed demented from the torture of his long captivity.

"Documents are not important now," the Ranger insisted.

"You don't understand. I need those documents to court-martial the man who ate my cat. He *ate* my cat."

"It don't matter now," the Ranger consoled him. "I'll personally get you another cat."

"Somebody'll eat it."

"Nobody will eat it. I promise."

Ranger Corporal Jim Herrick came across a POW who had fallen out of his bed and couldn't get up.

"Come on, pal," he said to the pitiful figure. "We've gotta get out of here."

"I'm a goner," the POW croaked. "Don't bother with me. Help get the other fellas out."

Herrick hoisted the naked bag of bones into his arms and started for the gate. Halfway there, he heard a faint gasp. The prisoner went limp in his arms, dead of a heart attack. The excitement was simply too much for him. Only one hundred feet from freedom and he'd died. Tears in his eyes, Herrick continued with his lightweight burden. None of these poor bastards was going to be left behind, not even if they were dead.

Backlighted by burning buildings, tattered skeletons and scarecrows began emerging from the inferno. Staggering and hobbling and crawling, like zombies emerging from catacombs and graves into unexpected light. Blinking, weeping, laughing, thanking God and their liberators in a repetitive heartfelt litany. All hollows and angles and stench and running sores and lost limbs . . . Like the gates of hell had been cast open. Dead men returned to life.

The sight broke PFC Kittleson's heart.

CHAPTER 32

Firing inside the compound slackened to an occasional rifle shot. The raid was over in twenty-eight minutes. The Japanese garrison was destroyed. The bloodied remains of some 250 Japanese soldiers lay scattered in the wreckage of the assault. Only a few survivors may have escaped and gone into hiding.

Eerie quiet settled over the stockade, broken only by the crackling of fire, the shuffling of feet, and the nearby sounds of the continuing battle at Cabu Creek. Captain Pajota was holding on, giving the Rangers their thirty minutes. There was still nothing from Captain Joson and his guerrillas down the opposite end of the road toward Cabanatuan town. Japs in the town probably didn't know what the hell was going on.

Other than the two Scouts and two Rangers wounded by mortars at the front gate, the raiders had suffered no further casualties. Luck was not to hold. Corporal Roy Sweezy, one of Lieutenant Murphy's squad leaders, was trotting along the inner rear fence headed for the front gate with his squad when two rifle shots cracked. Both bullets ripped through Sweezy's chest, toppling him. Silence returned. Corporal

Francis Schilli took out his canteen and administered a Catholic's last rites to his dying friend. The squad then hoisted the body and carried it toward the river.

POWs on bare, swollen feet continued to pour out the front gate in a crunch of pitiful humanity. Gentle hands lifted and carried them when they fell. Tearful POWs hugged and kissed their saviors. "Bless you! Bless you! Thank God you came."

Kittleson escorted one group of prisoners across the fields to the carabao carts on the other side of the river, then returned for a second while the battle continued inside the camp. He helped a man who had fallen in the road drainage ditch and couldn't get up. The man had no muscles at all. Only a rattle of bones crammed into dry skin. Kittleson's hand completely encircled his upper arm. Tears of pity welled in the young Scout's eyes.

Released physically, the POWs now began releasing themselves emotionally. Even while bullets ricocheted around their heads, it was like they had to tell somebody about what they had endured. It simply couldn't wait.

"We worked in these fields when we were too sick to stand up," a POW who happened to also be from Iowa narrated in a weak voice as Kittleson hurried a group toward the river. The man could hardly walk now. The Scout threw an arm around his bony waist and half-dragged and half-carried him. Asis and Cox and several Rangers were similarly escorting others in the long weeping column. "Raising crops for the Japs. They made us stay bent over all the time. If we even looked up, they beat the hell out of us. I still can't hardly straighten my back."

Most of the prisoners wore only dirty white underwear, which reflected intermittent moonlight like pale ghost parts. After a couple of bullets fired by holdout Japs hissed through Andy Smith's column, the Scout crawled along the prone line of frightened skeletons.

"Take off all your white clothing," he ordered. "They make good targets."

Prisoners promptly removed their underwear. They got

up naked and barefooted, clutching wadded underwear in their hands, and continued toward the river. They were not shot at again.

After all the POWs were removed and the camp burning, Captain Bob Prince entered a final time and shouted into each structure, "Anybody here?" Then he took out his Very pistol and fired into the clouds, the signal to withdraw.

Masses of mostly naked humanity waded the muddy Pampanga River to where carabao, hitched to more than two dozen two-wheeled wooden bull carts, lowed mournfully in the night. Solemn, silent Filipino farmers and armed guerrillas attended them.

"If they're too bad off to walk," came an order, "put 'em in the carts."

Kittleson carried a naked man to a cart and lowered him tenderly on a grass mattress. The guy weighed no more than a child. The man sobbed with gratitude as the Scout walked away to help with other prisoners.

Colonel Mucci fired his flares to signal the raid completed and to let Pajota at the bridge disengage from a battle he was doomed to lose if he stayed with it long enough. As the bull carts, the walking dead, and their protectors, a procession a mile long, pulled out in the dark with shuffling feet and rattling carts, Lieutenants Nellist and Rounsaville assembled their Scout teams to form a stay-behind blocking force at the river. Once a Ranger medic had removed the shrapnel shard from Rounsaville's backside, he insisted on reentering the fray. That meant the Scouts were short only one man, the seriously wounded Alfonso.

Pajota's partisans lured the Japanese after them while the POWs made a break for friendly lines. Scouts burrowed into clumps of cogon grass and arranged extra magazines and grenades within easy reach—just in case the Japs weren't fooled and came after them. The wide sheet of the river lay to their front, lighter from moon reflection than the surrounding terrain. The Cabanatuan camp burned with a smudged red glow. The rattle of bull carts soon faded into the night.

Kittleson lay next to Willie Wismer. His eyes strained to pick out any hostile movement on the dark opposite edge of the water. Bullfrogs freely distributed their bass mating calls. Mosquitos buzzed. The air was muggy. Kittleson sweated.

"I heard we lost a Ranger," Wismer whispered.

"Don't talk now."

"He was killed. Alfonso looked real bad when we put him in a cart, but I think he'll make it."

Wismer hushed for a few minutes. He sounded elated when he spoke again. "Kit, I was scared shitless. But, Kit, goddammit, Kit, we *did* it. We got our boys back."

Kittleson kept his gaze fixed on the opposite shore. "Not yet," he said.

They were far behind enemy lines with a long way to go to reach home, burdened now with 516 enfeebled men who would have to be carried out in carabao carts through enemy land.

CHAPTER 33

After a tense two hours, during which there were no indica-
tions of Japanese pursuit, the Scouts withdrew to the tiny
village of Balincarin. It lay in silence and darkness, both
near total. The only remaining signs of the passage of the
POWs and the bull carts were deep ruts in the road through
town, footprints, and water buffalo dung. Some townspeople
working without light were scuffing the road with shovels
and feet to get rid of the evidence. One of them silently
pointed the Scouts toward a nipa hut on the outskirts.

The Scouts automatically formed a perimeter to keep
watch around the hut. A blanket had been drawn across its
door, around which the only illumination in town seeped
dimly. Nellist and Rounsaville, a little stiff from his wound,
went inside.

After a while, they came out again with the skinny. Some
one hundred of the most frail of the POWs were hidden in
buildings around the village. The main body had proceeded
toward American lines at Sibul. It simply made good sense to
leave the weak behind rather than slow down the entire cav-
alcade and make it more likely that the Japanese would catch
it. Better to risk losing a few POWs than to lose them all.

"*We're* to escort out the last one hundred?" Kittleson guessed.

"Right."

Only, they could not depart right away. Captain Jimmy Fisher, the wounded Ranger battalion surgeon, and Scout Sergeant Alfred Alfonso were inside the hut undergoing emergency surgery. Fisher especially was in a bad way. The released POW doctor, Lieutenant Merle Musselman, had selflessly sacrificed his place on the bull cart train in order to stay behind to treat the wounded. Fisher was the only doctor who had accompanied the raiders. Two other POWs wouldn't leave without Musselman: Army Chaplain Hugh Kennedy and Dr. Herbert Ott, an army veterinarian.

"Those guys got balls," Corporal Gilbert Cox conceded. "Imagine: Being this close to getting out and then risking it all to help somebody else."

Major Stephen Sitter from the Ranger platoon had also volunteered to stay behind.

"We'll be leaving within an hour," Lieutenant Nellist promised. "Barring further complications."

"Further complications?" Wismer snorted. "Let me get this right. We're behind Nip lines being chased by about a million Japs. We have with us one hundred guys who can hardly walk and two stretcher cases. But that's okay because we also got twelve Scouts and a Ranger officer. Does that mean we have them outnumbered? And we're talking about further complications."

Wismer wasn't bitching. It was merely in his nature to point out the obvious. Then he fell to in helping fashion a pair of wooden doors into stretchers for the wounded men.

"I'm sorry you have to carry me," Alfonso apologized when Cox and Kittleson lugged him from the surgery hut to give the POW doctor more room to work with Fisher.

Cox dismissed it with an easy, "Forget it. Next time you might have to carry me—and I'm a helluva lot heavier than you."

An hour passed. Then two. Doctor Musselman and the scarecrow chaplain pushed aside the door blanket and stepped outside. Attention focused on them instantly. The waiting was making everyone jittery. Each passing minute brought the Japanese nearer to discovering them.

The flush of escaping light revealed ragged men so painfully thin they resembled yellow parchment drawn over bone frameworks.

"There's nothing else I can do for him here," Doctor Musselman said. "He'll die if we try to move him in a cart."

"It's in God's hands now," Chaplain Kennedy added.

"Not yet," the Ranger major protested. "If we can get an airplane in here . . . They're doing it in Burma—using airplanes for medical airlifts. There's a big field outside the village. It wouldn't take much to turn it into an airstrip. We can radio for an airplane . . ."

It was worth a try. General Kreuger at 6th Army promised to dispatch a plane before dawn. Scouts and Filipino villagers collected axes and shovels and hurried into the field which they began desperately hacking into a landing strip. They labored until an hour before dawn. Then they stepped back and watched the skies. Time was wasting.

Lieutenant Nellist brought the news. "Too late," he said.

Captain Jimmy Fisher died quietly while still unconscious. The POWs for whom he had sacrificed his life reached Sibul and freedom at almost the same moment he died. Chaplain Kennedy still wore his rags from prison as he stood at Fisher's grave to deliver one more eulogy after the countless he had recited over the dead generated by the prison camp at Cabanatuan. Alamo Scouts and Major Sitter lowered their heads.

"O God, we commend to You the soul of a very brave man . . ."

Filipinos later erected a marker changing the name of the little cemetery at Balincarin to *Doctor-Captain James C. Fisher Memorial Park*.

"Amen," Kittleson said. When he lifted his eyes the sun was rising red in the east.

A bad omen?

*   *   *

Moving so many noncombatants in broad daylight was risky and foolish business, but the Scouts had little choice. Filipino irregulars collected more bull carts into which the remaining frightened and helpless prisoners were cast. The string of carts with its wretched cargo and the small band of valiant Scouts eased out of the village and stuck to the edges of forests and to lowland drainages as they labored beneath a cruel sun toward American lines. Scouts ranged ahead or paralleled the slow convoy's flanks for security.

Kittleson and Sabas Asis on point observed a Jap patrol working its way through a copse of forest on the other side of a field of grass. Their green-brown figures flitted in and out of trees. Asis scurried back to warn Lieutenant Nellist while Kittleson hid and kept watch. Nellist halted the caravan. An expectant hush fell.

The enemy patrol continued at right angles, unaware of the cart train nearby.

To Kittleson it almost seemed that they were on a charmed march, like they were on a direct mission from God. They were pushing directly through the center of enemy territory teeming with Jap soldiers—and the Japs, it appeared, were blind to their presence. Maybe God thought the poor POWs had already lived through enough of hell.

By noon, the stragglers were within ten miles of Allied troops. Word had been passed all along the line to keep a sharp eye out for them. Wismer went up and down the string of carts joking with the POWs to keep their spirits up.

"Steak and ice cream tonight," he promised. "A soft bed and a pretty nurse."

Some prisoners wept just thinking about it. They grinned back at him with mouths missing teeth. Haunted eyes dared harbor the light of hope.

The Scouts vowed *nothing* would stop them from returning with their precious freight, short of their own deaths—certainly not the motley collection of communist guerrillas that suddenly materialized to block a fork in the road outside a friendly village. The leader was a squat, flat-faced Filipino wearing jeans and a castoff U.S. Marine blouse. He wore a fierce scar on one cheek and a bandoleer of .30-cal ammo across his chest. He carried an American M-1 Garand. About a dozen or so of his equally scruffy followers arranged themselves behind him in support.

Hukbalahap, led by Luis Taruc, an ardent Stalin communist, was one of the largest guerrilla groups in the Philippines. Although the Huks (Peoples Army to Fight the Japanese) were created to fight the invaders, their ideology led them into more clashes with other guerrillas than with the common enemy. Major Lapham had had his own skirmishes with the Huks. They had ambushed and shot Lapham's executive officer.

Most partisan commanders saw the Huks as better assassins than soldiers, more occupied with furthering communism than ridding the country of a conqueror. Huks routinely plundered from ordinary Filipinos and tortured any who resisted. They murdered Filipino landlords and drove many to the comparative safety of Manila. They were a treacherous lot, not to be trusted.

What they were doing now was trying to run a shakedown on the Alamo Scouts: Money or weapons in exchange for safe passage through Huk-controlled territory.

"You cannot pass," Scarface said, tilting the muzzle of his M-1 threateningly at Lieutenant Nellist.

Kittleson and big Gilbert Cox, both armed with Tommy guns, arranged themselves off to Lieutenant Nellist's flanks as the tall officer glared down upon the shorter Scarface. The Scouts had traveled two ways through Jap country and conducted a successful raid to free 516 Yank POWs. They were in no mood for some puffed-up Pancho Villa no better than a common street mugger.

"Let us through, you little sonofabitch," Nellist growled. "We're the goddamned U.S. Army and we're going through. Get the hell out of the way."

Kittleson charged his Thompson with a ratcheting sound hard enough to shatter tension. The tilt of his muzzle let it be known who would be first if shooting started.

"Move aside, Bill," Kittleson said to Nellist. "I'll cut 'em all to hell."

Scarface's eyes shifted uneasily from Nellist to Kittleson standing spread-legged to the side, Tommy gun ready. The big man on the other side, Cox, appeared equally prepared to give an accounting of himself. More Scouts slowly moved up, all stone-faced and gripping their weapons. Things were getting nasty.

No one moved. Everything stood still while Scarface considered his options.

He had to realize he would be the first to die. The short Yank with the big Thompson would see to it.

Turmoil warred on his ugly face, a mixture of rage and apprehension. Then, begrudgingly, he stepped aside. His band moved with him. Kittleson and Cox stood across the road, eyes and weapons aimed at the Huks, until the cart caravan passed safely. Kittleson chucked Scarface a mock salute and swaggered off down the road. By God, and with God's help, they were going home and taking the last of the POWs with them.

Get the hell out of the way.

PART II

*"... To proclaim liberty to the captives, and the opening of
the prison to them that are bound."*

Jeremiah

Galen Kittleson during World War II, shortly before the raid on Cabanatuan to free American Death March Survivors. *Photo: Galen Kittleson*

Kittleson (TOP ROW, LEFT) is shown with other Alamo Scouts in the Philippines in 1944. *Photo: U.S. Army*

General Walter Krueger (LEFT), commander of Sixth Army, congratulates Alamo Scout Galen Kittleson following the raid of Cabanatuan that liberated survivors of the Bataan Death March. *Photo: U.S. Army*

General Douglas MacArthur inspects dead Japanese upon returning to the Philippines as he promised to do. Alamo Scouts acted as his personal bodyguards. Sergeant Kittleson is the last man on the right. *Photo: National Archives*

Colonel Arthur D. "Bull" Simons, a legend in Special Forces, on the night of the raid against the Son Tay POW camp. *Photo: Galen Kittleson*

CSGM Kittleson prepares for an equipment parachuted jump at Fort Bragg, NC. *Photo: Galen Kittleson*

SFC Kittleson in Vietnam around the time he attempted to rescue Mike Rowe from a Viet Cong POW camp. *Photo: Galen Kittleson*

CSGM Kittleson (UPPER LEFT) with a Special Forces "A" Team. *Photo: Galen Kittleson*

Kittleson at a bunkered "hooch" at his Special Forces camp in Vietnam, shortly after his attempt to rescue Mike Rowe from a VC POW camp. *Photo: Galen Kittleson*

Col. Arthur D. "Bull" Simons (LEFT) and Master Sgt. Galen Kittleson in formation at Fort Bragg, NC, as the raiders return from their assault on the Son Tay POW camp. *Photo: Galen Kittleson*

Special Forces soldiers stand at attention to salute the Son Tay Raiders as they return to Fort Bragg after the raid. *Photo: U.S. Army*

Secretary of Defense Melvin Laird presents SGM Galen Kittleson with the Silver Star medal for heroism following the Son Tay raid on North Vietnam to rescue American POWs. Other Son Tay raiders stand in formation. *Photo: U.S. Army*

CSGM Galen Kittleson, Command Sergeant Major of the 7th Special Forces Group (Airborne). *Photo: Galen Kittleson*

CSGM Kittleson receives the Legion of Merit medal upon his retirement from the U.S. Army Special Forces in 1978. *Photo: Galen Kittleson*

Retired CSGM Galen Kittleson and family as they appear today. *Photo: U.S. Army*

CHAPTER 34

Dairy farmer Galen Kittleson—he was no longer "Kit"—swung wide the barn doors and let the Guernseys out. They lowed contentedly, having been fed and milked to relieve the pressure on their udders. The little farmer stood quietly and watched the cows crowd the open gate from the lot, before sorting themselves out and squeezing through in bunches to disperse below the red sky of the sun setting over northern Iowa's corn and dairy belt. Lush pasture spread out from the barn and lot, touched softly by the sky's paintbrush, blending into it. It edged into a fence and a corn field beyond. The growing corn was waist-high and green and silent in that time of twilight when there was no wind and the world breathed quietly.

Kittleson had filled out some through the chest and shoulders, mostly from the labor of making a go at farming, but he remained a modest five-four in height. He always joked that he had grown up in the army, but he hadn't grown *up*. Besides, it wasn't height that made a man a big or a small man; stature came more from what was inside him.

A rueful smile insinuated itself onto his broad face as he

watched his cattle going back to grazing. He had everything
he wanted in life. Didn't he? He should be content.

"What are you going to do when it's over?" Willie Wismer had asked him as the war was winding down. Hiroshima
and Nagasaki had been A-bombed. Would you believe that
that had been over ten years ago?

Kittleson thought about it a minute, simply relishing
the thought of home. "Cows and corn," he replied presently.
He thought about Darlene, his pen pal throughout most of
the war, and he wondered. "Settle down," he elaborated.
"Raise cows and corn back in Iowa—and maybe a kid or
two, God willing."

He *was* content. He *was* a happy man.

But sometimes, *sometimes*, he let his thoughts drift.

*We know not in what dignity these heroes were born,
but we know the glory for which they fought.* Ringing words
by General Walter Kreuger about the Alamo Scouts over a
decade ago.

How could he possibly miss something as horrible as
war? the farmer scolded himself.

But sometimes he did. Not the killing. Not the war itself.
But there was a comradeship, a brotherhood, among men at
war that he had not experienced before or afterward. *That*
was what he missed. He missed being *Kit* Kittleson. He
missed being part of something bigger than himself, of participating in grand events and being at least a cog in the
moving wheels of history.

The liberation of American POWs from the Japanese
prison compound at Cabanatuan on the night of 30 January
1945 was the largest and most successful raid made by any
nation in any war throughout history to free prisoners captured and held by an enemy. And *he*, Galen "Kit" Kittleson
from Iowa, had been a part of it. He had been *there* to help
rescue 516 POW survivors from the Bataan Death March.
That was *something*.

Only one prisoner had been left behind, an elderly Brit
who had gone nearly blind and stone deaf due to maltreatment. He had dozed off in an outdoor latrine a few minutes

before the attack and slept through the raid. When he awoke, he found everyone gone and the camp abandoned. A Filipino scavenger found the old man in the ruins a few days later and escorted him to his village. He was later picked up by a U.S. tank destroyer outfit and taken to an American hospital.

None of the POWs were killed during the action, although one died of heart attack during the raid and another had a heart attack and died on the arduous cart trip back to friendly lines. Two U.S. Rangers died from hostile fire: Captain Jimmy Fisher, the battalion surgeon, and Corporal Roy Sweezy. Two Scouts and two other Rangers were wounded in action but recovered. Captain Pajota, who had held his ground to give the raiders their thirty minutes, lost twenty-six of his guerrillas during the fight at Cabu Creek Bridge, but the partisans took a toll from the Japanese that numbered in the hundreds. More than 250 enemy soldiers were slaughtered at the camp.

General Kreuger personally awarded medals to Scouts who participated in the raid. All received the Presidential Unit Citation. Enlisted men were presented Bronze Stars with a V device for "Valor." Lieutenants Bill Nellist, Stud Rounsaville, and Jack Dove received Silver Stars with V. At the end of the war, Kit Kittleson ended up with three of the nation's highest awards for valor in combat—two Silver Stars and a Bronze Star. He won two of the medals for action involving the rescue of POWs at Oransbari and Cabanatuan. In constant combat for two years, he had not suffered so much as a scratch.

"I owe it all to God," he would say in his modest, down-to-earth manner.

Lieutenant Hollywood Jack Dove, whom Kittleson later learned became a minister, used to watch Kittleson drop to his knees and pray before every mission. Then the kid would go out and fight like a Viking warrior.

"If this young kid is praying," Dove once commented, "then there must be something to it."

Rescued POWs publicly verified reports of Japanese

atrocities against those they captured in battle, hardening Allied resolve. Their stories contributed to President Truman's decision to develop and use the atomic bomb.

From February 1944 to September 1945, Alamo Scouts conducted 106 missions behind enemy lines, including the two prison camp liberations. Not a single Scout was killed or captured. They in turn killed some five hundred enemy soldiers and captured sixty. Through their intelligence efforts, they assisted Allies in achieving important victories on Los Negros, Biak, and Noemfoor Islands; and at Hollandia, Aitape, Ormoc, Leyte, Luzon, and elsewhere.

PFC Kittleson was promoted to sergeant following the Cabanatuan raid, skipping over the intermediate rank of corporal. Lieutenant Nellist tried to persuade him to go for an officer's commission, maybe even apply for West Point. Kittleson vowed to fight the war until it ended and then go home.

"I might *really* have something to go home to now," he said, thinking of Darlene.

They were historic times. Sometimes, now, Kittleson the farmer dug out his old war diary recording them in his terse style. The ink was fading.

February 14. Went with General Kreuger to Bataan. Played cards after supper.

February 15. Went with General MacArthur to Bataan.

February 25. Lt. Nellist, Capt. Hanosak, two Scouts and myself sniped at Japs in Bulan.

April 3. At 158th RCT (Regimental Combat Team). Japs shooting German-made rockets. Scream in flight.

May 22. Listened to Japs on highway. Japs passed by within 50 feet of us with bull carts.

June 22. Lt. Nellist was wounded while he and I sniped at 15 Japs. Got Nellist to 48th Hospital.

August 14. Birthday, 21 years old. Japs accepted peace terms set down at Potsdam Conference.

September 2. Listened to official signing of treaty—heard Truman's address to nation. Also Nimitz's and MacArthur's.

"Gay? Galen?"

A woman's voice calling from the back door of the white, two-story farmhouse interrupted Kittleson's war reveries. He had spoken to Bill Nellist via the telephone that afternoon. That was what had brought back all the memories of days when a man lived on the edge and was therefore more *alive* than he would ever be again. They laughed together and remembered the old days. Then Kittleson went outside and let the cows into the barn and milked them.

What glory was there in herding mindless cattle into milking stalls morning and evening?

Time, for him, had assumed a sameness after the war. Everything had slowed down. If only *something would happen*—something to jar his daily routine.

Was there something strange about him? Did other veterans feel this way?

"Galen? Supper's ready, honey."

Kittleson shook his head slightly to clear it, to bring himself back.

"Be right there, Darlene."

He turned and went into the barn to lug the full cans of raw milk to the cooler before making his way to the house. There would be homemade bread for supper. There was always homemade bread; Kittleson's mother had made bread at home.

"Gay is used to homemade bread," Darlene's aunt had said to her. "It's up to you to learn how to make it before you get married."

After the war, Kittleson had had enough money saved to buy a new Chevrolet and a John Deere farm tractor. He still had it in the back of his head that he was born to be a farmer, like his father before him and his father's father. The first thing he did when he got discharged was drive his new car the twenty miles from St. Ansgar to Toeterville where Darlene lived in the two-story ancestral home with her family.

One thing followed another, as it will in life. A year and a half later, Kittleson and his wartime pen pal Darlene Bruggeman were married on the stairway of her house; her

mother was an invalid and couldn't easily leave the house.
Darlene told her mama that Galen could be as brusque and
hard as any man could be, but with her he was never anything but quiet and gentle. During the hard times when the
farm was getting started, the little veteran had a general response to cover any disagreement or difficulty: "Darlene,
honey, I never promised you a rose garden." It always made
them laugh. They used the phrase to soften any discussion.

Son Bruce came along on 3 October 1948. The Korean
War began with North Korea invading the South on 25 June
1950, a year before Darlene gave birth to son Lance on 4
July 1951. Kittleson read newspapers and listened to the war
news on the radio. He felt almost guilty for staying home on
the farm while other men shipped overseas to fight for their
country.

"Maybe I should enlist again," he suggested.

That frightened Darlene. "You've done more than your
share for your country," she scolded. "You have a wife and
two little boys to think about now."

Kittleson was always a quiet, introspective man, but as
the years passed, he was often even quieter than usual. He
had everything he wanted, everything he had dreamed about
in the trenches and jungles of the wartime South Pacific.
Then why wasn't he satisfied?

"Gay, what's wrong?" Darlene asked when he came in
from the barn after milking.

"Nothing's wrong, Darlene. Why do you keep asking?"

"I catch you staring out at nothing. Like you're thinking.
Like you're missing something or have something weighing
on your mind. Is it about Bill Nellist?"

"Really. It's nothing."

Occasionally, Kittleson thought of reenlisting in the
army. He *missed* the army. It wouldn't be so bad on the family, he thought. The U.S. was in between wars at the moment. The Korean ceasefire had been signed and while there
was some rattling and noise in a place called Vietnam, he
doubted anything would come of it. It would be just like
having a job, wouldn't it?

Except Darlene was a homebody. She had roots and she wanted their children to share those roots. Everything she knew and loved existed within 50 miles of Toeterville.

"It's *really* nothing," insisted Galen, shaking the mood, then grinned at the two boys tumbling in for supper.

He was living the American Dream.

In 1956, as the spring crops were being laid by, Galen's brother Norman was about to be drafted into military service. The Kittleson patriarch, Floyd, came to Galen. "I need your brother bad on the farm," he said. "Will you take him to the National Guard and see if you can get him enlisted?"

Galen, who had tried the Army Reserve for a few years after the war, took young Norman down to the National Guard armory. Norman did not enlist; Galen did. Six months later he reenlisted in the Regular Army with his old wartime rank of buck sergeant and was assigned to the 101st Airborne Division since he was already parachute qualified.

He caught a train to Fort Campbell, Kentucky. Darlene stood tear-stained on the platform holding the hands of nine-year-old Bruce and five-year-old Lance as the train pulled into the station to take her husband away.

"I'll send for you as soon as I can," he promised. "Darlene? Look at me. I never promised you a rose garden."

This time she forgot to laugh.

Kittleson stared out the coach window until his family disappeared from view.

"God? What have I gotten myself into?"

CHAPTER 35

After returning to the army, Sergeant Kittleson knocked around in the 101st Airborne for a couple of years before receiving orders to the 3rd Infantry Division in Germany, a nonairborne "leg" outfit. It was shortly after he arrived in Germany with Darlene and his sons that he heard of a supersecret unit, not yet more than a half-dozen years old, that was taking the concept of partisan guerrilla warfare to a new scientific level.

"What's Special Forces?" he asked.

Special, elite units like Alamo Scouts tend to flourish in wartime out of necessity. When the war ends, however, they are confined to the dustbins of history. Most military officers, especially of high rank, are ultraconservative, ultraconventional. They think in terms of mass infantry, more armor, and bigger guns. That was the emphasis after the World War: big war and tactical nukes. The 82nd Airborne at Fort Bragg, North Carolina, conducted training jumps from huge, two-level C-124 aircraft. Paratroopers joked about a new jump command: "Everybody downstairs, outside! Everybody upstairs, downstairs!" The advent of the Cold War, however, kept alive the idea of guerrilla warfare, *unconventional* warfare as a substitute for all-out war that might lead to total destruction of the earth through nuclear conflict. A few men kept taking unconventional warfare down from history's shelves and dusting it off.

Within the Pentagon's Psychological Operations Staff Section existed a Special Warfare Division in which General Robert McClure collected a small group of men who had seen and recognized the value of guerrillas and guerrilla activity during WWII. Commanding this SWD was Wendell Fertig, who had commanded guerrillas on Mindanao in the Philippines. Among other veterans of unconventional warfare on Fertig's staff were: Colonel Russell Volkman, a commander of guerrillas on Luzon; Colonel Aaron Bank, who had parachuted three times into occupied France and once into Indochina with the OSS (Office of Strategic Services); Joe Waters of Merrill's Marauders and the OSS; and Bob McDowell, who had been with the OSS to work with partisans in Yugoslavia.

After many bitter battles, McClure and Fertig finally sold their concept of unconventional warfare when, in early 1952, the army reluctantly allotted 2,500 personnel slots to the program. What emerged was Special Forces and the guerrilla mission, born out of the fear of a universally expected World War III and the need to devise an alternative to nuclear holocaust. The mission of the newly formed unit could be condensed as: To seek out, train, and support men capable of becoming effective guerrillas; to seek out, engage, and neutralize other guerrillas—that is, both guerrilla insurgency and *counter*guerrilla insurgency.

In an obscure corner of the post at Fort Bragg, a Psychological Warfare Center was established, to which Colonel Aaron Bank was assigned. On 20 June 1952, the 10th Special Forces Group (Airborne) was born with a strength of ten men. More OSS and Ranger veterans were gathered. Every man had to be a triple volunteer: He had to be a volunteer in the army—no draftees; a volunteer for parachute training; and a volunteer for Special Forces.

The 10th moved to Germany in 1953 with five hundred

men. Those who stayed behind reorganized into the 77th SF Group (Airborne). Eventually, some dozen SF Groups were to operate in hot spots around the globe.

In the spring of 1962, President John F. Kennedy awarded Special Forces its distinctive headgear, the green beret. "The Green Beret," he proclaimed, "is again becoming a symbol of excellence, a badge of courage, a mark of distinction in the fight for freedom." It was an unconventional outfit for unconventional times.

Perhaps it was inevitable that the former Alamo Scout who had operated clandestinely behind enemy lines during World War II, who had fought one of the nation's first modern unconventional wars, should gravitate toward that kind of action when the opportunity arose. Alamo Scouts was, after all, one of a number of those elite WWII units—including the Office of Strategic Services (OSS), the 1st Special Service Force (Devil's Brigade), and the 5307th Composite Unit (Merrill's Marauders)—that led to the formation of the U.S. Army's "first unconventional warfare unit" to be adopted as an integral part of the army. Like Sergeant Galen Kittleson, the men who volunteered for U.S. Army Special Forces, which became popularly known as the Green Berets because of their headgear, were as unconventional as the wars they were commissioned to fight. Many were mavericks, even quiet mavericks like Kittleson, who chafed at the rigidity of the regular army, who were imaginative and innovative and wanted to try something new and challenging.

The men who joined the Alamo Scouts and OSS during the World War had much in common with those who signed up for Special Forces when it came along. Columnist Stewart Alsop could have been speaking of any of these units when he described in OSS the presence of "missionaries and bartenders, polo players and baseball pitchers, millionaires and union organizers, a human fly and a former Russian general, a big game hunter, and a history professor."

"*Naturally*," Darlene complained mildly, "Galen *had* to volunteer."

Kittleson was readily accepted with 10th Group in Germany because of his service and reputation with the Alamo Scouts. "For Christ's sake, the little man was on *two* raids behind enemy lines to rescue POWs." Kittleson had "toted the rucksack." He might be pushing forty years old at the time, but he remained in excellent physical condition and had expertise in combat that Special Forces needed. But even though SF soldiers were on the average older and more mature than other soldiers, the new sergeant boosted considerably the average age of any operational detachment to which he was assigned. While the amicable little war hero might have been "Kit" in the Pacific when he was twenty years old, he now became known among his younger cohorts as "Pappy."

Soldiers of 10th Group trained and exercised with airborne, commando, ranger, raiders, special forces, militia, and clandestine organizations all over Europe, Asia, Latin America, and the Middle East. They adapted quickly to operating across cultural and linguistic barriers. The men were tough, proud, intensely trained, and competent specialists in guerrilla warfare.

While the *insurgency* part of guerrilla warfare was well understood and practiced by SF, *counterinsurgency* had to wait until the Vietnam War. It was the Vietnam War, America's most controversial foreign involvement, that catapulted Special Forces into the eye of the American public.

Although SF detachments had been in Vietnam as early as 1956, they operated with their customary secretiveness and attracted little attention. SF wives were sometimes asked, "Oh? Your husband is in Vietnam? Where is that? Is he home on weekends?" In the early 1960s, however, that changed. Robin Moore wrote an action thriller, *The Green Berets*, based on early SF activities in Vietnam, and John Wayne starred in a movie of the same name. Sergeant Barry Sadler followed with a hit song, "The Ballad of the Green Berets." The Green Berets were suddenly America's heroes.

Working in twelve-man "A-Teams," or Operational Detachments, early MTTs (mobile training teams) in Asia helped develop Vietnam's special forces and ranger battalions. As the pattern of the war grew and became more complex, SF found itself taking on a number of different roles and missions. It became involved in every conceivable aspect of counterinsurgency: military, economic, psychological, and political. It involved hundreds of U.S. Special Forces soldiers spread out into more than one hundred camps from the Demilitarized Zone to the Gulf of Siam. Its was a history of mostly small skirmishes with a few big battles: of carving isolated camps out of jungle and Delta swamp; of teaching Vietnamese how to shoot, build, farm, care for the sick, or run ambush and combat operations against the enemy.

The nucleus of the Vietnam effort was the CIDG (Civilian Irregular Defence Group), composed of a U.S. SF A-Team and local Vietnamese or ethnic minorities such as the Montagnards. Working out of primitive camps, the CIDGs were charged with detecting North Vietnam infiltrations, keeping an eye on enemy movements, conducting reconnaissance, and making clandestine hit-and-run forays across the border into Laos and Cambodia. The first Medal of Honor of the war went to a Green Beret; seven more followed.

In the spring of 1967, "Pappy" Kittleson, now a balding, tough-as-rawhide master sergeant with 6th Group at Fort Bragg, was due for rotation. Command Sergeant Major Dunaway summoned him.

"Where do you want to go, Pappy?" he asked gruffly.

"Sergeant Major, I was under the impression the army put a guy where it needed him."

It was a vintage Pappy Kittleson response: Do the job, wherever, whatever.

Dunaway let a smile crack his granite face. "Damn right. That's what I wanted to hear."

Orders came two weeks later: 5th Special Forces Group, Republic of Vietnam. After the passage of more than two decades, Kittleson was going back to war.

Darlene expected it, but she had turned into a good soldier's wife. She tried not to let her fears show. The army was Galen's life; Darlene loved him enough to want what he wanted. Up to now, in fact, the small-town girl from the corn fields had also learned to enjoy the more-or-less nomadic life of servicemen and their families in the years after World War II and Korea. American soldiers were being sent all over the world in the hands-to-throat struggle of the Cold War. She had seen things and places she might only have heard about had Galen and she remained back on the farm.

Bruce, the elder son, was in college at Iowa State. Darlene and Lance decided to stay at Fort Bragg while Galen was overseas. Here they had all their friends and the support of other Special Forces families whose men were also at war.

Kittleson tried to make light of it. "I never promised you a rose garden."

"That's just not funny, Galen. You have to come back. Who's going to make you homemade bread?"

CHAPTER 36

The OD-green Caribou circled the Mobile Guerrilla Force camp at Tau Chau. As it leveled out on low-altitude downwind, Master Sergeant Pappy Kittleson got a good buzzard's-eye view of a slum behind barbed wire. The camp was set next to a beach of the South China Sea, with a dirt road running between the front gate and the beach. Driftwood, rotted sampans, and other debris from the hootches along the road lay strewn next to the water.

Barbed wire and carelessly placed concertina formed a rectangle around a dozen or so bamboo hootches with tin roofs. Kittleson noted that earthen bunkers at each corner of the compound were above ground, fairly open, and not sandbagged. More earth had been pushed up here and there along the perimeter to fashion defensive berms. Clothes flapped on the barbed wire to dry.

An asphalt runway unadorned by hangars or other buildings separated the Special Forces camp from the little village of Tau Chau. Overlooking this Vietnam ghetto were three tall mountains, one of them cone-shaped and not more than one hundred meters outside the fort's wire. A half-dozen enemy soldiers strategically placed on either of these three modest peaks could pin down the garrison. A few mortars on the hills might pound it back to dirty South China beach.

Not a few Special Forces camps had been overrun by Viet Cong within the past few years. Most of those were farther north and not in IV Corps' Mekong Delta region, but that didn't make Tau Chau immune to the threat.

The plane came in on final and touched down. Halfway up the runway, several American troopers in tiger stripes and carrying weapons lounged about, members of A-Team 502 ready to greet their new operations sergeant—Master Sergeant Galen Kittleson, the team's newest ranking enlisted man. He and the team's commander, a First Lieutenant Ochoa, would lead the Mobile Guerrilla Force in Mekong Delta operations for the next year.

Mobile Guerrilla Forces had been created by 5th Special Forces Group in late 1966. They were like ready-reaction MIKE Forces, only larger and with more-specialized missions. Each Mobile Force was composed of a 150-man CIDG company; a 35-member reconnaissance platoon, all members of which were Vietnamese, Cambodian volunteers, or other ethnic minorities; and a twelve-man American Special Forces command element. Their job was to conduct guerrilla warfare using the enemy's own guerrilla tactics inside enemy territory outside the AOs (areas of operation) of CIDG camps. This included interdicting enemy lines of communications, conducting surveillance of enemy base camps and way stations, destroying food and ammunition caches, prowling enemy-used trails for ambush opportunities, intercepting courier and small troop units, performing civic action in nearby villages, acting as an immediate reaction force, and setting booby traps and delayed-fuse demolitions. In short, they were to raise hell, spread chaos, and kill VC—in no particular order. The missions were called "Black Jack" missions in deference to 5th Group's commanding officer, Colonel Francis "Black Jack" Kelly.

Kittleson had been in-country two days. Those days were spent in orientation at 5th Group Headquarters in Nha Trang where Colonel Kelly himself welcomed Special Forces replacements. He was a huge, Irish Catholic ex-cop from Boston who spoke with fire and intensity.

"While I am Group commander," he thundered, "none of my camps will be taken by the enemy. If any of my camps are threatened, day or night, we will parachute MIKE Force or Mobile Forces on them immediately. Men, welcome to the Republic of Vietnam where the name of the game is: *Kill VC! Kill VC!*"

Kittleson wondered if Black Jack Kelly had visited this shantytown of a camp with its surrounding overpowering peaks before he vowed that none of his camps would be overrun.

He grabbed his CAR-15 carbine and rucksack and jumped out the door of the Caribou as soon as it rolled to a stop. He was the only passenger getting off at Tau Chau. The airplane turned back down the strip to take off for its next leg. A narrow-chested lieutenant ran up to shake Kittleson's hand, introducing himself as Ochoa. He was in his thirties, slender and light olive complexioned. Kittleson later learned he had been a member of the Cuban brigade that attempted to invade Castro's Cuba during the botched Bay of Pigs invasion. He still spoke with a thick Latin accent.

He looked over the stocky little Iowan in fatigues still pressed from the Outside World. The new sergeant had short gray bristles around his ears and, Ochoa noticed when he took off his beret to replace it with a narrow-brimmed bush hat, his pate was so bald that it was tanned the same color as the rest of his face. The face looked weathered around the eyes.

"Jesus to God," he blurted out. He pronounced Jesus the Spanish way—*Hey-sus*. "What in Hey-sus's good name are you doing in this shitbag country? How old are you, *viejo*?"

"Forty-three," the sergeant responded in that quiet, imperturbable way of his. He added with a trace of amusement, "You can call me Pappy."

The three other SF troopers with Ochoa were the skinny commo specialist, Sergeant Morin, who wore what his compadres called a "little cocksucker mustache"; Godsey, who carried around on his hulking frame the look of a Nebraska swine farmer; and the Irishman Burdish, a slab-sided weapons specialist with a receding hairline.

All five piled into a Jeep quarter-ton, Ochoa driving. They whisked down the runway to the yellow road and weaved through a squatters' settlement of thatched-roof hootches to reach the front gate. Naked kids, chickens, pigs, and dogs scurried to get out of the way. Ochoa kept his foot pressed on the gas.

"Dependents' camp," Ochoa explained before returning to his discourse on the conditions at the camp. "Our soldiers' wives and *niños*."

There were two Mobile Guerrilla Forces at Tau Chau, he explained. Roughly 350 Vietnamese and Cambodians. The Viets and the Cambodes couldn't get along in the same outfit, so the outfits were segregated. Two Forces meant two A-Teams—501 and 502. Team 501 had lost its operations sergeant, so Kittleson would be in charge of both teams' enlisted.

"We will build an empire, you and I, Senor Pappy," the Cuban joked.

The Jeep screeched to a halt in front of a long building with upright bamboo walls and the inescapable corrugated tin roof, the team house, where the Americans quartered. A dog as yellow as the road lay in the dirt licking its balls. Ochoa sat behind the wheel while the others climbed out with a "See ya, Pappy," or "Later, Sarge." The lieutenant wasn't through talking.

"Pappy, this war is really getting fooked-up what with air-conditioned trailers and steaks being airlifted in for high-ranking officers' quarters and messes. I do not know what the propaganda is back home, but I would imagine it is more of the same old water buffalo bullshit—winning hearts and minds and all that. 'If you do not give me your hearts and minds, I will blow up your village.' Senor, the truth is, we are being out-guerrilla'd by the VC guerrillas.

"We control nothing in the Mekong Delta but what you

can see at any particular moment. We are the cocks of the yard when it is daylight. But when it comes dark, seven or eight VC come into a hamlet and they give their speech. They say, 'We are noble liberators who fight to free the people from the oppression of absentee landlords and corrupt government officials. Once inevitable victory is in our grasp, you will no longer be plagued. But, of course, we need the help of all patriotic citizens. We will take with us five young men to participate in the people's glorious struggle. In three days we shall return and your contribution to the cause will be one water buffalo, six chickens, and eight bags of rice. You will report to us all enemy movements. Mr. Elder of the Tribe, what are your comments?'

"Should the poor sonofabitch's comments be negative, the elder gets his throat cut. The VC disembowel his wife and children and water buffalo, then politely ask who is the next-ranking elder. The new chief is likely to understand the logic of the VC's arguments. It is very effective. That village is not apt to be won back by American candy bars and sick call."

In the Philippines during *that* war, terrorism backfired on the Japanese and made the Filipinos more determined to resist. Kittleson recalled delighted cries of "*Liberator! Liberator!*" and the sweet refrain of the American anthem whenever Americans entered a village. Of course, the Japanese had been foreign invaders, not guerrillas from within. In Vietnam, terrorism seemed to be brutally effective. Americans here were made to seem the invaders. The quickest way to get dead was to trust the Vietnamese.

In Vietnam only three days, Kittleson was already troubled about what he was learning of the war and how it was being conducted. He had never doubted the rightness of the cause while fighting the Japanese.

But the commies had to be stopped, didn't they? If not now, *when*? If not here, *where*?

There was much of the patriotic midwestern farmer remaining in the little Iowan-turned-professional-soldier. To him, it was America, right or wrong. He stepped before a formation of troops and he automatically heard the "Star Spangled Banner" playing. America was more than a country; it was an inheritance, a symbol of liberty and justice, shined upon by the face of God. It was worth fighting for.

"We are Black Jacking out of here at Zero-dark-thirty in the morning," the Cuban lieutenant said. He gave a snort of amused cynicism. "Some headquarters types want to make a combat parachute jump, but they desire us to secure the drop zone so nobody shoots at them. Master Sergeant, you have just arrived. You need not accompany the Mobile Force if—"

"I'll go," Kittleson interrupted. "As team sergeant, it will be my policy that when the teams go out, I go out with them."

The Cuban lifted one arched brow and nodded approval.

"*Verdad*," he exclaimed. "That is also my personal policy to go whenever the teams go. Cubans have proved themselves classic in fighting for lost causes."

CHAPTER 37

The jungle was a mean place to fight, made even meaner by the VC. A grunt from the 173rd Airborne told Sergeant Kittleson while they were waiting for a flight out of Nha Trang that Vietnam had 133 species of snakes, 131 of which were poisonous. In January, the young GI said, he had participated in Operation Junction City, the only combat parachute jump to have been made in Vietnam so far. On the back of the helmet he carried was scrawled "If I die here, bury me face down so Vietnam can kiss my ass."

"Master Sergeant," he said, "the snakes is mean, but there must be about 200 species of VC and NVA—and they're all meaner."

Lieutenant Ochoa, Kittleson, Morin the radioman, and about sixty Vietnamese Mobile guerrillas, which was all they could round up on short notice, trucked out of Tau Chau in deuce-and-a-half trucks to the Seven Mountains area near Nui Giai. Ordinarily, Special Forces carefully planned its missions and gave briefbacks to superiors to hone that readiness. This time, however, the entire operation was conceived and put into effect in only thirty-six hours. By the time A-502 received mission orders, the team had little more time than to grab rucks and head for the trucks.

The concept of the mission called for companies from the 5th Mobile Strike Force to parachute from six C-130 aircraft onto a DZ (drop zone) near Nui Giai. On the ground, they would form an anvil for a much larger hammer of CIDG surrounding a VC stronghold on one of the Seven Mountains. Ochoa and Kittleson's Mobile Guerrillas would secure the DZ for the drop, then pull back toward the mountains to search for a reported enemy ammunition depot hidden in a cave.

The parachute jump went off without a hitch. Old, dry rice beds and short grass hummocks covered the DZ and there were no injuries. Charlie failed to show up for the party. A-502's Mobile Guerrillas pulled back into the foothills, away from all trails, to hole up until morning. Ochoa and Kittleson found a slight rise in the ground with plenty of cover and concealment, established a defensive perimeter, and set up 50 percent alert. The ARVN (Army of the Republic of Vietnam) lieutenant, Tee Wee Chong, was nervous. Kittleson joked with him to allay the Viet's fears and to judge his abilities at the same time. The American was not impressed; he had heard too many tales of ARVNs bugging out on U.S. GIs in the middle of a firefight.

The sun went down quickly, as it had in the Philippines. Darkness took away sight, the most important of the senses. Then it rained—rain drops so big they hurt. They drummed on the foliage and it was like the jungle roared. Only someone who has tried to eat a cold C-rat can of sliced pork as rain poured into it, mixing water with grease, can appreciate a meal in the jungle.

Sleep was tortured and intermittent—and dangerous. Kittleson slept with one hand on his weapon and the other near a claymore clacker ready to detonate mines encircling the company's position. Ghosts of enemy soldiers he had killed seldom haunted his dreams; his nightmares, when he had them, were filled with his *trying* to kill the enemy only to have his rifle jam.

At daybreak, they breakfasted while Morin set up his PRC-10 with a long antenna and tried to bump a signal back to Tau Chau. "Rattlesnake Nest, Rattlesnake One," Morin chanted. "How do you read?"

"Are you getting through?" Lieutenant Ochoa asked.

"Short count follows," Morin said into the headphone. "One, two, three, four, five; five, four, three, two, one . . ."

"Tell Nest we're prepared . . ."

"Fuck, Lieutenant. This ain't no goddamned telephone."

Airwaves in Southeast Asia were often cluttered with interference, much of it enemy jamming.

"Keep trying," the lieutenant said patiently.

"Roger that."

Mornings after a night spent in the jungle made men stiff and surly. Kittleson felt little aches and pains that would never have bothered him twenty years ago. He had almost forgotten how many fetid smells the jungle produced—odors from stagnant pools, rotting vegetation, and unwashed bodies.

He bowed his head and gave thanks for the food he was about to partake; pound cake and peaches, a feast from OD cans. When he looked up, he found Tee Wee Chong watching him. The tee wee smiled and looked away.

It was a Vietnamese custom, even among soldiers, to hold hands and chatter. This morning, however, the Vietnamese were conspicuously silent as they burned chips of soft C-4 explosives to heat their tea and rice. They glanced about apprehensively.

"Beaucoup VC," said the ARVN tee wee. He looked at Kittleson as though daring him to try to allay his fears.

The company moved out single file, Ranger style. Two shotgunners armed with 12-gauges and double-aught buck traveled about twenty yards ahead on point. Double-aught could really sweep a trail in case of ambush. Another man traveled between the main body and any trail they paralleled.

This terrain lay on the edge of the Delta, making it higher and drier, especially in the rocky foothills as they stepped into the Seven Mountains rising in the background. Still, it was jungle, though not impenetrable. Tumbles of moss-covered rocks made footing underneath the trees perilous. There were low hills and gravel washes and fast-running streams. Humping in such terrain meant constant agony, discomfort, and fear. Minor problems like jungle sores and insect bites never healed. Ants were torture, always crawling, always biting. Leeches went beyond torture; grunts said if you didn't watch out, the little bastards crawled into your penis, swelled up with blood and gave you the grandest but most painful diamond-cutter blue boner of your life.

Perspiration coursed down Pappy's face and arms, making his grip on the black plastic stock of his CAR-15 slimy and slick. The weapon felt like a toy compared to the heavy wood and steel of the Thompson he'd carried in the South Pacific. He wished he had Tommy now. The CAR fired a tiny 5.56 cartridge a fraction of the size of the .45 slug pumped out by the Thompson submachine gun. When you held a .45 bullet in your hand, you *knew* you were holding stopping power.

Plainly, they were in the enemy's backyard. Saigon had exerted so little military presence in the area that the local VC took few precautions. Trails through the foothills avoided dense underbrush, and there were sneaker prints in the mud. Most VC wore either sneakers or sandals. They came upon VC campsites and rest areas at trail intersections near streams. According to the intel provided Ochoa by Group, the cave and its cache of munitions should be nearby. Lieutenant Ochoa and one of the Viet troopers scouted ahead to take a look while Kittleson stayed with the main body.

Maybe it had been over two decades, but Kittleson felt his battle senses sharpening.

A single thought occurred to him: *This is what you were born to do.*

Soldiering, not farming.

CHAPTER 38

Grunts had a saying about how bad things could get: "Bad as a day in Vietnam."

From what Pappy Kittleson had learned, secondhand so far, a day in Vietnam could go *real* bad. Viet Cong were apparently far more wily and treacherous in guerrilla combat than the Japanese had ever been. The Japs were never true guerrilla fighters. The VC were that and much more: flitting among shadows, striking and withdrawing, only to strike somewhere else. It was like attempting to capture wisps of smoke.

The Japanese must have looked upon the Alamo Scouts as wisps of smoke.

The Viet at the head of the column with Lieutenant Ochoa called a halt and summoned Kittleson to go forward.

"Beaucoup VC," the tee wee whispered, his eyes rolling.

Were those the only words he knew?

Ochoa crouched among some boulders. He held up a hand for caution. "Watch it! Watch it!" he mouthed, pointing.

The sergeant spotted it: a trip wire about shin high tied off to a sapling at one end and then stretched across the trail to the pin of a grenade attached to another sapling. It was a highly effective man trap, especially at night. Humans hunting humans meant it was sometimes difficult to determine which were the hunters and which the hunted.

Kittleson stepped over the wire. Ochoa peered down into a wide gulch and he pointed again. Below stood two Vietnamese among moss-crusted boulders as big as houses. The black hair on their bare heads gleamed; they wore the dirty gray coarse cloth of farmers rather than traditional "black pajamas." They stood there bullshitting while their AK-47 rifles leaned against a rock.

They were either guarding something—the ammo depot?—or they were an outlying OP/LP (observation/listening post) for a larger element somewhere ahead. The two Americans carefully scanned the gulch but spotted nothing resembling the mouth of a cave. If there was a cave, it was hidden somewhere in the boulder field.

The lay of the terrain on this side made a stealthy approach nearly impossible. The gulch wall sheered off on a landslide of rock scree entangled in new undergrowth. The opposite wall seemed a gentler slope and provided more cover and concealment.

It took the company nearly an hour to drop back, maneuver across the lower gulch, and approach on the opposite side. Ochoa and Kittleson deployed their understrength company in a simple assault line once they were fifty yards short of the enemy position. The object was to catch the sentries and the main VC body by surprise: Kick ass and take names later. Tee Wee Chung looked uncertain about the kick ass part. *Beaucoup VC! Beaucoup VC!*

Cover here was not so thick and entangled as to cause serious impediment. The Mobile Force weaved forward on line, the Americans a few paces ahead to lead the way. Kittleson's eyes and rifle adjusted together as he worked his way down toward the boulder field. His heart pounded with excitement.

A shape ahead suddenly darted in the treeline. The split second it took Pappy to align the barrel of his weapon was a split second too long.

They had been detected.

The suspense of the stalk erupted in violence. Hidden VC opened up almost point-blank from among the boulders with a withering hail of automatic rifle fire. It seemed like the earth was screaming, the sun was screaming. The air exploded with resonating energy. Lead chewed into foliage, snapping loose a storm of leaves, twigs, and bark. Bullets spanged screaming off rocks.

Two troopers were hit in the first burst. One's face blew up like a watermelon whumped by a sledgehammer. The force of the blow threw him ten feet backwards into some bushes. He thrashed the bushes as he died, spewing blood and flopping his legs and arms like a chicken with its neck wrung. The second guy merely walked over and sat down against a tree after he was hit. Jagged bones protruded from shredded flesh. He blinked rapidly, as though trying to focus.

The wall of lead halted the advance. Viets dropped where they were and scrambled around looking for cover. Hardly anyone returned fire. They were dead men if they remained in the open.

"Charge! Charge!" Pappy bellowed, sweeping an arm forward while he one-handed the CAR-15 in three-round bursts, shooting point-blank at enemy muzzle flicker. "Kill the gooks! Kill the little bastards!" He led the assault down the slope, weaving among the rocks like a broken field runner. Supersonic green fireflies flickered all around him—tracer rounds from a light machine gun.

Emboldened by the American's example, a number of the braver ARVN soldiers lunged to their feet to follow. Others at least blasted back high-velocity M-16 chatter. Morin the radioman, a young kid, got caught up in the adrenaline surge and raced past Kittleson, screaming and shooting.

Ochoa stayed behind and ran up and down the stalled line, throwing and dragging troopers from hiding. "Move, goddamnit! Move, you fooking *cobardes*! Get your asses down that hill! Do you wish to die like chickenshits?"

The company stirred. Then it pulsed, everybody yelling

and screaming and shooting to build courage to a crescendo. The charge had everything except fixed bayonets.

Morin disappeared around a boulder. *Crazy damned kid!*

Kittleson darted among the boulders. A muzzle flickered ahead, from *underneath* a big rock, and what felt like a bee stinging numbed his nose and upper lip.

The motherfuckers had shot off his nose! Pappy hurled himself to one side and scrambled to the cover of a stone shelf. He felt his face. His nose remained attached to it, but blood filled his mouth and streamed off his chin.

He peeped around the end of the shelf. The guy under the boulder stitched a row of geysers along Pappy's rock. Pappy ducked back.

He waited a second. He heard the guy shooting again, but he was shooting at a fresh target. Pappy had the gook's location pegged. He guessed the VC to have dug a fighting hole behind the boulder, leaving a firing port underneath it.

Okay. Sayonara, motherfucker.

Kittleson twisted from cover with the CAR to his shoulder and his eyes already aiming down the sights. He squeezed off rounds into the VC's firing port until the carbine snapped empty. He rolled onto his back and slapped in a fresh magazine. No more firing came from the boulder.

He jumped up and continued the attack. By this time, Mobile Force soldiers were swarming like ants through the rocks, shooting at anything that moved. The enemy gave way, running uphill toward the Seven Mountains.

Vietnam firefights followed a common pattern. Action broke loose; the sun exploded. Over here thirty or forty guys shooting; over there thirty or forty guys shooting back. Then somebody decided he had had enough and it ended, returning to stalemate. Seldom did anyone win anything or permanently move any lines. It was not a war of lines and fronts and ground held; it was a war of body bags and body counts.

An eerie emptiness crawled out of the jungle at the end of the firefight.

Beyond, uphill, the VC were regrouping, preparing for a

counterattack. They were shouting and making noise running about.

"Motherfuckers are coming back," Morin shouted, appearing out of the rocks.

"You dumbass," Kittleson scolded. "What did you think you were doing, running out in front like that? Trying to get yourself killed?"

"Trying to keep up with an old man, Pappy. I'm not doing that anymore. You're hit."

"I'll live." He wiped away blood. The bullet had gouged a shallow groove across the flat part of his nose above his lip.

He had gone through World War II, including two behind-the-lines POW rescue missions, without sustaining even a minor wound. Now, here he was on his first mission in Vietnam, three days after his arrival, and the enemy was already starting to chip away his flesh. He hoped this wasn't precedent-setting.

"*Hey-sus*, Pappy," Ochoa exclaimed, rushing over. "If you had sneezed, the bullet, she would have chopped off your entire nose."

The little Viets, expressing the high that followed combat once you realized you had survived, were shouting and laughing and making insulting gestures up the hill at the VC. They appeared eager to chase the enemy now. Ochoa nixed pursuit.

"We are under strength and we are directly in the middle of an enemy stronghold," he reasoned. "We are retreating. Morin, radio for a helicopter extraction. Do you concur, Master Sergeant Pappy?"

"Leave me one squad to hold them off until you're clear," Kittleson replied.

Ochoa looked at this FNG, this *fucking new guy*. It was clear the old man had seen combat before—and lots of it.

There was trouble over the casualties. One was dead, the other alive, but only barely so. Their comrades didn't want to carry them out. This would slow down the withdrawal. Viets shrugged their shoulders and motioned with their hands as if saying, "So what? The one who is alive will soon be dead. There is nothing we can do for the dead, but the dead can make us all dead."

Kittleson took Tee Wee Chong aside and spoke in his steady, soft voice. "Lieutenant Chong, assign men to carry the casualties. We don't leave them behind. I will personally shoot any man who refuses the order. Tell them that."

Lieutenant Chong believed him.

Ochoa withdrew the main body in the direction of the DZ. Litter bearers carried the two casualties in folded ponchos. Kittleson distributed his squad of eight soldiers in cover below the rocks. Soon, VC crouching bent-kneed, AKs at the ready, crept out of the woods above the boulders.

Wait. Wait.

"*Now!*"

The squad opened up with such ferocity that the VC hastily retreated into the foothills.

That was Master Sergeant Galen Kittleson's introduction to war after a hiatus of twenty-two years. It was a scene that, in one variation or another, was to replicate itself often during the year ahead. Vietnam, compared to World War II, was a strange war. There were no Philippines to retake, no Tokyo to march toward and conquer to end the war, no Hitler to get rid of, not even a world to save or a people to liberate. It was a strange war whose only objective seemed to be to fight on and on, back and forth, like *Spy vs. Spy* in *Mad* magazine, until one side or the other got tired, bagged up all its dead, and went home.

CHAPTER 39

January 1968.
Americans had been in-country in force for three years. During that time, they had grown accustomed to everything becoming quiet by 30 January, the beginning of Tet, the Vietnamese lunar new year. People in Vietnam stopped fighting and started partying with their families and friends. ARVN soldiers took holiday leave and the cities became crowded with celebrating civilians. A cease-fire was declared and even Americans went on stand down and took R&R.

This year was going to be different. The siege of Khe Sanh started on 21 January, before Tet, which diverted attention from the 84,000 VC and NVA troops moving into position all over South Vietnam. Before dawn on 30 January, communist soldiers who had mixed with peasants coming into Hue, Saigon, Bon Me Thuot, Da Nam, Nha Trang, Pleiku, and dozens of other provincial capitals and cities violated the traditional holiday truce and started attacking government buildings and military posts with mortars and machine guns. Towns the length and breadth of South Vietnam exploded in violence. It was the largest and most violent offensive of the war. General Westmoreland placed all U.S. forces in South Vietnam on full alert.

Tet battles raged for over a month. VC sappers attacked the American embassy in Saigon and actually breached U.S. Marine security to get inside. In Nha Trang, home of 5th Special Forces headquarters, MIKE Forces fought all over the city and repelled attacks against headquarters. In the old imperial capital of Hue, ARVN defenders were overwhelmed. U.S. Marine reinforcements entered a nightmare of house-to-house fighting during which they suffered many casualties. Pinned down at the Citadel, it took them until 25 February to retake the city.

U.S. Special Forces Teams A-501 and 502 in Tau Chau spent hours in the operations center gleaning what they could of the situation from battle chatter on the radios. All over IV Corps, up to within a few kilometers of the Mobile Guerrilla Force camp, VC and NVA attacked. Bien Hoa, My Tho, Phu Vinh . . . All almost within hearing range of Tau Chau.

During the year since his arrival as team sergeant, Pappy Kittleson had directed the repair and strengthening of the Tau Chau camp. Bunkers had been sunk and sandbagged. Berms were raised and hardened with bamboo. A few critical buildings inside the wire were now constructed of reinforced concrete. Additional concertina and moats had been added to the perimeter. Kittleson sometimes stood outside and looked up at the cone-shaped peaks glowering down upon the camp and shook his head. He expected Tau Chau to be hit. Colonel Black Jack Kelly was going to be damned disappointed.

The camp was almost identical in personnel composition to the Special Forces camp at Lang Vei located only twenty miles south of the DMZ and four miles southwest of the Marine stronghold at Khe Sanh. Like Tau Chau, Lang Vei was defended by twenty-four Green Berets and about four hundred irregulars. The siege of Khe Sanh had been going on for nearly two weeks when shortly after midnight of 7 February, a descending trip flare lit up an observation post at Lang Vei. Startled, Sergeant Nick Fragas squinted his eyes against the blinding flash. He couldn't believe what he was seeing.

He radioed his command bunker: "We have tanks in the wire!"

"Say again?" came the response.

"Tanks! Damnit. That's right—*tanks*!"

It was the first time the NVA had deployed armor—Soviet-made PT-76s. Fragas was about to be run down by tanks, something that no other American soldier in Vietnam had yet experienced.

The battle raged most of the night before the camp fell. Sergeant Fragas, team commander Captain Frank Willoughby, six other Green Berets, and twenty-five irregulars ended up isolated in the depths of the command bunker. The twenty-five irregulars surrendered to the NVA, only to be mowed down as they dashed out of the bunker with their hands up. That left eight Americans, six of whom were wounded, to fight on until repeated U.S. air strikes permitted their escape from the battle-scarred compound. Over two hundred of Lang Vei's original complement ended up dead or missing in action.

Special Forces was a relatively small, tightly knit outfit. Kittleson knew several of the Green Berets at Lang Vei; a few were his friends. That Lang Vei had fallen under so brutal an attack, from *tanks* no less, added to the anxiety of other SF camps all over Vietnam. Kittleson and Lieutenant Ochoa's replacement, Captain Dan Hendricks, placed combat outposts on the three peaks, but they were not foolish enough to believe that Tau Chau could hold out under an all-out assault.

The expected attack never came.

In March, the surviving VC retreated to lick their wounds while antiwar protesters in the U.S., incensed by what they viewed as an escalation, renewed their howling. Captain Hendricks was summoned to Nha Trang. When he returned, he called a meeting in the team house around the little

French-made cooking stove. All Vietnamese were excluded—for security purposes, he said.

He draped a poncho on the wall, upon which he taped a map of IV Corps. Kittleson glanced at the map and upended an ammo crate to sit on. Out through the door of the team house he watched an old man in a cone hat driving a water buffalo along the beach. The setting sun hung red behind him. It looked like a scene from a postcard a tourist might send home. *Having a great time; wish you were here.*

Captain Hendricks pointed to the map.

"This is Tan Phu," he said. "Two companies of CIDG being advised by Team A-23 were all but wiped out in a fight out on the canals between Tan Phu and Le Couer. Three Special Forces advisors—Lieutenant Rocky Versace, Lieutenant Nick Rowe, and Sergeant Dan Pitzer—were captured by the VC. Gentlemen, that was *four* years ago."

He paused. Contemplation of being captured by the VC always produced silence. Death might be preferable.

"The VC are odd little bastards," Hendricks continued after sobering reflection. "We don't know what's happened to Versace. Pitzer was released in Thailand last November to that commie prick antiwar activist Tom Hayden. Three days ago an ARVN POW escaped from the Vietcong. He saw Nick Rowe last week. He is being held in a camp alone somewhere in this vicinity."

His finger stubbed at the edge of the U Minh Forest a few miles west of Le Coeur.

"They've kept him all these years in the same area where he was captured instead of sending him north to a regular POW camp. He's not in good shape. They've beat him and half-starved him. He was in a bamboo cage when he was last seen. All we know so far about his location is that the camp is in a wooded area near a stream. We're trying to develop more intel."

Terrible conditions in the Delta camps had caused the deaths of several American POWs. Prisoners held in the U Minh "Forest of Darkness" faced worse treatment than others elsewhere. Versace, as it turned out, had already been executed with a bullet to the brain. The American Joint Personnel Recovery Center had made several raids attempting to locate and rescue Rowe, but all targets resulted in dry holes.

In the fall of 1967, SOG (Studies and Observations Group) had led one operation into the Delta, but again turned up nothing. SF Medic Dan Pitzer, released in November of that year, later explained how he heard firefights on that occasion.

"Several months before I was released," he said, "I was taken to a hidden bunker when troops air landed. I had a cocked pistol held to my head. I heard people walking around searching the area. After that, I heard an American voice on a radio requesting helicopters for extraction. I heard the choppers come in, pick up the troops, and leave. I cried."

That was always one risk of attempting to rescue POWs; that their captors would shoot them first. It had been a risk when rescuing prisoners held by the Japanese; it was a chance that had to be taken in Vietnam.

Captain Hendricks looked away from the map and his eyes fixed on Sergeant Kittleson.

"Ask Pappy what it's like to see the faces of liberated American POWs," he said. "The old man has been there."

A vision of the skeletons who removed their white underwear to avoid being targeted as they straggled pitifully from the Jap POW camp at Cabanatuan flashed before Kittleson's eyes. He would never forget those tear-streaked faces.

"Bless you. Bless you. Thank God you came."

"We owe it to Nick Rowe to rescue him if we can," Captain Hendricks said. "Pappy, we're going to ask you to do it one more time. We're sending you on another POW raid."

CHAPTER 40

Lieutenant James "Nick" Rowe was executive officer of U.S. Army Special Forces Detachment A-23 at the Tan Phu camp. Tan Phu was located not much farther south than Tau Chau, but away from the seacoast, deeper into that swamp and rice paddy domain of the Mekong Delta's Vietcong legions. Americans in 1963 were in theory still "advisors." The twelve soldiers of A-23 "advised" four companies of CIDG, about 380 Vietnamese and Cambodians trained to resist Vietcong in their home villages.

Tan Phu—Special Forces camps were named after the nearest hamlet or town—was an isolated fortress, a Fort Apache in Indian country. In many ways even more primitive than Tau Chau, it was a cluster of bamboo-walled hootches surrounded by a chest-high mud berm; a narrow, yellow-water moat; and barbed wire. Its defenses included machine gun bunkers at each corner, scattered rifle positions along the walls, a watch tower, and a concrete ammo bunker that still bore bullet scars from when the enemy had overrun the camp the previous year. Move away from the camp and the nearby village in any direction by one klick, one kilometer, and you were in hostile country. Here, night *and* day belonged to Charlie when Charlie wanted to claim it.

In those early years before Marines landed at China Beach, before fast-moving air cover, artillery support on demand, and American infantry, the war consisted mainly of VC night assaults, ambushes, and chance daylight encounters. VC gunners routinely lobbed mortar rounds into the camp every afternoon about sundown, just to let the Americans know they were still out there, lest they forget.

On the night of 28 October 1963, A-23 planned an operation against the small hamlet of Le Coeur, located eight klicks to the northeast on the bank of one of the main canals leading into the dreaded VC sanctuary of the U Minh Forest. The enemy was supposedly establishing a command post in Le Coeur to support large concentrations of main force VC moving northward from rest areas deep in the mangrove swamps near Camau. Destroying the command post called for two CIDG companies from Tan Phu to link up with a militia company from Thoi Binh. One company would hit the ville while the other two established an ambush between Le Coeur and the U Minh Forest to catch VC when they cockroached out of the village.

Rowe; Captain Humbert "Rocky" Versace, an intelligence advisor from MAAG (Military Advisory Assistance Group) in Saigon; and team senior medic Sergeant Daniel Pitzer would go along with the assault company. Everyone expected the mission to be more than another walk in the sun.

"I don't like this one, sir," Rowe confided to Captain Al Penneult, the team commander.

He had this *feeling.*

Captain Penneult was a bull-necked former college football jock. His neck muscles bunched. "If you don't like it, Rowe, stay home. I'll take the walk."

"That's not what I meant, Cap. No sweat. It's my turn. I'll go."

"Okay. Everybody going on the op tomorrow go ahead and sack out. Get some rest before you leave."

First Company and the militia company pulled out of Tan

Phu first, just after midnight, to set up for the ambush. Third Company would be the hammer. It saddled up at 0200 hours, accompanied by the three Americans.

Scuttling clouds played tag with a bright moon, which made walking easy across the terrain of rice paddies studded with scattered banana and coconut groves and small hamlets. Rowe took along three additional bandoleers of ammo for his M-1 carbine. Pitzer armed himself with an M-79 grenade launcher and extra 40mm bandoleers in addition to his medical aid bag.

When first light showed at 0540, brightening the sky, a wide rice paddy some seven hundred meters across lay ahead. A tree line marked the village of Le Coeur. Rowe reached down with his bush hat and scooped up water as the company formed a skirmish line and started across the flooded rice field. He put the hat, water and all, back on his head. It was going to be another typical scorcher of a day.

Walls and roofs, thin spirals of cooking smoke, and split bamboo fences showed in the tree line. Versace and Pitzer walked next to Rowe. *Ti-uy* Tinh, the lieutenant who commanded Third Company, and his platoon and squad leaders worked hard to keep the attack line straight. As they drew near the village, weapons went to on-guard positions. Ungainly bazooka tubes—World War II weapons—bounced onto shoulders. Excitement mounted until the morning air almost crackled with it.

Two reports banged from the village. VC sentries were awake and firing the alert. Black-clad figures began tumbling from hootches. Third Company howled like a pack of wolves and lumbered into a slogging run that got faster the nearer it came to the trees. Scattered shots snapped and whined from the ville across the rice paddy. It was not a defense, only an attempt to slow down the charge.

The VC broke and ran—but instead of running toward the U Minh Forest as expected, they headed for the canals and *away* from the ambush rigged by the other two companies. Tee Wee Tinh yelled orders sweeping his right flank ahead to cut off the fleeing VC and drive them back toward the ambush. A bazooka gunner let off a round. The back-blast sprayed Rowe with water. The Willie Pete (White Phosphorus) shell crashed into the trees and puffed up a plume of white smoke.

CIDG strikers entered Le Coeur running. Chickens, ducks, and pigs scattered. Little remained of VC presence except red-and-blue flags with yellow stars in the centers and a 7.62 round from a Russian-made Mossin-Nagant rifle. Strikers on a high laughed and pantomimed the running VC. It was a glorious day for an outing; they had chased off the enemy like the coward he was.

"We will rest here until First Company comes from ambush position," Tee Wee Tinh decided. "Then we shall go to find VC."

Restless, Rowe and Pitzer crossed the freshwater canal on a monkey bridge behind the village and peered into lush banana groves so thick you couldn't see more than a few feet into them.

Rowe still had that *feeling*.

The militia and the two CIDG companies pursued the retreating VC for a klick or so, but the enemy continued to melt away just out of reach. Occasionally, a sniper popped a few rounds, then ghosted out. Rowe recognized it as a VC trick to lure an enemy deeper into his territory. Lieutenant Tinh was having none of it.

"We are strong and VC stay away from us," he declared. "But it is danger that we go further. We will return to camp now."

Splitting the companies, Rowe realized in retrospect, was their first mistake. The militia veered off on a direct route back to Thoi Binh. First and Third Companies separated to sweep separate parallel canals back to Tan Phu, now only four or five klicks to the southwest. Third Company, and the Americans with it, followed a feeder canal toward the main canal, which led back to base camp. All three companies were soon widely separated and out of each other's sight.

Houses thinned out on either side of Third's march.

Fields were uncultivated. Clumps of reeds and dead trees made isolated islands here and there. Tall, leafy trees and palms lined the canal banks. There was no further sniper harassment fire. Apparently, Charlie had given up his baiting.

Lieutenant Rowe, Versace, and Pitzer marched about midway of the column, which now stretched out along the feeder canal for nearly two hundred yards. An advisor's role was merely to tag along in case the shit hit the fan. Rowe began anticipating an iced glass of tea when they reached camp. He hoped nothing happened to delay them.

A disturbance on point halted the march. Rowe and Versace made their way forward to where excited strikers, shouting and gesticulating, pointed left across a broad paddy that banked up against the main canal a kilometer away. Black-clad figures were running along the banks of the canal. Tee Wee Tinh dragged his radio bearer with him. He gripped the radio handset in indecision.

"VC run to get ahead of us," he opined. "They try to cut us off."

The battery of 155mm Howitzers at Thoi Binh was well within range. "Can you get Thoi Binh on the radio and request artillery cover?" Rowe asked.

Lieutenant Tinh looked harried. "I cannot reach Thoi Binh," he said.

Radio waves were being jammed by the VC.

"I will contact First Company and have Sergeant Canh relay the request."

He couldn't raise Sergeant Canh either.

Rowe glanced across the rice paddy. Charlie was hauling ass over there, trying to cut the route back to sanctuary.

"Let's get the fuck out of here," he said. "*Di-di mau!*"

The column lurched into a dog trot. The enemy had the advantage. He knew the terrain and he had already pinpointed CIDG locations.

"Lord, please let me get back to that iced tea," Rowe prayed uneasily.

The small canal they were on T-junctioned and angled off to the right through a thick grove of coconut palms. On the other side of the T, a reed-bordered irrigation ditch beelined eight hundred meters across the rice paddy to the main canal. The ditch offered some cover in traversing the rice field to reach it.

The company splashed into the water and crawled out on the other side into the ditch. Mud sucked at boots and in places there were puddles of thick brown water. Strikers picked up the pace; the main canal and the relative safety it offered lay almost within reach.

Charlie recognized Third Company's intent. Muzzle flashes suddenly flickered and sparked along the canal ahead and to the left. The rattle of automatic weapons shattered the morning calm once again. Green tracers waved almost lazily across the rice paddy and scythed at the reeds lining the drainage ditch.

Strikers returned fire. The firing by both sides was ineffective at such long ranges. Rowe knelt in the ditch with the other two Americans next to him.

"They're trying to fix us in place," Versace shouted above the din of rifle fire.

Rowe looked desperately about. *This* surely qualified as shit hitting the fan.

Or, he thought, *they're trying to stop us long enough for their blocking force to get ahead of us and into position.*

He crawled to Lieutenant Tinh. "The range is too long, *Ti-uy,*" he shouted. "They're attempting to cut us off. Get our guys moving!"

Tinh understood. Fear flashed across his face. Rowe pointed toward the thick grove of coconut palms on their right flank. He saw thatched roofs among the foliage. Heading for the little hamlet and the palms increased the distance between them and their harassers; continuing on the same azimuth toward the canal only brought them into closer VC contact and exposed them in the open field.

Tinh jumped up on the mud bank and waved his arms and shouted for the frenzied strikers to cease firing and move out. He pointed toward the palms. The Americans ran up and down the ditch and threw Viets out in the direction of the village.

Firing came to a ragged halt on both sides as the VC realized their ploy had failed and the CIDG concentrated on getting the hell out of Dodge. Strikers stampeded, bent over and
eyes white-rimmed.

Mortar rounds thumped into the rice two hundred meters
short, exploding clumps of mud, rice plants, and whizzing
shrapnel. VC gunners didn't yet have the range. The dreaded
Car-r-rup! Car-r-rup! of the exploding shells was like
adding fire to the tails of the running CIDG troopers.

Rowe's stomach knotted. Water wouldn't have gone
down his throat, as parched as it was.

"Keep 'em moving, Tinh!" he yelled, unnecessarily.

One group of strikers broke away from the main body
and headed for the canal. A murderous barrage of mortar
shells chased them and marched over them like a freight
train. The earth underneath and around the strikers belched
violently in series. Bodies and parts of bodies flew like
shredded rag dolls through their screams.

The earth smoked.

The foolish strikers' unintentional sacrifice allowed the
rest of the company to reach the palms that marked the little
hamlet. The column raced past the palms and through the
gathering of hootches. Too late. The VC blocking force had
already moved into position with machine guns. The guns
opened devastating fire on lead elements.

The head of the column turned back on itself like a
threatened snake.

VC were crowding in on all sides now.

Mortars fell in the treeline, shredding palms.

Townspeople either were forewarned and skipped out, or
had taken to their bomb shelters. Rowe and the *ti-uy* threw
the company into a hasty 360 defensive perimeter around
the palms and part of the hamlet. Did they have another
choice short of offering their bodies to the mercy of enemy
machine guns?

"If we have to stop anywhere, it may as well be here,"
Rowe rationalized as Tinh crouched with his radio handset,
still trying to raise First Company.

"VC jam radio signal," Tinh said, looking up anxiously. "I cannot talk with First Company."

First Company had to have heard the firing. Surely Sergeant Canh was on the way with reinforcements.

"For the first time I know how Custer felt," Pitzer cracked.

Sounds of firing increased all around as VC shock troops launched their attack. Everywhere around the perimeter men were banging desperately away while they tried to burrow into the ground.

The VC main effort seemed directed at the treeline. Rowe made a dash for that section to check it out. Bullets slashed through the palms, creating a rainstorm of shredded fronds. CIDG soldiers sprawled behind mounds of earth and tree trunks, firing into black-crested waves of VC swarming over the rice paddies like hordes of warrior ants. Dead and wounded commies piled up on the opposite bank of the shallow canal in front. More stiffs lay scattered in unnatural positions all over the field.

But still they came screaming and firing in a solid wall of black-clad bodies. Floppy bush hats. Muzzle blasts almost point-blank. Distorted faces. Moaning. Gunfire like sticking your head inside a tin bucket while two hundred pygmies beat on it with steel pipes.

Rowe dropped behind a fallen palm. He emptied a clip into the rushing hordes. He pushed another clip into his carbine and continued firing, piling up dead and wounded VC. Water in the canal turned a bright pink from the blood. Rowe picked among the attackers with his rifle sights.

"You die! Piss on you! You die!"

They beat back the assault.

"Hold your fire!" Rowe shouted. "Save your ammunition."

Lieutenant Tinh ran up with bad news. "First Company has likewise been ambushed," he reported, panting. "They are dead. They will not come to help us."

Rowe dropped his head on folded arms. He looked up. "How about our casualties?"

"Many wounded. I do not know how many dead."

"Ammunition?"

"There is enough for one more assault, perhaps a little more."

"What about commo?"

"We have lost all radio contact."

Talk about a lost patrol.

"We gotta bust out of this cul-de-sac," Rowe decided.

Their only chance, as Rowe saw it, depended upon their breaking through the blocking force on the other side of the village toward the main canal and then hauling ass for the SF camp. He talked it over with the other Americans, who agreed with him.

"What have we got to lose?" was the way Versace put it.

They were going to die if they remained here.

The withdrawal began by thinning the ranks and gathering the men for an assault on the blocking force. The ranks were already thinned; every other man, it seemed, was either dead or wounded. The wounded would have to stay behind. Those were the cold, hard facts.

What began as a controlled maneuver disintegrated into panic and a rout during the next VC assault. Men simply deserted their posts and ran for it. Some threw away their weapons and started stripping out of their uniforms as they ran.

Rowe snapped off a few shots across the gore-filled canal ditch. When he saw the Viets jumping up to flee, he dived back through the trees toward the village with Versace and Pitzer. The medic fired a 40mm grenade round into the chest of a charging gook. The VC's upper body disintegrated with a brilliant blush of wet scarlet. What was left of him took two more steps before collapsing.

Chunks of flesh, body parts, and blood littered the ground.

The three Americans, fighting together, made their way through the village, dancing past mortar explosions and ribbons or tracers. They had given up the idea of a breakout in force. It was now every man for himself. Commies were already sweeping into the village, shooting CIDGs at will where they hid or knelt pleading for mercy.

In still another drainage ditch on the other side of the hamlet cowered the pathetic remnants of the Tan Phu strike force. No more than a dozen of them in the reeds and weeds. Firing slacked off everywhere as the VC probed for survivors.

"It is finished, *Trung-uy,*" mourned a CIDG sergeant dubbed Pee Hole by the Americans. "It is finished."

Rowe's frantic glance fell upon a large field of tall reeds growing out of the drainage ditch and skirting rice paddies in the direction of the canal.

"Into the reeds," he ordered. He shook a stunned Tee Wee Tinh by his shoulders. "Get the men into the reeds."

The VC closed in. Only a couple of strikers too terrified to move remained behind in the ditch. They had stripped naked, ready to proclaim themselves frightened villagers whenever enemy soldiers appeared. Hardly had the Green Berets slipped into the reeds than Rowe heard screaming in the ditch and then gunfire. Poor scared *dead* bastards.

A group of enemy appeared trotting across a small clearing. The leader carried an AK-50 submachine gun and wore a camouflaged bush hat pulled down hard on his head. Rowe burst the guy's head with two hasty shots.

He shifted to the second man. He missed his first shot. Then a heart-stopping *Ping!* as the empty clip ejected.

The VC fired back. A round struck Rowe's carbine and knocked it spinning from his hand. Instinctively, he dived backwards for the weapon, grabbing for it in a puddle of muddy water. The VC's remaining shots went over his head. Rocky Versace sprayed him and the man behind, knocking both down.

The two Americans ran through the reeds together.

"Where's Dan?" Rowe puffed.

"Ahead, I think."

The bolt in Rowe's carbine was smashed. Useless. He flung it down.

Unseen automatic fire ripped into them. Rocky moaned

and slumped to his knees. Rowe grabbed him and dragged him into the thickest clump of reeds he could find. He straightened the broken grass to conceal their position, then examined Versace's wound. Blood seeped from three neat little holes in the lieutenant's abdomen.

Rowe then noticed he had also been hit—a flesh wound to the thigh.

He was kneeling over the MAAG officer, bandaging him, when a sharp command from behind froze his blood. "*Do tay len!*"

He finished tying the bandage before slowly turning his head to peer into the tunnel of an American carbine's muzzle. Behind it were two VC. They pounced on the American and quickly tied his arms behind him, once at the elbows and once at the wrists, cutting off circulation. They jerked him to his feet.

"God bless you, Nick," Versace groaned before Rowe was led away.

"God bless you, Rocky."

CHAPTER 41

Sergeant Kittleson enjoyed being aloft. When the doors of the UH-1B "Huey" helicopter were closed, the essence of the chopper was a combination of hot oil, gasoline, grease, sweat, and stale cigarette smoke. But when they were open, as now, clean, cool air rushed in. On the ground the air was thick and laden with moisture the temperature of hot soup. Up here, the war seemed distant and he breathed air that did not seem recycled so many times through lungs of fear and anger.

He rode the chopper easily. The rucksack on his back pushed him forward in the back-to-back canvas seating. He leaned toward the door with his elbows resting on his knees, a carbine in his hands with its buttplate resting on the Huey's metal floor. The gunner in the doorway swayed, balancing himself on the M-60 machine gun hanging on a bunji strap.

Out of the habit of constantly checking his men, the little sergeant let his eyes move to Captain Hendricks next to him. The captain was an undersized man not much taller than Kittleson. He looked back at his sergeant, took off his patrol cap, and ran a hand across the sandy burr of his crewcut. He nodded.

In the other seat, backs to them and facing the other door, rode Burdish, the Irish weapons man, blank faced and going along with the flow; Morin, the skinny commo man with the cocksucker mustache who had been with Kittleson in the Seven Mountains fight; and Pogue, the medic, a young, freckled, red-headed kid with a detached manner. Pogue came along in case Nick Rowe needed medical attention when they rescued him.

Morin gave Kittleson thumbs-up and readjusted the heavy ruck on his back. Burdish jerked his bush hat tighter onto his forehead against the whistle of wind and gazed out and down at the lush green terrain of Vietnam. He carried an M-60 machine gun. Bright, raw bandoleers of linked ammo hung Pancho Villa-style across his chest. The boyish Pogue, who was a damned good medic, calmly gazed out the open door to the earth below.

Five men on a rescue mission to save one POW. It was nothing like the other POW missions in which Kittleson had participated. The team went out and practiced in a chopper with the McGuire Rig and rope, in case they had to be extracted out of trees, and then they sat around for a couple of days until the brass made up its mind.

Now they were going. There was no need for words. The chopper was noisy and they would have had to shout anyhow, but there was no need for it.

"Pappy, that's all the intel MAAG can furnish," Captain Hendricks apologized before the team choppered out of Tau Chau. "The camp is in this vicinity."

He always had his map handy.

"That's a big vicinity," Kittleson said, not criticizing or protesting, merely stating a fact.

"Yes," Hendricks agreed. "Rowe is supposedly the only prisoner, with perhaps three or four guards at most. Pappy, we have to try."

Kittleson nodded. They had to try. He recalled the comment he had made over two decades ago in the Philippines: "If I was in that camp, I'd sure hope there'd be volunteers to come get me."

The camp where Rowe was being held consisted of three or four hootches for the guards and a bamboo tiger cage for the prisoner. It was supposed to be next to a stream in an isolated patch of woodland surrounded by large fields of grass. The question was, how the hell did you tell one batch of hootches from another and determine which was the right patch of woods? Clusters of bamboo huts bordered by coconut palms, banana and mango trees, bamboo stands, and elephant grass were pegged all over the Mekong Delta. Thick growing reeds and clumps of trees grew in uncultivated fields where, this time of year, fetid water stood at constant flood stage.

"It'll be like looking for a needle in a mountain of needles," Morin commented.

"Poor bastard," Burdish said. "Imprisoned in that cage for four years, like a pet monkey."

"He's going to die," Hendricks said.

They were all going to die. Some day. But not like that: not as a POW where each breath was torture, each day a new punishment; not knowing *when* or *if* it would ever end.

"Our POWs have to know they're not forgotten," Kittleson observed in his simple, straightforward manner. "*We* wouldn't want to be forgotten."

"We think the most likely spot is here," Hendricks said, pointing to a location on the map west of Le Coeur on the edge of the fearful U Minh Forest, the so-called Forest of Darkness. "Pappy, we'll insert two klicks north of it."

Kittleson's eyes searched the myriad of unmapped waterways as the chopper and its cargo of would-be rescuers flew over Vietnam's rice bowl. Things hadn't changed much from when Lieutenant Rowe was captured in 1963. VC still ruled the Delta. Wherever government forces landed, it was like sticking a fist into a bucket filled with water. As soon as the fist was withdrawn, water rushed back in. Most Vietnamese homes possessed two sets of flags—one for when the VC were in town, another for the benefit of government troops. Interchangeable loyalties.

"We are loyal to our buffalo and our rice," an old papasan

had once told Kittleson. "The buffalo and the rice are a part of the earth and do not change. All else is temporary and the people can endure."

The chopper had scheduled seven insertions. Six of them would be fakes to confuse observers. The rescue team would un-ass on the fourth.

Kittleson held up three fingers and made sure everyone saw as the bottom dropped out of the Huey. The bird lazily auto-rotated, circling like a vulture over a carcass. It dumped the last one thousand feet of altitude rapidly. It didn't do to dally within small arms range. Its skids kissed the earth lightly in a stand of high elephant grass next to a weed-choked drainage ditch. Rotor wash whipped the grass flat. The Green Berets remained seated, looking out. Blades clawed and jerked the OD-green bird back into the sky.

The next one was it.

From aloft, the countryside was lovely and deceptively peaceful, an illusion easily shattered by dropping to within small arms range. Farmers in cone hats worked the thigh-deep water of their rice paddies. Water buffalo oblivious to all around them wallowed in mud to ward off flies and mosquitos. Cooking smoke squeezed out of fires in front of some of the thatched huts. A graceful "spirit bird" suspended on a rising air thermal floated motionless in its own lonely world undisturbed by the passing helicopter or the war below.

On the fourth set-down, the team tumbled out the door while the chopper momentarily hovered. Rotor blade wind whipped at an enormous field of reeds and grass. Kittleson sank up to his knees in brackish water as warm as a bath. The Huey leaped back into the air. Grass and reeds straightened and closed above the heads of the five heavily armed invaders.

The world narrowed. There was the buzz of insects and birds doing balancing acts on the ends of reeds and the sun straight overhead and turned up to boil. Captain Hendricks and Kittleson consulted the map. Then the captain took a compass reading and jabbed an azimuth with a straightened arm and his flattened hand.

"Rowe, I hope you're there," Pogue murmured as they began fighting their way through grass as thick as a wall.

In the distance, off to the left rear quarter, two rifle shots sounded.

"They know we're here," Morin assessed, his voice sounding grim.

CHAPTER 42

Hendricks and Kittleson rotated in leading a pace as fast as stealth and the terrain permitted. It was exhausting work with the mud and water sucking at their boots, the sun stewing them, and grass blocking every breeze and retarding progress. Kittleson assumed the rifle shots they heard simply placed everyone in the vicinity on notice that a helicopter had landed, not necessarily that troops had been put down. Still, scouts might be sent out to investigate.

They left a broken trail, but Kittleson took some solace in knowing that it would not be one easily located in this stuff, not even by experienced trackers. They pushed on to put as much distance as they could, in as short a time as possible, between them and their insertion point.

Traveling along canal banks or even in rice paddies would have been easier, but the risk much greater. Encountering a peasant or blundering into a hootch in the trees meant VC quickly received news of the intruders. Nick Rowe needed American company back in the Real World, not in a bamboo tiger cage next door.

There were no further shots. The raiders paused frequently to listen and observe their back trail.

"I don't think they picked us up," Pogue declared, his face so red from heat and exertion that his freckles almost disappeared.

Kittleson nodded noncommittally. "Let's keep moving."

They drove on as the sun lowered in the west. Their stomachs sunk with it. With the sun went the light and the most vital of their five senses. Nothing was more intimidating than a night in Indian country. Kittleson was watching the blood-red sun, as though willing it to hang suspended for a little longer. He glanced away, glanced back, and the sun had sneaked away to Acapulco or somewhere. Within a surprisingly short time darkness ended all progress.

They were still among the reeds, a field as thick and vast, it seemed, as the wet grasslands of the Plain of Jars. They were an hour or so short of the hummock of trees next to the stream where Nick Rowe must be about to go into restless and tortured slumber. Hopefully it was Nick's last night sleeping on the ground in a bamboo cage.

The plan had appeared so simple and direct at Tau Chau: Find the camp, charge in and kill the guards, snatch Rowe, radio for a chopper to come taxi them all out. The plan on the ground, however, lost its simplicity in the warm swampish bath of reality. Even the eternally optimistic veteran sergeant of the Big War began to have doubts. Admittedly, the plan had not been as complete as it should have been before committing men's lives to it. *In the vicinity*, the captain had said . . .

That could mean almost any damned thing. Vietnam was *in the vicinity* of Red China.

"FUBAR," grumbled Pogue. *Fucked Up Beyond All Recognition.*

Fearful purple shadows oiled through the reeds like melting snakes. The Green Berets squatted on their haunches close together for support and comfort. They couldn't sit down or lie down because water rose past their ankles. Droves of vicious mosquitos turned into a plague. A swipe of a hand across the face produced a handful of the little bloodsuckers.

Maybe it wasn't so much the actual rescue that counted as it was the *attempt*. Any effort to reassure increasingly disgruntled troops in the field that if they were captured they weren't forgotten. Liberating POWs, even a single man, meant a big public relations coup back home where the war was generating riots and draft resistance.

"If we're going to go after POWs," Morin whispered, "we ought to raid the Hanoi Hilton or one of the big camps. Make it worthwhile."

"A single American's life *is* worthwhile," Captain Hendricks said.

"I'm sure bigger POW raids are in the works," Pappy Kittleson reasoned. "Our mission is to get out one Special Forces soldier—Nick Rowe. He'd be in our wet boots now if the tables were turned."

Life seemed to stop for the night. The giant heads of the reeds and grass closed suffocatingly above them. They stared hard into darkness so complete it was like they had to touch their eyes to make sure they were still open; they startled at the crack of a cane reed as some animal of the night passed through. Thoughts invariably turned to the world outside where people actually walked around in open view of other people without being afraid. Kittleson thought of Darlene, and of homemade bread.

Dozing off still squatting on their haunches. Catching themselves before they toppled over into the water. Shivering as the water turned cold. Legs cramping and going stiff. Afraid to speak because voices carried so far at night, and the night belonged to the bad guys. Reaching out to touch the other men huddled there in order to reassure themselves that they were not alone.

Kittleson knew daylight was finally coming when he made out Captain Hendricks scraping a leech off his arm with a knife. Blood gushed and the captain looked disgusted and flung away what was left of the parasite. His eyes caught Kittleson's. They both nodded. Far from refreshed, they nonetheless stood up slowly and stretched life back into their cramped limbs.

Within two hours after dawn, the sun again beat down hard on their heads. Visibility for any distance was restricted, but if their azimuth was correct and had been held, the wooded hummock and stream should lie directly ahead. The exhausted patrol pushed on, slowly.

Morin spotted it first. He pointed at the tops of trees sticking up above the grass ahead. That had to be the camp. It wasn't more than one hundred meters away. The team stopped to shuck and cache their rucks and check weapons. Morin held on to his PRC-10 radio; the radio was their lifeline to escape this shithole. Once they hit the camp and grabbed Rowe, it would be balls to the wall to get the hell out.

Dogs barked lazily from somewhere in the distance. A "spirit bird" hung high on a thermal and calmly surveyed his domain, in which lesser creatures fought each other and died. Three jet fighter bombers returning from an air mission to save GI or Marine asses screamed northeast toward Saigon or Da Nang. It was another *normal* day in The Nam where men were dying or about to die. When the rescuers came upon the camp, they would have to go in quick and violent to prevent Rowe's captors from either slitting his throat, putting a bullet into his brain, or whisking him away out the back.

Kittleson took point. He was the best and quickest shot at Tau Chau, plus he had had lots of experience at it in two wars.

Excitement mounted as the patrol advanced through the grass, pausing often to listen, taking one careful step at a time to prevent alerting the enemy by splashing water or cracking a bamboo stalk. Sweat, anticipation, the jitters combined to soak and make fetid their clothing.

The hummock rose comparatively dry out of the swamp, like a tropical island covered with coconut palms. The patrol eased into an assault line and escaped the sea of grass like shipwrecked sailors washed ashore. It was a relief to walk on solid ground again, even though tension increased.

Eyes darting, scanning through the trees, weapon muzzles sweeping to follow the direction of their eyes. Searching for a glimpse of a hootch, a wisp of smoke from a dying breakfast fire. Listening to the silence underneath the velvety hum of insects.

Captain Hendricks looked at Kittleson and shrugged. Where *was* Rowe?

Tension slowly dissipated as the raiders gained the center of the island without incident. It was the highest point from which the earth sloped back into the water in all directions. Rowe's tiger cage should have been *right here*. There were no fire ashes, trash, nothing.

Shortly, they came out on the other side where the grass sea murmured in its eagerness to re-devour them. In the distance, across the tops of the gently waving grasses, rose more hummocks. Captain Hendricks hunkered the patrol close around him.

"It's a wooded area," he acknowledged. "There's plenty of water around, but where's the stream?"

"There is no fucking stream," Pogue said. "Those chickenshits at Group sent us on a wild goose chase to make themselves feel like they're doing something for POWs."

"If I was a betting man, which I ain't," Burdish said, "I'd bet Rowe was where we heard the rifle shots."

The little ops sergeant kept his own counsel, as he was wont to do. However, it did seem to him that there might have been better air reconnaissance to more accurately pinpoint Rowe's location. Had that been done, they could have airlifted in the entire Mobile Guerrilla Force on a successful surprise raid.

But, it was easy to quarterback a play after it was all over.

Kittleson slowly stood up and gazed off thoughtfully toward the next hummock. "If I was Rowe," he said softly, "I wouldn't want us to give up easily."

That took all the wind out of the bitching. The raiders returned for their rucks and then set out for the next hummock, approaching it with equal caution. It was a repeat of the first: nothing there—not even the cold ashes from an old cooking fire.

Same thing for the next two islands.

"If there was even one small chance of finding him, Pappy," Captain Hendricks finally sighed, "I'd be willing to keep us out here til Jane Fonda's commie-loving ass dropped to her ankles. But I don't want us to suffer another night in this shit when there's no need to."

They were pushing luck to the edge. The men looked fatigued and haggard, on the breaking point from heat, stress, effort, and lack of sleep. They couldn't wander around in enemy country indefinitely without being discovered.

Pappy remembered eyes hollow as caves, yellowed teeth falling out, amputated arms and legs, the stench of disease and gangrene and starvation and despair. He remembered *"Thank God! Thank God you came!"*

He was two for three when it came to POW rescues. He had hoped to make it three for three.

He turned to Morin the radioman. "You heard the Cap. Call in our grid for extraction. Tell 'em," he said, and he looked out over the grass, "Tell 'em we didn't find the egg."

Underneath his breath, he murmured, "Don't give up hope, Nick Rowe. I'm praying for you."

CHAPTER 43

During Nick Rowe's long captivity, his keepers had moved him numerous times to prevent his rescue, in and around the U Minh Forest, the Forest of Darkness. The rescue attempted by the Tau Chau Special Forces camp was one of nearly a dozen such attempts made throughout the years. Intelligence sent down from MAAG and 5th SF Group headquarters turned out to be accurate in content; the only error was in his precise location. Kittleson's Green Beret patrol was, in fact, within one or two kilometers of the prisoner's tiger cage—almost within shouting distance.

By December of 1968, a few months after this latest rescue endeavor, Lieutenant Rowe had been a prisoner of the Vietcong for five years, one month, and two days. That month a joint U.S.–ARVN operation waged against VC forest strongholds in the Le Coeur region almost caught his guards and him. American airpower ripped hell out of the enemy refuge. Air mobility forces struck in lightning attacks that scattered VC units all over the Delta. Rowe's hopes sometimes surged when he heard firefights in the distance, then plummeted immediately upon realization that guards had orders to kill him rather than let him escape or be rescued.

His days and nights melded into one confusing cycle of constant movement to evade attacking American and ARVN units. His guards hid him in patches of reeds or forest during the day, then shifted him elsewhere at night to avoid air strikes by B-52 bombers and helicopter gunships. His life, these days, hung by the proverbial thread. For five years the VC cadre had attempted to break him, force his "cooperation" in making of him a propaganda tool to further fuel the antiwar movement in the United States. He had held out until, even he had to admit, he was more of a liability than an asset to his keepers. That he remained alive was due more to the immutable nature of the communist mentality than anything else. Any changes that had to be made went through so many layers up and down that by the time a decision was made somewhere it was lost before it got back down the chain. His keepers, as a GI saying went, were content to keep on keeping on.

On 30 December, Rowe and his guards, seven of them, avoided American Cobras and Huey gun ships during the day and burrowed like rats into the reed-covered banks of a small canal to sleep after nightfall. The guards seemed more surly than usual, as though they blamed their prisoner personally for the plight in which they found themselves. They gave him almost nothing to eat, even in comparison to the little he had lived on over the years. Rice was apparently scarce, almost nonexistent, possibly because the region had been sealed off to resupply.

Physically, what remained of the prisoner was only a figment of his former self. The lining of his stomach gnawed at itself. The guards cast him in heavy leg irons and shoved him into the middle of cattails and bamboo reeds to sleep. One of them pulled watch while the others slept. They did not move again that night.

The return of daylight on 31 December brought back the helicopters. A guard kicked Rowe in the stomach to awaken him. The others hid underneath a tree and stared at a Huey circling high above the terrain to the south. Rowe assumed it was a command ship.

Accompanying the Huey were helicopters Rowe had never seen before. Slim olive-green airframes with shark-like noses, long tail sections, and huge rotor blades. They were Cobras, fearsome machines capable of dramatic aerobatics at treetop level. As Rowe watched, a pair of them zipped across the sky underneath the Huey and darted out of sight below the skyline. He heard brutal bursts of fire—piercing foghorn-like blasts from 20mm miniguns, the ripping screams of multi-barreled machine guns. He imagined how all that fire ate into the earth and obliterated everything within the impact zone.

One of the guards climbed a tree to take a look. He sounded agitated as he reported troops being landed to the southeast. The frantic guards cached most of their equipment, keeping only light packs and their weapons. Then they dragged Rowe to his feet, removed his leg irons, and pushed him across the canal and into another field of reeds.

They hurried in the opposite direction from the troop landing. Cobras continued to skywalk across the area, hurtling down bright death upon hapless targets. The VC withdrawal more resembled an exodus than a retreat. Everywhere, black-clad units of frightened troops scurried about like rats in a burning barn. Discipline appeared to be collapsing as individual survival instinct took over.

Rowe and one of the older guards he had nicknamed Porky trailed the guard contingent. Porky appeared dissatisfied with the direction his leader had chosen. Whether deliberately or not, Porky and Rowe became separated from the others while traversing a thick patch of jungle. Rowe recognized the moment as the best opportunity he had had to escape in years. He dared not let it pass.

All he had to do was get rid of Porky and attract the attention of the helicopters. That meant, of course, that he would incur a great risk to his own life. His uniform had worn out years ago; he now wore VC black pajamas. His face was sunburned. American pilots might not even notice his beard until they had already unleashed their rain of destruction.

Still, he had to try. He slipped his mosquito net from his pack in order to have something white to wave at helicopters when the time came.

In front of him, Porky slung his weapon on his back so he could use both hands to clear a pathway. Rowe reached quickly and tripped the flange release to let the ammunition clip drop from the tiny submachine gun. He ground the magazine unnoticed into the mud with his heel. Since a burp gun fired from the open-bolt position, there was no round in the chamber. The VC now carried an empty weapon and had no spare magazines. Rowe noticed he had taken none with him when the guards cached their equipment.

So far, so good.

He sought the right opportunity as the guard broke brush for their passage. In his weakened condition he dared not grapple with the Viet face to face. As he walked, he picked up a short club about two inches in diameter and concealed it along the back side of his leg. Porky was too busy trying to escape to notice.

Soon, opportunity presented itself. Porky became entangled in wait-a-minute vines and thrashed around trying to dig out. His back was to Rowe and he was paying no attention. It was too late for reconsideration. The American lunged forward and swung his club with all the strength he had left. It connected with the base of Porky's skull just below his floppy bush hat. The Viet dropped as though poleaxed, which he had in effect been.

Rowe pounced on the body like a wild animal, judo-chopping at Porky's neck with short vicious blows. He didn't necessarily intend to kill the VC, only to incapacitate him, but when he stood up, Porky lay still with blood leaking from his mouth and nose. He looked like he was dying.

"Sorry."

He turned and ran. It was too soon to be exhilarated, but he felt it building.

He leaped a narrow ditch and ran for about fifty meters before he came to a relatively clear area. He set about frantically tramping down the weeds to make himself more visible. He heard a chopper coming.

Lord, let it see me now.

He waved his white mosquito net wildly. The Cobra passing overhead banked sharply and circled. Cobras generally worked in pairs. The second warbird appeared, flying hard. Rowe's heart was beating so fast it almost knocked him off his feet. He waved his net even more frantically.

The pilot of the first Cobra radioed his wingmate. "There's a VC down there in the open."

"I see him," the other ship responded. "What the hell is he doing? Is he crazy?"

"It might be some kind of a trick."

"Gun him down."

Rowe waved and waved. "They've seen me! It's okay. They've seen me!"

Just as the Cobra lined out to make a firing pass, a voice blasted over the net from Major Dave Thompson in the command Huey: "Wait one. I want a VC prisoner. Cover me. I'm going down."

Sergeant Mike Thompson, the Huey's door gunner and no relation to Major Thompson, flight commander of B Troop, 7th Armored Regiment, 1st Air Cavalry Division, leaned out the door over his M-60. Finger on the trigger, he tried to get a look at the crazy VC as the chopper spiraled down. The guy was jumping up and down in exuberance. Then Thompson spotted the beard.

"God Almighty, sir. That's an *American*."

Automatic rifle fire spat at the helicopter from the treeline, but failed to deter it. The chopper swung tight and low and pulled up in the clearing like a running horse reined to a sliding halt. It settled not fifteen meters away from Rowe.

Tears flooding his eyes, Rowe ran stumbling and slipping toward it, dragging his mosquito net. He tumbled onto the cool metal floor.

"Go! Go! Go!" he shouted.

The bird leaped into the air, rising fast and high and circling. And now it all—all of it—was below Lieutenant Nick Rowe and behind him. He was free.

CHAPTER 44

The first combat deaths and captures of Americans in the Indochina conflict occurred not in Vietnam but in neighboring Laos during the fighting between the communist Pathet Lao and Royal Lao government in 1961–62. American clandestine support for the Royal Lao government included sending roughly four hundred U.S. "advisors" under a program code-named White Star. A civilian associated with White Star who worked for the American Embassy became the first American POW in Indochina.

Endowed with an adventurous spirit that caused him to disregard the turmoil in the country, Charles Duffy left on a hunting trip from the Lao capital of Vientiane in a rented Jeep with a Lao guide on 13 January 1961. The guide returned several days later and informed the American Embassy that Pathet Lao had captured Duffy and taken him away.

Duffy never returned; his body was never found.

The Soviets weighed in on the rebels' side against the American-backed Royal government. On 23 March 1961, Soviet-supplied antiaircraft guns fired upon a U.S. Douglas C-47 cargo aircraft used as a surveillance plane, bringing it down. The only survivor was Army Major Lawrence Bailey, who parachuted out. Too seriously injured to escape, he was captured by the Pathet Lao, at whose hands he suffered disease, hunger, and solitary confinement.

The number of POWs in the theater continued to grow. On 22 April, communist forces ambushed a team of American Special Forces advisors in the battle of Vang Vieng. Team commander Captain Walter Moon, who suffered a bad head wound, and Sergeant Orville Ballenger were captured. Moon apparently never recovered from the head wound, which caused him to behave erratically. When Ballenger was finally released, he reported having heard several rifle shots one night and seeing Pathet Lao guards carrying Moon's bloodied body from the prison where they were being held. Moon's body was never returned.

Prisoners taken by the Pathet Lao who remained alive were eventually freed with the signing of the Geneva Accords on Laos in August 1962. However, the war in the region and America's involvement in it were just beginning. The years ahead only exacerbated the POW problem for America.

To George F. Fryett, Jr., fell the dubious distinction of becoming Vietnam's first U.S. POW. He was a young enlisted man who worked the Top Secret document control desk for U.S. Military Assistance Group in Saigon. On Christmas Eve 1961, he was riding his bicycle enroute to a swimming pool in Thu Duc on the outskirts of Saigon when two VC, also on bikes, surrounded him. One struck him on the head with a hand grenade, knocking him cold. He was whisked away to the main communist POW camp near the Cambodian border, where he was held in severe privation for six months before being released.

As in Laos, the POW saga in Vietnam was only beginning.

Three months later, 8 April 1962, four U.S. Army Special Forces sergeants—George Groom, Francis Quinn, James Marchand, and James Gabriel—were on a training patrol with a platoon of South Vietnamese Popular Forces in the province of Quang Nam.

"We broke all the rules," Groom was to comment in describing the catastrophe. "A couple of natives from the nearby village of An Chau came over to our camp. Marchand and the interpreter were talking to the villagers about buying some food, when suddenly the VC opened fire on us. We retreated with the platoon to a tiny wooded area that offered the only cover in the immediate area. Gabriel was on the radio, trying to call in that we had been attacked. Then he was shot on the right side by someone. Marchand picked up the radio next, and then he was hit in the leg. By this time we were surrounded by VC holding rifles pointed at us.

"The VC cleaned up the battlefield quickly, and when they left they made Quinn and I carry the two wounded Americans. We carried them for about one half-mile before they ordered us to leave them by the side of the trail. I set Marchand's leg, which was broken. He told me that our radio operator was the one who had shot him in the leg. I had also seen some of our platoon helping the VC carry equipment away. Quinn tried to patch up Gabriel, who was in much worse condition. We didn't want to leave them, but they insisted and told us that other VC would come by later and pick them up. We had no choice, so we left them by the trail. A little while later, Quinn told me he heard shots."

Later that day, a rescue party from Special Forces Combined Studies Division, forerunner of SOG, found Marchand and Gabriel dead, each with a bullet through his skull.

The surviving two SF troopers were marched for two days to a camp in the mountains near Cambodia where they were interrogated while VC made attempts to "brainwash" them. They were set free on 30 May on condition they carry communist propaganda leaflets back to be distributed to South Vietnamese troops.

Contrary to popular belief, North Vietnam *was* a signatory of the Geneva Convention and its requirements for humane treatment of prisoners and for making reports on identities, location, and treatment of POWs. The communists routinely, even deliberately, ignored these requirements and attempted, successfully in most cases, to keep their prison camps secret. It was difficult for Americans to comprehend the communist methods and motivations for handling POWs.

The Communist Party dominated all aspects of the war. The North Vietnamese military and its guerrilla army, the Vietcong, were merely "tools" of the party. Although communist POW policy encouraged taking prisoners and forbade killing them, those rules fell subordinate to whatever propaganda value could be elicited from the captives. Torture, maltreatment, and death were dark companions of every American captured. It was not enough that a soldier merely surrender physically; he had to also surrender his will, his mind, and his thoughts. This was accomplished through a process called "proselytizing." An Enemy Proselytizing Officer accompanied each NVA unit down to battalion level. Political officers handled prisoner duties at levels lower than that.

Proselytizing consisted of a series of crude propaganda acts directed at motivating civilians to change sides and at modifying the belief systems of the POW, by whatever means necessary, so that he became a supporter and propaganda tool for the communist cause. When it came to changing the minds of POWs, the campaign included "brainwashing," lecturing, study sessions, deprivation, starvation, and torture.

The POW issue was used to foment and drive antiwar sentiment in the United States. "The problem of POWs and defectors is important and complicated since it is the basic content of our political offense against the enemy," stated a captured North Vietnamese document on POW policy. "The policy essentially aims at attacking the enemy's morale. To implement the policy well is to contribute actively to the destruction of the enemy's idea of resistance and to introduce the idea of surrendering into the enemy ranks. . . . The proper implementation of our policy toward prisoners can also exert a great political influence on enemy soldiers' dependents, the people in South Vietnam-controlled areas, the American people, the people of satellite countries, as well as the people of the world."

Invariably, captured American prisoners were pressured—read *tortured*—to sign propaganda statements or to make radio broadcasts denouncing the United States. In these statements and broadcasts, they were to make political declarations praising "revolutionary forces" for their humane treatment, condemning U.S. involvement in the war, and extolling the communist cause. Even though the proselytizing campaign was almost entirely unsuccessful—one American pilot batted out *T-O-R-T-U-R-E* in Morse Code with his eyelids when forced to make a TV appearance—it continued under the momentum of its own weight throughout the war. If anything, methods became more brutal and inhuman as time passed.

While early in the war American POWs were frequently released within weeks or months after capture, the policy changed as the war escalated. Some Americans were to be held in captivity longer than any other U.S. POWs in history.

Unfortunately, U.S. ability to launch effective POW rescue operations was almost nonexistent in the early stages of the war. That changed somewhat by September 1966 when the Joint Personnel Recovery Center (JPRC) became operational as a section of SOG (Studies and Observation Group), one of the most top secret and elite American military units in Southeast Asia. CIA operatives and Special Forces soldiers made up its ranks.

SOG was an intelligence and commando unit specializing in quick-strike raids, clandestine guerrilla activities, and reconnaissance against enemy supply columns on the Ho Chi Minh Trail. JPRC handled POW intelligence and aimed at retrieving Americans held in communist prison camps. It maintained intelligence data on the locations where POWs were kept and their status, developed various Escape and Evasion programs, and launched a number of "Bright

Light" raids to free POWs using Special Forces troops.

JPRC seemed jinxed from the beginning. Its first major POW raid on 18 October 1966 resulted in a bloodbath.

To begin with, SOG and JPRC intelligence was unable to pinpoint the precise location of the camp near Soc Trang that purportedly held Army Sergeant First Class Edward R. Johnson, who had suffered immensely during his captivity. Army Captain Frank Jaks was to lead a hundred-man Nung company on the operation. Two other Americans went with him—Sergeant First Class Fred Lewis and Sergeant First Class Charles Vessels.

As Huey helicopters filled with the rescue force came in to set down on target, enemy machine gun fire suddenly exploded from the trees. Chunks of metal flew from one helicopter as bullets ripped into it, sending it crashing to the ground in a fiery burst. Sergeant Lewis leaped from the door of his chopper, only to be cut nearly in half by a burst of enemy machine gun fire. Shortly afterward, Vessels was also killed.

Casualties in Second and Third Platoons were relatively light, but only six men out of forty in First Platoon survived the ambush. It turned out that POW Johnson had probably already been moved from the camp.

The American count of POWs and MIAs lost in Vietnam rapidly increased over the next several years. The bombing of North Vietnam by American warplanes contributed considerably to North Vietnam's prison population. By the time President Lyndon Baines Johnson ordered a total bombing halt on 31 October 1968, communist gunners had bagged 927 American warplanes and captured 356 POWs. By 1970, there were 1,463 U.S. POWs or MIAs listed in Southeast Asia.

And in spite of efforts by JPRC, SOG, and the CIA—some forty-five rescue attempts between 1966 and 1970—not one single American prisoner had actually been rescued from a POW camp.

CHAPTER 45

Colonel Arthur Simons seeks volunteers for moderately-
hazardous mission. Volunteers report to Brigade Theater . . .

These unobtrusive notices appeared on bulletin boards and
in Daily Bulletins throughout the U.S. Army Special Forces
section of Fort Bragg, North Carolina, in late August 1970.
Out of mild curiosity, Master Sergeant Galen "Pappy" Kittleson, now a team operations sergeant with 6th SF Group,
nosed around trying to come up with some skinny on what
the Bull, as he was respectfully called in SF, was up to.
Everyone speculated on what the mission might be, but no
one seemed to know. Whatever it was, it was being kept a
closely guarded secret.

"It's gotta be something good if the Bull wants guys,"
was the common assessment.

Pappy thought about it. He went to his off-post home in
Fayetteville and tended his backyard vegetable garden.
While you might take the man out of the farm, you could not
take the farm out of the man. Darlene sometimes boasted
that they were the only family at Fort Bragg who had home-
grown radishes, organically grown no less, at Christmas. So

Pappy weeded his garden and watered it in the cool of approaching evening. And he kept thinking.

At his age, 46, Darlene had started expecting him to take it a little easier, run no more risks, eat homemade bread, and ride out his last few years to retirement. The minor nose wound he had received during the Seven Mountains fight, the only injury he'd incurred during two wars, had won him his first Purple Heart and another Bronze Star for valor, but at the same time had exerted a sobering effect on him. He was still a devoutly religious man.

"Remember how guys in foxholes pray to God, then forget and backslide when it's over," he once remarked. "Well, I'm not forgetting."

Maybe the wound was God's way of telling him not to push his luck *and* his faith.

"Let the younger guys take over," Darlene encouraged.

"Honey, I'm not *that* old."

He might be losing his hair—hell, it was about lost—and, an old warhorse from a different era, he might be pushing the half-century mark in age, but he was still healthy and kept in top physical shape. He was even a bit proud of being called Pappy. The other men meant it as an affectionate tribute to his seniority. He was still a good soldier. He had a little left in him.

Besides, he was becoming a little tired of and bored with hanging around Fort Bragg training and training, "picking up pine cones" just to keep busy, and then waiting. Bull Simons's clarion call seemed to promise some action, a chance to do something. Kittleson assumed it would be testing new combat equipment or trying out new tactics or techniques.

Sometimes Darlene was simply *too* damned perceptive. "Okay, Galen. What is it?" she asked, sighing.

"The tomatoes are really growing," he said.

He had done his single tour in Vietnam, going on one raid to free a POW, and then took his rotation back to the U.S. to run SF missions in other parts of the world. He was attending French language school in California when news came of Nick Rowe's escape. The aging sergeant rose silently from his seat in class and walked outside. He looked up at the sky. "Thank You, God," he said.

After washing out of French school because of poor hearing—too much gunfire, artillery, and aircraft engine roar at close range—he volunteered for an MTT (Mobile Training Team) assigned to Iran where he taught mortars and machine guns to the Shah's special forces.

Then he came back to Bragg to grow onions, tomatoes, and radishes and chafe underneath the monotonous yoke of garrison duty. Nothing but paperwork, bullshit training, and pine cones.

Although Pappy wasn't personally acquainted with Colonel Bull Simons, he had naturally heard of him. Simons was with 7th Group. The man was virtually a legend. Kittleson and he had even been in the Philippines at the same time in 1945 and had almost worked together. As a company commander with the 6th Ranger Battalion, Simons would probably have gone on the Cabanatuan raid if he had not already been on another combat mission.

Simons, it was said, not only looked mean, he *was* mean. At slightly less than six feet tall and at almost two hundred pounds, he was thick-necked, bushy-browed, and barrel-chested. Time and combat in World War II, Korea, and Vietnam had gouged deep trenches in the granite out of which his face was carved. He possessed less hair than Kittleson, but he *was* six years older, after all.

What harm, Kittleson asked himself, could it do to simply show up at the theater and hear what Colonel Simons had to say?

Nearly five hundred Green Berets packed the theater for the same reason. They fell silent when the colonel lumbered onto the stage at the front of the auditorium. He was the kind of man who demanded respect. A half-chewed stogie protruded pugnaciously from his lips. It was his trademark. It was said he never bought new cigars, only used ones. His philosophy on war and leadership was well known around Bragg:

"The guy who carries the gun wants to know what the hell kind of guy you are, and he wants to know you're there with him. Not up front, necessarily, but that you know your business, you've got control of the sonofabitch, and if the thing really goes sour, that you are going to be there with him when it's time to have it out. If history is any teacher, it teaches you that when you get indifferent and you lose the will to fight, some other sonofabitch who has the will to fight will take you over."

The Bull chewed on his stogie and kept things pointedly brief. He growled, "I need some men for a hazardous mission that involves a long period away from home and no extra TDY (temporary duty) pay. Anyone interested report back to the theater after lunch with your 201 personnel file. If you're not interested, don't worry. I made sure no one takes roll of who comes back and who doesn't."

He glowered out over the audience before he turned and stalked off.

What harm, Kittleson asked himself, could it do to come back after noon?

He needn't tell Darlene—not just yet. He might not even be selected.

Speculation ran rampant over the noon hour.

"It has something to do with Vietnam," some guessed. "What else could it be?"

"The Middle East . . ." was offered.

"South America, Central America . . . The world's about to go to hell in a wheelbarrow."

Someone even suggested a *space* mission.

"Pappy, are you volunteering?" a 6th SF trooper asked.

"I'm considering it."

He considered it some more. His radishes didn't need him; he could do without Darlene's bread for a while. Bruce and Lance were out on their own and Darlene could take care of herself. Self-sufficiency was the trademark of an SF trooper's wife. Darlene was accustomed to her husband's being gone for long periods of time, then coming home only long enough to empty a ruck of filthy clothing and have a quick romp in bed before skying up to fly to some other forgotten armpit of the world.

He picked up his 201 file from Personnel and returned to the theater. Only about one hundred troopers were there this time. Colonel Simons glared out over the depleted congregation.

"Hell, I guess they wanted TDY pay," he rumbled. "The screening process starts this afternoon at the Little White House." That was what SF soldiers called Special Forces headquarters.

"Colonel? Sir, can you give us an idea what this is all about?" a voice asked.

Simons mangled his cigar some more. "It'll be worthwhile," he said.

Whatever it was, Simons certainly wasted little time in assembling his force. Within two days, start to finish, the selection board consisting of Simons, two sergeants major, and a Special Forces surgeon named Lieutenant Colonel Cataldo, gleaned eighty-two enlisted men and fifteen officers from those who volunteered. Men under consideration waited nervously among the pines outside until they were summoned one at a time into headquarters. Doctor Cataldo looked up from his desk and eyed the stocky little master sergeant who stepped crisply up to his desk and snapped a salute. The sergeant had a broad weathered face and thin gray bristle around the edges of his otherwise slick pate.

"How old are you . . . uh . . . ?" He looked at the 201 file on his desk. "Master Sergeant Kittleson, is it?"

"Yes, sir. Forty-six years old, sir."

"Isn't that getting a bit old for volunteering?"

"Colonel Simons apparently volunteered. How old is he, sir?"

Cataldo chuckled. He was a dark-complexioned man with black hair and intense brown eyes. He could have passed for any nationality from Latin to Middle Eastern. Kittleson liked him right away.

"You got me on that one, sergeant," Cataldo said. "The Colonel has to be *ancient*."

He remained thoughtfully silent while he perused Kittleson's 201. His brow lifted with interest. "You have commendations for participating in *two* raids to free POWs?"

"Actually, sir, there were *three* rescue attempts. We couldn't find Nick Rowe."

"*Why* are you volunteering, master sergeant?"

"Damn, sir. It might be interesting."

Cataldo chuckled. "It might be at that."

The screening began. Later, Kittleson learned the surgeon had a rare perspective on selecting applicants. More times than not, he admitted afterwards, he chose men whom he considered average. His reasoning was that the mission needed common sense and "real smart guys don't always have it." Kittleson wasn't sure if he should feel complimented or insulted.

"Can you ski?" Cataldo asked.

"Have you had SCUBA training?"

"How long can you walk in the desert without water?"

"Do you sunburn easily?"

"Do you panic working alone?"

"Any objection to living in crowded confines with a bunch of garlic-loving Arabs who never take showers?"

"How much weight can you carry?"

Where the hell were they going anyhow?

"Pappy? Is that what they call you?"

"Sometimes, sir."

"Pappy, I think we might use you in Support."

"Sir, if it's all the same to you, I'd rather be on the operation."

"Support is all we can offer."

Kittleson tried to hide his disappointment. "If Support is all you have, I'll give it my best."

He had just volunteered and been accepted—and he still had not the foggiest notion of what he had volunteered for.

He was going to have to tell Darlene now.

CHAPTER 46

The planning stage of the operation for which Colonel Simons was recruiting had already been completed. Planning began in May 1970 after the Interagency Prisoner of War Intelligence Committee (IPWIC), a step higher than the JPRC in Vietnam, identified two active POW camps in the Red River Valley in North Vietnam, the only two known to exist outside Hanoi. They were: Son Tay, twenty-three miles west of Hanoi at the junction of the Song Con River and the Red River; and, seven miles farther west, Ap Lo.

An NVA soldier captured near the DMZ first brought attention to the camps. Under interrogation, he said he had been drawing water from a well near the walls of Son Tay prison when he saw what he assumed to be American prisoners working inside the compound. SR-71 "Blackbird" overflights revealed increased activity at the camp, while other intelligence sources confirmed that from fifty-five to seventy POWs were being confined there. One photo reconnaissance flight discovered laundry displayed in such a way as to spell out SAR, an obvious plea for "Search and Rescue." Near another building, someone had stomped into the ground the number 8 and an arrow, which apparently indicated the direction and the distance to the fields where the POWs labored.

On May 25, Air Force Brigadier General Don Blackburn, former SOG commander and now head of IPWIC, briefed Army General Earl Wheeler, outgoing chairman of the Joint Chiefs of Staff, and Wheeler's successor, Navy Admiral Thomas H. Moorer, on the situation and presented a tentative plan to free the POWs at Son Tay. Rescue would be a challenge, but IPWIC believed it could be accomplished.

Son Tay camp itself was small and set in the open surrounded by rice paddies. Three observation and guard towers and a stone wall seven feet high encircled four large buildings in which the POWs were believed confined. Trees forty feet tall obstructed any clear view of the courtyard.

Although removed from Hanoi, Son Tay was by no means isolated. Not far away were an enemy air defense installation, a supply depot, an artillery school, and the 12th NVA Regiment with about 12,000 troops on a twenty-minute daylight reaction time. Phuc Yen Air Base was only twenty miles northeast of Son Tay. Five hundred yards south was a "secondary school" compound, an administration center believed to house forty-five guards.

For any raid to succeed, it would have to be executed swiftly and violently. Wheeler and Moorer agreed with General Blackburn that it could be done. They appointed a fifteen-man group headed by Blackburn to come up with a plan.

Once the plan was completed and approved, it was time to begin the second phase of the operation, code-named Ivory Coast.

In July, Brigadier General Leroy J. Manor, the forty-nine-year-old New York-born commander of the Air Force's Special Operations Force at Eglin Air Force Base, Florida, received phone orders advising him that he had been designated to command a special mission for the Joint Chiefs of Staff. He was to fly to Washington by courier plane for briefing. On the way he would pick up Army Colonel Arthur D. Simons at Fort Bragg. While Manor, a precise organizer, was to be "overall commander," Simons would be deputy commander and actually lead the operation in the field.

Manor, like Bull Simons, had seen more than his share of combat—70 air missions during World War II and 275 in Vietnam, where he commanded the 37th Tactical Fighter Wing at Phu Cat. Whereas Simons was outspoken and somewhat of a brash rogue who gave his superiors heartburn, Manor was quiet, serious, and competent when it came to putting together an operation.

Simons, 51, had joined the army in 1941 as a slick-walled second lieutenant fresh out of ROTC. Four years later he commanded Bravo Company, 6th Rangers, during the retaking of the Philippine Islands. By 1960, he was already embroiled in Indochina, as commander of White Star teams tasked with training soldiers in Laos to repulse North Vietnamese cross-border operations.

Laos had so little muscle in its armed forces that Simons decided to build an army on his own—by kidnapping recruits. His men impressed into uniform twelve battalions whom he tossed behind barbed wire and trained to soldier. They proved to be such tough opposition that North Vietnam soon lost its appetite for cross-border raids.

After Laos, Simons joined Colonel Don Blackburn's SOG in Vietnam. "The more improbable something is," he would say, "the surer it is that you can pull it off."

Manor and Simons were both enthusiastically receptive to a POW raid. Bull Simons only mused gruffly, "You have to find a place where in fact it is feasible, and that's, I suppose, a matter of location, tactical situation, garrison, and things like that. I think everybody in the military feels that those people who are in there are kind of their brothers in arms, to put it perhaps a little dramatically, but that's the way it is and that's the way I do feel, as a matter of fact. And, yes, of course you want to get them out of there. But it has to be tactically feasible in order to attempt it."

Son Tay, he thought, was "totally feasible."

The Joint Chiefs of Staff set a timetable for planning, organization, training, and the operation. They would reconvene in Washington on 8 August for five more days of detailed planning, during which a special security section would be organized to develop cover stories and prevent leaks. The actual operations plan had to be finished by 28 August. Training would start by 9 September. Deployment was set for 10 October or before, with the raid to come off during the first good weather window between 20 October and 25 October.

Manor returned to Eglin Air Force Base to begin picking experienced combat pilots to fly the raider helicopters. Simons corralled his key subordinates and men at Fort Bragg. The first two soldiers he wanted were Lieutenant Colonel Elliot "Bud" Sydnor to act as his deputy and Captain Dick Meadows to head the compound assault element. Both were presently stationed at the Infantry School, Fort Benning, Georgia. Simons, Sydnor, and Meadows were old war buddies, having served together with SOG in Vietnam.

Sydnor was described as "lean, mean, and tall . . . gung ho, brilliant, competent, sensible, fearless." Colonel Blackburn, his old SOG commander, said of him, "You ask him to do something and he doesn't react. He just *does* it. . . . He's fantastic in combat. The tougher things get, the cooler he is. *Nothing* flusters him. I've never seen another soldier like him in my life."

Meadows was dark with a crop of black hair. He was also lean, but without Sydnor's long-boned angles. He was described as a "real life Jack Armstrong." As a sergeant working SOG crossborder operations into Laos, he once captured an entire battery of Russian artillery from a North Vietnamese storage point. General William Westmoreland, commander of U.S. forces in Vietnam, awarded him the first battlefield commission of the Vietnam War. Bull Simons pinned on his bars.

Simons needed a third senior officer—a full-fledged doctor to go on the raid and care for the prisoners and, if required, any of the raiders wounded during the action. Simons asked the Army Surgeon General to recommend a surgeon, but neither the Surgeon General nor the doctor could know why. A few days later, Lieutenant Colonel Joseph R. Cataldo strolled into Simons' office.

"I'm Doc Cataldo. I understand you need a doctor."

Simons stood up and studied the dark-eyed man. The guy had quick, precise movements; a steady, open gaze; and a firm handshake.

"Do you know why?" Simons asked him.

"No. The Surgeon General sent me here to see you about some kind of special assignment. I'm available."

Cataldo had been chief surgeon for Special Forces at Fort Bragg before graduating from the Command and Staff College at Fort Leavenworth and being reassigned to Washington D.C. He and his wife and four small children were just getting settled in D.C. He was parachute qualified and had worked with Green Berets in the field.

Simons came right out with it. "We're planning a POW rescue raid into North Vietnam," he said bluntly. "The risk can be great. We need a doctor to go along."

Without blinking an eye, Cataldo responded, "I'm your surgeon."

Some critics would later describe Cataldo in conflicting ways. He was earnest and competent, but also "a self-centered publicity seeker."

"Bullshit!" Simons rumbled. "The guy is a funny guy. He *is* hyperaggressive and some people don't care for him. But some people don't care for me either, and I really don't give a shit. He had the guts to do the job and he was intensely interested in doing it well. I don't give a damn about his motives, to tell the truth. From his point of view, the risk was great. But he volunteered. Just remember *that*."

Of the ninety-seven volunteer officers and men of Operation Ivory Coast who loaded aboard a C-123 on 8 September 1970 to fly south into isolation training at Eglin Air Force Base in the Florida panhandle, only three knew the nature of the mission: Lieutenant Colonel Sydnor, Captain Meadows, and Doc Cataldo. Colonel Simons was already at Eglin preparing to receive the raiders.

Darlene Kittleson took her husband's departure in stride.

She had come to accept over nearly twenty-five years of marriage that her quiet, unassuming little farmer was going to be a warrior. That was his cut in life.

"How hazardous is this . . . this whatever it is? Mission?" she had asked, otherwise nursing her fears inside.

"I don't know anything else," he said.

"Will you let me know as soon as you can?"

"Sorry, honey. We've already been cautioned. We can't tell *anyone*, not even our families, *anything* until it's all over."

"How long will it be?"

He didn't know that either. "Keep the bread warm."

"I know. You didn't promise me a rose garden."

CHAPTER 47

Where Master Sergeant Pappy Kittleson stepped off the C-123 the sun burned hot and bright and the climate was tropical. He might have been back in Vietnam had he not known better. Buses hauled the jungle fatigue-clad special troopers out to Eglin's Auxiliary Field Number 3. Captain Meadows pointed out that the Doolittle Raiders had trained on this same field twenty-eight years earlier for the first daring air raid on Tokyo. It was a huge training area, fenced off with guards at the gate.

Eglin itself, half as big as the state of Rhode Island, was the largest military base in the United States. It was home to the Aerospace Rescue and Recovery Training Center and the U.S. Air Force Special Operations Wing, from which General Manor had selected pilots for Operation Ivory Coast. With the U.S. involved in Vietnam, it was bristling with training activities. On one of the base's out-of-the-way areas had been constructed a full scale Vietnamese village used to develop and evaluate new techniques and devices for the war.

The buildings and barracks were all World War II era—double-storied, narrow-sided, painted white with green composition shingles—without the coal-burning stoves.

There were six barracks; a mess hall; motor pool; long, low headquarters building with barred windows; classroom buildings; a small theater; and an even smaller post exchange, snack bar, and beer hall.

"Welcome to Paradise, your new home," quipped lantern-jawed Sergeant First Class Lorenzo Robbins, stepping off the bus and looking around. Florida's flat wet scrublands of pine and cottonwood trees crowded up to an immense concrete parking apron upon which rested several UH-1 Huey helicopters and three or four more HH-53 rescue choppers, long-range heavy birds sometimes called Super Jolly Green Giants and sometimes BUFFs for "Big Ugly Friendly Fuckers." It depended upon who was doing the calling and whether the company was mixed or not.

"This place is a piece of work," Robbins went on, sweeping his arm across the tableau of the terrain. "You get up close to the DMZ in Vietnam and this is what it looks like."

You couldn't have proved it by Pappy. He had never gotten out of the Delta's swamps.

Bull Simons stood up front in the little theater, biting on his cigar. "If you need a cover story, it's this," he rumbled: "You're in training to rescue missionaries or foreign service hostages. Where? You don't need to know. Don't speculate. Just accept it. One thing I will tell you is, don't breach security. You're going to be tested. Don't be a shitbird and fuck up. You can call your wives on telephones provided, but the calls are being monitored. One slip of a loose tongue, and you're out of here on your red ass. You'll be held in confined isolation at Fort Bragg until this is all over. Understand? If anybody breaches security and it gets to the bad guys and they're waiting for us, we're all dead."

Kittleson tossed the old parachute bag containing his personal gear on a bunk in his assigned barracks. Robbins sank onto the next bunk and a tall, lanky kid not many weeks out of Training Group, Buck Sergeant Patrick St. Clair, took the bed on Kittleson's other side. Like Kittleson, St. Clair was in Support, which meant he wouldn't go on the raid either.

"We're going to Cuba," Robbins declared.

Pappy merely shrugged.

"Home sweet home," the kid St. Clair said. "But for how long?"

"Until it's over," Pappy Kittleson said. Patience was one thing the old master sergeant possessed in abundance.

Approximately fifty men would be selected out of the one hundred in isolation. That meant Support people hadn't been ruled out of the game entirely. Eliminations would continue right up to the end. Every man had to do his job or his speciality the best he could. If somebody else proved he could do it better, he got the job.

The selection process started the next morning with calisthenics led by Colonel Simons himself, then a tongue-dragging three-mile run behind Captain Dick Meadows. It was a ball-buster, uphill and through woods and then down along the beach in deep sand. Kittleson was the shortest man and the oldest on the run. The youngest was twenty-year-old Buck Sergeant Terry Buckler, who was a year younger than St. Clair. Kittleson relied on sheer bottom and spirit to bring him across the finish line with the much younger soldiers. He tried not to show how much he was hurting. Colonel Sydnor, who was about forty, took another look at the oldest man on the raider team, not counting the Bull.

"Pappy, you do pretty good for an older fella," he said. "You're in good shape."

Kittleson wanted to say that it damned near killed him. Instead, he said, "I want to go on the raid."

Sydnor nodded, noncommittal.

That started the routine for mission training. Pappy realized that because he was older, he had to try harder. He rolled out of the sheet before "Drop your cocks and grab your socks!" and went out for long, dark solitary runs, building up his wind and legs. Because he was in Support, helping in Supply and Administration, he and the other Support personnel weren't expected to conduct regular training with the other raiders. On the second or third morning, Kittleson returned from his run while Captain Meadows was forming the group for its ball-buster workout.

"I just finished it," Pappy alibied.

"Run it again."

Pappy did. Afterwards, he went to Meadows, who was more approachable than either of the colonels, Simons or Sydnor. That made him and Doc Cataldo the intermediaries between the soldiers and the ranking leaders.

"The way I understand it," Pappy began in his mild way, "final selection hasn't been made for the assault teams?"

Meadows nodded assent.

"Those of us on Support are to be backup in case something happens to somebody or he can't cut it?"

Again, Meadows nodded.

"Doesn't it make sense that Support should do all the same training as everybody else?"

And that was what happened. Support people handled their regular duties *and* trained. Pappy Kittleson had been there many times before, starting with Airborne training and A.S.T.C. with the Alamo Scouts: cross-country movement and compass courses, radio procedure and practice, helicopter orientation, demolition drills, patrolling, survival, escape and evasion. There were building searches and clearing; immediate action drills; village surveillance of the mock Vietnamese hamlet; use of star clusters and other pyrotechnics; and, always, night firing—target acquisition and recognition, burning up ammo, chewing up silhouette targets.

As Kittleson had attended one of the first M-60 machine gun schools at Fort Benning when the army switched from the .30-caliber to the M-60, he volunteered to train the raiders when it came to maintaining and shooting the gun. He did his job and controlled his envy of the younger men who would go on the mission. He sometimes found it difficult to accept that he had gone from being the knight to being the horse holder for the knights who went into battle.

The little veteran's reputation, bolstered by the fact that "that old man" had been on *three* POW raids, grew far out of proportion to his modest size as the training routine progressed. He busted ass not only to keep up, but to lead. Quiet, modest, even-tempered, he was nonetheless extremely proud and competitive. He became the training motivator, short legs pounding across the sand, balding head browning in the sun, eyes clear and steady and purposeful.

"If Pappy does it," went the rallying call, "then I can do it too."

Only in his letters to Darlene did he ever express his frustration. He sometimes regretted not having continued his diary from WWII.

"I'm only forty-six years old," he wrote his wife. "I've proved I can keep up and do the job. I don't know what the mission is yet, but whatever it is I don't want to wake up some day and find out I was left behind on one of the biggest operations in history."

"Galen," Darlene wrote back, "you've gone on more than your share of big missions."

One evening the platoons were night firing for record. Sergeant First Class John Jakovenko, a big, brash Polack who could almost play Beethoven on a machine gun, was shooting in the lane next to Kittleson.

"Leetle man," he taunted Pappy, "I v'ant you to v'atch this v'ith envy, the v'ay I shoot this leetle gun."

"I can outshoot you, Polack," Kittleson challenged.

"Ah-hah! Make eet a case of beer?"

"You're on."

Red tracers waved and arced downrange. Jakovenko stood up and thrust out his chest, swollen by his remarkable 81 hits. "Top that, leetle Pappy."

"That is pretty good," Pappy acknowledged. He settled down prone behind the M-60 and eased in the trigger with three-round bursts, tapping out a rhythm.

"I don't give a damn how many I hit, Polack, as long as I got one more hit than you," he said.

Captain Tom Jaeger, an assault element team leader, returned from the target trench after counting the bullet holes. He grinned at Kittleson. "You shot one less, Pappy," he said.

"Bullshit. I shot one more."

"That's right—82. You outshot him by one."

Not only had Kittleson topped Jakovenko, he'd also fired

the highest score of all the raiders for night record. Then he shot the highest day record. Captain Meadows drew him aside.

"Pappy, we need somebody really good with a machine gun to ride the assault helicopter. You want to try out for the assault team?"

"You bet, sir."

Knight once again. He wrote Darlene, "I won't be left behind."

CHAPTER 48

One late afternoon Bull Simons had choppers pick up the raiders to introduce them to the mission target. They flew out over the Florida scrubland to circle a "mockup" constructed of two-by-fours and target cloth to represent walls and buildings. Windows, gates, and doors were painted or cut into the cloth. Huge trees had been dug up elsewhere and transplanted inside the mockup enclosure. The helicopters landed nearby.

"You've seen what it'll look like from the air," Simons growled, leading the way. "Now you get the goddamned twenty-dollar tour."

Apparently, either Blackbird high-altitude surveillance photos or inside informants had provided the model dimensions and details for the mockup.

"It's made to exact scale," Simons explained. "Everything in the real target is represented here as nearly as possible."

The walls were seven feet tall enclosing an area Kittleson estimated as roughly 125 feet by 140 feet. The main gate was on the long east wall, outside of which were guard quarters and administration and logistical buildings. Three guard towers, much like those at Cabanatuan, studded either corner of the west wall and the main gate.

"A river flows close outside and along the west wall," Simons pointed out.

There were four large buildings inside the compound to house the prisoners. One nestled in the southeast corner parallel to the east wall. The second, longer and lower than the first, bisected the compound from the east wall to the west. The other two were snugged up close and parallel to the north wall. Man targets were scattered throughout. Some represented good guys; others were "enemy" soldiers.

Simons explained the general concept of the operation. The raid would consist of three main elements: a Support Group of approximately twenty-two soldiers headed personally by Colonel Simons; a Command and Security Group of twenty commanded by Colonel Sydnor; and the Compound Assault Group of about fourteen Green Berets led by Captain Meadows.

Tentatively, Kittleson was Meadows's machine gunner and a member of a five-man rescue element under team leader Captain Dan McKinney, a tall, thin blond officer of about thirty.

This was how the raid was supposed to go down:

Six helicopters would be involved in the assault, along with various jet fighters and C-130 flare ships to provide air support and diversions. A four-engined C-130 would drop flares over the compound to light it up, as the raid would be conducted under cover of darkness. Two HH-53 Super Jolly Greens would circle the target to act as backup flare and rescue ships. A third Super Jolly would spearhead the assault, coming in with a 7.62 minigun mounted in each door and at the open tailgate to take out the northwest guard tower. It would then withdraw to a location a half-mile west of the compound to set down and wait until it was recalled to pick up raiders and rescued prisoners.

Captain Meadows's Compound Assault Element would be first on the ground in an HH-3, a smaller version of the

HH-53. The HH-3 wasn't simply to be landed; it was going to be *crash-landed.*

"Because of the trees, there's not enough room to land it in the compound quickly enough at night," Simons explained. "We have to be in like lightning to prevent harm to the prisoners. A Huey could land, but it's not big enough to carry all of us and it doesn't have the range we need. Obviously, we're not going to crash Uncle Sam's helicopters during drill, but we're going to be setting down pretty hard to give you the feel of it."

The second element, Colonel Sydnor's Command and Security, would land just outside the compound to the south and blow a hole through the wall to permit Sydnor's men to reinforce Meadows inside. Prisoners would be whisked out through the hole.

Bull Simons's third Support Group element would also land outside the south wall. These men and some from Sydnor's command were to take care of the guard quarters outside the front gate and block off the area to enemy reinforcements.

The two choppers would scoot out to a holding area to wait for the call to return with the first gunship.

"The entire operation must go down in less than a half-hour," Simons warned. "We're all going to get creamed if we're in there longer than that. The raid has to have exact timing and placement. If you stray from where you're supposed to be by as much as a yard, or lose your timing by as much as a second once the action starts—you're mince-meat."

Where *in hell* were they going?

Although the plan of action continued to be modified by training experiences, it remained basically as Colonel Simons outlined it.

At first, the elements went through their mockup assignments at walk speed on the ground. As they mastered each step, the next stage was added to make it increasingly more complicated. In order, step by step, came helicopters flown from the aprons at the post. They landed and the men jumped off and walked through the mission with empty weapons. After that came blank-firing rehearsals at walk speed, then run speed timed by Colonel Simons himself. Live fire followed on the walk during daylight hours, gradually speeding up to real time. Last came night live-fire rehearsals with the helicopters following courses similar to the ones they would fly during the actual mission.

"There's no room for error," Simons and Sydnor both stressed.

The men napped during part of the day. As soon as the sun reddened over the Gulf of Mexico, they stirred in their barracks and prepared for the long night's drills. Same thing, night after night.

Like the Green Beret raiders, Air Force pilots began with fundamentals and added new tasks gradually. Four-engined turbine-propped C-130s would escort the raider choppers to the target and refuel them en route. Pilots started out flying low over the Gulf, then graduated to NOE, nap of the earth: low-level, terrain-hugging flights twisting and turning over Georgia and Tennessee, then flying treetop level back to Florida. Most of the flying occurred at night in close formation; aerial refueling added to the risk.

Soon, choppers joined the C-130s, flying with them in "draft" formation tucked in close behind the wings to be sucked along in the airplanes' vacuums as a means of gaining speed and conserving fuel. Raiders were added and, as Lorenzo Robbins put it, "stir well, salt, and see what happens." What happened were nearly exact simulations of the actual mission played out in real-time, live-fire action. All totaled, flight crews logged 1,017 hours of flying time during 368 sorties preparing for a mission whose destination was still kept a closely guarded secret by a few planners at the top of the rank structure.

It didn't take the men long to notice that flying time from *liftoff* to *mission complete* burned no more than four hours. That one fact provided endless hours of speculation.

"It makes sense," Robbins insisted. We're flying four

hours. It's a three-and-a-half-hour flight from Homestead Air Force Base in Miami to Cuba and back.

"We don't have POWs in Cuba," Kittleson pointed out.

"What makes you so sure this is a POW raid? Maybe we're going in to kidnap some of Castro's political prisoners."

"The training has the feeling of a POW raid," Pappy said mildly, and left it at that.

It wasn't enough to have a single plan and practice it enough that the men dreamed about it at night and could have worked through it start to finish with their eyes closed. They also played "What if?" which required alternate and backup plans. What if Colonel Simons was shot down en route? That called for *Plan Green*. What if Captain Meadows's team aborted or was lost? *Plan Blue*. What if Sydnor's and Doc Cataldo's chopper went down? *Plan Red*.

Pappy Kittleson focused on his job. Flares at a distance from the compound simulated a diversionary attack as raiders neared the target following a four-hour, rough, low-to-the-ground flight. A chopper hovered high to provide the light of a quarter-moon with its floods. Then the mockup burst into flickering illumination as a C-130 dropped its flares and the assault choppers circled and came in on target one behind the other, low, skimming the Florida scrub brush.

As Meadows's smaller HH-3 trailed the minigun ship, flying in low toward the west wall next to the simulated river, Kittleson balanced himself at the chopper's left window with a mounted M-60 machine gun. Ahead, the ripping rattle of the miniguns took out the northwest guard tower. Kittleson lay on his trigger, pouring in a stream of red tracers as soon as the southwest guard tower came into his sights. It had to be taken out too.

Meadows's ship "crashed" inside the compound. It came down slowly, carefully, in order to avoid the trees, but then the Air Force pilots, Lieutenant Colonel Herb Zehnder and Major Herb Kalen, dumped it hard enough the last few feet to approximate a real crash landing. The tail ramp fell and

Captain Meadows ran out with his bullhorn, shouting for the prisoners not to panic.

Captain McKinney's five-man team, of which Kittleson was a member, cleared the west end of the long, low building that bisected the compound before moving on to the two small buildings on the north wall. Pappy abandoned his M-60, leaving it in the ship, and grabbed his CAR-15. The assault team selected carbines because they were lightweight and provided a lot of firepower.

Rushing across the camp was so familiar by now that Kittleson knew exactly how many steps it took him to go from the downed helicopter to the building. Not only that, but the raiders had crawled and walked and run through the mockup so many times on both dry and live-fire runs that they knew exactly where every friendly bullet was going. The attack had to be swift, violent, and, most of all, lethal for the bad guys.

They practiced streaking into the make-believe buildings, busting down doors, breaking hasps and hinges, cutting chains with bolt cutters, rounding up "prisoners"—played by Support people—and hustling them to the hole in the wall Sydnor's men would have blown. At the same time that McKinney's team cleared their buildings and parts of buildings, two other assault teams led by Captain Tom Jaeger and First Lieutenant George Petrie were rescuing captives from the remaining buildings and taking out the tower at the main gate. This tower could not be neutralized from the air because of a small shed below it that was probably used by the enemy as an isolation and torture chamber.

Simons and Sydnor were omnipresent at every drill—cajoling, evaluating, urging, encouraging.

"Pappy, that's damn good shooting."

"Erickson, get lower when you go through the door."

"Faster, Tapley. Move it! Move it!"

Colonel Simons personally counted bullet holes in the targets. If they were not riddled to his satisfaction, he ordered the raid reenacted immediately.

M-60 ammo belts were normally loaded one tracer to four regular rounds.

"I'd like every round in the belts to be tracer," Kittleson requested. "We can adjust fire a lot faster."

The next night, steady red streams of fire poured from the black choppers flying over Eglin, all over again.

As part of training security measures, workers with Secret clearances arrived to disassemble the mockup before daybreak. It would then be reassembled that night. The Soviet Cosmos 355 spy satellite passed over every twenty-four hours at an altitude of seventy miles. It could spot and identify a single outhouse nearly anywhere in the U.S.

One morning, Captain Meadows announced with a half-grin that a new member was being assigned to the raid. "Her name is Barbara," he said. "Barbara has never slept alone, and she won't sleep alone here. Somebody will guard her day and night. She's really quite handsome, amply endowed and really put together."

"We don't give a rat's ass what she *looks* like at this point," someone blurted out. "We've been in isolation for over a month. What we want to know is, does she *fuck*?"

Barbara turned out to be a $60,000 table-sized replica of the target compound built by the CIA. Each detail proved exact. She was equipped with special devices that allowed a viewer to see what the compound would look like the night of the raid. Simply by adjusting the viewer, the model could be lit by a quarter- or half-moon, or by flares, or she could remain in near-total darkness. Little palm trees grew all over Barbara.

"Don't surmise anything by that," Bull Simons cautioned his soldiers. "There are palms in South America and the Middle East as well as in Southeast Asia."

Near the end of September, Colonel Sydnor posted a first list of men chosen for the mission and their team assignments. Some of the men crowding around looked at it, then walked off trying to conceal their disappointment. Kittleson's name was on the list. So was SFC Lorenzo Robbins's.

They were on Captain Dan McKinney's team along with stocky SFC Bill Tapley and another sergeant, who would not make it to the end of training before his complaining and bitching got him excised and returned to Fort Bragg. Pat St. Clair's name was not on the list. He walked out onto the grinder and stood alone looking at the HH-3 parked there.

"These men are so familiar with that camp," Colonel Sydnor reported to Simons, "that they can fight their way into those cells even if they're blind, half-dead, or full drunk."

CHAPTER 49

Coaches and other fashioners of muscles and tools understand that professional athletes and fine steel reach a point beyond which further work can actually be detrimental. The trick is to hone the knife and then use it before further sharpening merely dulls it.

"Get up, fly out, shoot . . . Get up, fly out, shoot . . . It's like living the same day over and over again," Lorenzo Robbins bitched as training bled from September into October, with no end in sight. None of the men knew of the 20–25 October "window," which at any rate came and went.

A few of the men got together and designed a shoulder patch for the force. It depicted a pair of white eyes peering out from the dark at the base of a mushroom. Underneath was the inscription *KITD/FOHS*.

Colonel Simons chewed on his stogie and glared at it.

"*Kept In The Dark/Fed Only Horse Shit*," Bud Sydnor explained.

Simons chewed on his cigar. Then he burst into laughter.

Kittleson sent one of the patches home to Darlene.

I can't tell you anything about where we're going, when, nor for how long, honey, he wrote, *even if I knew, which I don't. I'm not sure if we'll be allowed to telephone before we go, but even if we can I don't think I'd want to worry you like that. Just know everything is okay.* He signed it with his usual, *Your husband, Galen.* During World War II when Darlene was his pen pal, he had signed off with, *Your friend, Galen.* Dramatic, Master Sergeant Pappy Kittleson had never been.

Pappy Kittleson, Captain Dick Meadows, and the personable Doc Joe Cataldo, surgeon for The Mushrooms, as the men sometimes jokingly referred to themselves, remained motivators for the other men. Whereas Kittleson was a steady, quiet inspiration and Meadows an unmoving, unchanging rock, Cataldo was as gung ho and aggressive as a boot camp Marine. He cross-trained with an ax to bust down building doors, as it might be necessary for him to personally get out wounded or ill prisoners. He constantly came up with new ideas. It was he who derived the notion that raiders of the assault party should all carry light cotton rope. Why? To bind prisoners' hands or to tie prisoners together should they panic and try to run off when the raiders landed.

The men started calling him Super Doc.

"None of the other goddamned pussy doctors wanted to get dirty," Bull Simons growled in approval.

Cataldo instructed the force in how to treat battle wounds, shock, and fractures and how to inject morphine and sedatives. He also taught them various combat carries.

"The people you rescue may be ill or wounded," he explained.

"Do the bad guys there speak Spanish, English, Chinese, or what?" soldiers probed.

It was understood that the surgeon was among the elite few who knew the nature and destination of the mission. Doc Cataldo merely grinned.

He presented a profile of what they might expect from the "hostages."

"Of the expected sixty-one hostages," he said, "we expect twenty-five will have or have had malaria, thirty-five intestinal parasites, fifteen dysentery, twelve tuberculosis, four goiter—and most will be suffering from primary malnutrition. Restriction of protein intake and physical inactivity will have caused marked muscular atrophy and a slow reaction to stimuli."

The same diagnosis applied to the POWs at Cabanatuan.

"Some of them still hope for liberation," the doctor continued. "Others will have given up all hope. The majority are probably unsure and live day by day, driven only by their natural desire for survival. To find they are suddenly liberated will be very shocking for them.

"What you'll see are stunned individuals. They are easily fatigued. They will have lesions and sores on their mouths and bodies. The skin on their arms and legs will irritate readily. Their tongues will be swollen, their speech slow and slurred. They'll bruise easily, walk unsteadily, and may burst into tears. Some of them may become terrified and try to run away, while others will have to be restrained or carried."

"I've changed my mind," Robbins said. "We're not going to Cuba. It has to be Vietnam."

Kittleson agreed. The conditions Doc Cataldo described could only belong to prisoners of war.

And the horseshit, as the raiders put it, continued. Training was very physical. Green Berets by nature were rough, physical men. Colonel Bull Simons once remarked that he hadn't asked for a bunch of Boy Scouts—and he didn't expect or get any. On the training schedule posted inside the barracks appeared the activity "Friday Night Fights," which was what occurred on stand down nights when the raiders all congregated boisterously at the little beer hall on post. For too long the soldiers had been restricted to that one piece of real estate in the Florida panhandle, cooped up together, training with violence. Drinking and a good fist fight let off steam.

Occasionally, U.S. Air Force females were granted access to the club with instructions to test security: Get the men drinking and talking and pump them for information. Women were a rare commodity. Even the *ugliest pig*, as Lorenzo Robbins put it, seldom lacked for attention. "If I was an *ugly* woman," he opined, "I'd spend the rest of my life in the army, where even a snake can get loving if somebody will hold its head."

Kittleson went over for a few beers with the guys, but he was a reserved little man who often found a corner to occupy while he observed and smiled with amusement. The Air Force ladies pretty much ignored the crusty old man while turning their attention and feminine wiles on the more vulnerable young studs like St. Clair, the kid Terry Buckler, or Lieutenant George Petrie, who was tall and fair and had an eye for pretty women. To their credit, however, not one word about the mission leaked out.

"This bitch keeps asking me what we're doing here," Lorenzo Robbins said to Pappy. "I told her to kiss my rosy red airborne ass and I'd bare it for her right there in front of God and everybody."

One Friday night a rawboned master sergeant with Sydnor's Command and Security group got tanked up at the club and began railing against Bull Simons's leadership. The training was going on and on and nothing was happening. The soldiers were being kept in the dark—*fucking mushrooms!*—like they were children or fools.

"I'm going to shoot the sonofabitch!" he threatened and staggered from the club.

He reached the barracks, grabbed his carbine, and started loading it. Kittleson, Lorenzo Robbins, and a couple of other GIs tackled him and tied him to his bed until he sobered up. The next day, Colonel Simons raked him up one side and down the other, then sent him back to his team.

"You're not firing him?" Sydnor exclaimed.

"The guy has a point. Goddamned politicians are dragging this on and on. I don't blame him for being pissed off and wanting to shoot somebody. *I* want to shoot somebody. Besides, that master sergeant is one hell of a soldier."

It was vintage Bull Simons.

Pappy Kittleson knocked on Captain Meadows's office door the next morning. The men had elected him to express their dissatisfaction. After all, they had been in training, *hard* training, for over two months.

"Pappy, what's on your mind?" Meadows asked.

"Cap, I think it's to the point we all need a kick in the ass. Let the Mushrooms out of the dark. We're getting sick of being fed horseshit. We're not going to get any better than we already are. We've been through the mockup 182 times already and still counting. Wherever it is we're going, whatever we're going to do, let's do it."

Meadows slowly rose from his desk. He walked to the barred window behind it and let his thoughtful gaze sweep over the tarmac apron separating headquarters from billeting.

"Pappy, I'll talk to the men and see what I can do to settle them down. You talk to them. They listen to you. I'm going to tell you the same thing Colonel Simons told me."

He turned and looked at the little sergeant. "Pappy, we don't have much longer."

CHAPTER 50

President of the United States Richard M. Nixon met in the White House Oval Office on 18 November 1970 with four of his closest advisors to listen to a dramatic briefing by Admiral Tom Moorer, Chairman of the Joint Chiefs of Staff. Secretary of State William P. Rogers was about to hear for the first time on that cold and bleak autumn day that an "invasion" of North Vietnam had been in the planning stages for nearly six months—and that everything was ready to go.

Only for Rogers would the briefing be a complete surprise. The others present in the Oval Office—Nixon, CIA Director Richard Helms, Defense Secretary Melvin Laird, national security advisor Henry Kissinger—knew that a POW raid was being planned; they just didn't know the details. What was conceived back in the spring and summer as a modest quick-strike from Laos using theater assets had ballooned into a large-scale rescue effort planned, trained, and rehearsed in the United States.

Public support for the Vietnam War had long waned or turned into outright resistance. A daring successful rescue of American POWs would be a morale booster for the beleaguered military and at the same time provide Nixon a political victory. The Vietnam War was the first in U.S. history whose tactics, and even strategies, often came down from Washington.

Admiral Moorer was ushered into the Oval Office at precisely 11:00 A.M. From a large map case marked Top Secret he removed a series of briefing charts and arranged them on an easel. Nixon gave him the nod to go ahead.

"Mr. President," he said, "the code name for this operation is Kingpin. It provides for a raid on North Vietnam to be conducted by Army Special Forces personnel assaulting the Son Tay prisoner of war camp twenty-three miles west of Hanoi in Air Force helicopters assisted by a Navy air diversion over Haiphong Harbor. The most advantageous period for this undertaking is between November 21 and 25.

"This is the only confirmed active POW camp outside Hanoi, Mr. President. The Son Tay camp has a prisoner population of seventy Americans. Of these, sixty-one have been tentatively identified by name and service. There are forty-three Air Force, fourteen Navy, four Marines . . . We propose to rescue them all."

Moorer, using a map of the Hanoi area, described in brief detail how the raid would be conducted.

"The ground commander is positive that the operation will succeed, Mr. President."

President Nixon leaned eagerly forward in his chair. "Sounds great, Tom. What else?"

"A final word, Mr. President. If resources in support of the operation reveal that the enemy may have determined our objective, the operation will be canceled."

"Damn, Tom. Let's not let *that* happen," Nixon exclaimed. "I know you guys have worked months on this. I want those POWs home too. . . . Hell, if this works, we could even have them here for Thanksgiving dinner, right here at the White House."

CHAPTER 51

On 16 November the mission alert funneled down the pipe to the men at Eglin Air Force Base. No one was allowed to call home with the news that Ivory Coast, now code-named Kingpin for the actual operation, was moving out within the next twenty-four hours. Equipment was crated for shipment—several tons of it: personal combat gear such as LBE fighting harnesses, special knives made from ground-down machetes for prying open doors, head lamps, ear plugs so the men would not be deafened by aircraft noise when they hit the ground, red goggles to prevent night blindness from explosions and flares, CAR-15 rifles, M-60 machine guns. There was team and mission equipment: satchel charges to blast a hole through the south wall of the compound; C-4 explosives and a thermite grenade stuffed into a length of fire hose to blow up the HH-3 after it crashed; Armalite night sights on CAR-15s; ninety-two radios ranging from "Handy-Talkie" individual radios and survival radios to command-sized AN-PRC-77s to be operated on eight separate frequency nets; bolt cutters; acetylene torches; chain saws; rope; cameras to document living conditions suffered by the prisoners; shotguns; Light Anti-Tank Weapons

(LAWs); M-79 grenade launchers; one hundred sets of pajamas, bathrobes, and slippers for the rescued captives; Heinz baby food in case the recovered Americans were unable to eat "real food"; Ketamine HCL, a fast-acting "knock-out" anesthetic; surgical instruments; ponchos . . .

The raiders were ready to go but waited twenty-four hours for the final word to come.

"Still Mushrooms," someone murmured. "It's been called off, but as usual we're the last to know."

Finally, Colonel Sydnor assembled the men. It was 17 November, shortly after noon meal. "We will be loading aboard a Lockheed C-141 Starlifter jet early tonight," he announced. "From that point on, we are 'sterile.' There will be no insignia of any kind on our uniforms. Be ready."

"We *have* been ready," said Sergeant Herman Spencer.

Kingpin raiders loaded aboard the C-141 and lifted off from Eglin in the dark. The aircraft offered comfort in the form of regular airliner seats instead of military canvas. All seats faced the tail section. Word passed that Colonel Simons and General Manor had preceded the raiders by nearly forty-eight hours.

One last change affecting Pappy Kittleson had been made two days earlier when the bellyaching sergeant was removed from an operation and sent back to Bragg. Backup Buck Sergeant Pat St. Clair, who had thought he was going to be left behind, took his place. The kid was excited as he climbed onto the Starlifter with Pappy and Lorenzo Robbins. Captain Dan McKinney's assault team now consisted of Kittleson, Robbins, Bill Tapley, and Pat St. Clair.

The jet landed at Norton Air Force Base in California for refueling.

"I guess we're not heading for Cuba," Robbins conceded.

The next refueling stop was at Elmendorf Air Force Base in Anchorage, Alaska.

Their destination had to be Vietnam. Pappy had taken a similar route to Vietnam in 1968.

In Japan when they transferred to another Starlifter, American Air Police surrounded the two birds and formed a lane from one aircraft door to the other. The precaution annoyed Kittleson.

After all the shit we've been through, Simons has to post guards on us!

"It's to make sure no one gets near us," Meadows explained easily.

"Do you know where we're heading, Cap?" Kittleson asked.

"The Colonel will explain it all in due time."

After twenty-eight hours in the air, Kingpin touched down at what was obviously an American Air Force base. They weren't in Kansas anymore, Toto. Kittleson looked out the window as the plane came in on final approach and observed flat terrain and what he took in the darkness to be rice paddies. He saw thatched huts on stilts. That meant Asia somewhere. Colonel Simons waited stone-faced on the apron in the 3:00 A.M. pre-dawn. It was 18 November, twelve hours ahead of Washington D.C. time. The raiders were already in place by the time Admiral Moorer briefed President Nixon and his advisors on the raid planning.

The weather was warm, with traces of the previous day's rain fresh in the air, and puddled on the tarmac runway and apron. Pappy took a quick look around between the time he was hustled off the C-141 and into the back of a sealed, windowless van. He saw only hangars and various war planes with both American and Oriental—but not Vietnamese—markings.

For weeks back at Eglin, the men had joked that each day was the "final rehearsal." It was quite evident now that the real show was imminent. Tension and excitement had everyone wide awake and quietly speculating about where they were. Kittleson dozed during the short van ride.

"This ain't your first county fair, is it, Pappy?" Robbins wryly noted.

The van disgorged the troopers in front of new air-conditioned billets, luxurious compared to what they had become accustomed to at Eglin. There was a tall fence around the barracks patrolled by guard dogs and Air Police. Doc Cataldo distributed sleeping pills.

"They'll help you with jet lag. You need to rest."

Colonel Simons gathered the men in a little theater for a thirty-minute briefing at 2:00 P.M. He introduced the man on stage with him as Brigadier General Roy Manor, the overall commander for the operation. It was the first time most of the men had ever seen the general. Simons told the raiders in his usual gruff manner that he thought they were ready, then provided a rough training schedule for the next few days. It was a light schedule, nothing like the grueling rehearsals the men had endured at Eglin since 9 September. Mostly, it consisted of test-firing weapons and assembling, maintaining, and checking equipment. There would be more briefings as required.

Nothing about where they were nor where they were going.

"You will learn what the target is," he promised, "as soon as—and *if*—we receive final mission approval from Washington."

"Is there a chance the mission can still be a no go?" someone inquired.

"There's still time for any of you to back out," Simons answered instead.

Chow was at 5:00 P.M., followed by a movie at 8:30. The movie featured Burt Lancaster in *Birdman of Alcatraz*. Restless, Kittleson got up and left halfway through the film. He and St. Clair walked back to the barracks in the clear tropical night.

"Any idea where we are, Pappy?"

"Asia."

"That's a big continent."

"I'd say wherever we are, Vietnam is not far away."

"Was it like this the last time you went on a big prisoner raid?" St. Clair asked.

"It was all over at Cabanatuan, from start to end, in four days."

The next day's schedule included a local Air Force SAR (Search and Rescue) commander who presented a class on survival radios and call signs for rescue aircraft. He issued signal flares fired by a small pistol. "It can double as a weapon to kill the enemy," he elaborated, adding on a more somber note, "Or, if you're about to be captured . . ."

No need to finish that statement. Back in the Scouts, Andy Smith always advised every GI to keep an extra bullet in his pocket.

A CIA operative then delivered a second briefing on escape and evasion. He handed out "blood chits"—small silk scarfs with maps and a microthin compass sewed onto one side and on the other side phrases spelled out phonetically in Laotian and Vietnamese: *Which way is north? I need water. I need food. Can you find me a doctor? I am an American. . . .*

Something was definitely up. It was coming down soon. The feeling was there.

After lunch on Friday, 20 November, Doc Cataldo came by with his bottle of sleeping pills. He personally stood by until every man, including Simons, swallowed his. He then returned at 5:00 P.M. to hold reveille for chow.

"Eat heartily," he warned. "This will be your last meal for twelve hours. We're taking off in five hours."

At 6:00 P.M., the men herded into the tiny theater. Doors were closed and guards stationed outside. The proverbial pin could have been heard dropping as Simons and Sydnor walked briskly onto the stage. They were finally going to reveal the raid's target, kept secret these several months.

"This is your last chance," Simons began. "You can still back out. Nothing will be said about it."

The Bull waited, heavy jaw thrust forward, chewing hard on his cigar. No one moved in the entire theater. It seemed the raiders were barely breathing. Simons nodded his approval. He turned to Lieutenant Colonel Sydnor, who stood up and pulled down a huge map of Hanoi. There was a big, red circle west of the city. Sydnor turned to the silent theater. There was still no reaction. Everyone sat too stunned to react.

"Gentlemen, *this* is where we're going in," Sydnor proclaimed in a ringing, dramatic voice.

That produced a reaction. Fear and anxiety suddenly released themselves in a surprising roar of laughter and cheering. Bull Simons stood there with his head up, proud of these magnificent bastards and plainly moved by their response.

"This," murmured Sergeant Billy K. Moore, without the usual sarcasm that accompanied the comment, "*is* the last rehearsal."

Simons preambled his own remarks by removing the cigar from his mouth. The theater fell quiet again.

"We are going to rescue seventy American prisoners of war, maybe more, from a camp called Son Tay," he said. "This is something American prisoners have a right to expect from their fellow soldiers. The target is twenty-three miles west of Hanoi."

Robbins, sitting next to Pappy Kittleson, let out a long, low whistle. St. Clair appeared frozen in place. Pappy stared deadpan at the map with its red circle. The Cabanatuan raid had been behind enemy lines, but it *hadn't* been in Tokyo.

Bull Simons batted his eyes hard. He was a man who never revealed emotion. He said, "You are to let nothing—*nothing*—interfere with the operation. Our mission is to rescue prisoners, not take prisoners. And if we walk into a trap, if it turns out they know we're coming, don't dream about walking out of North Vietnam—unless you've got wings on your feet. We'll be one hundred miles from Laos; this is the wrong part of the world for a big retrograde movement. If there's been a leak, we'll know as soon as the second or third chopper sets down. That's when they'll cream us. If that happens, I want to keep this force together. We will back up to the Song Con River and, by Christ, let them come across that goddamned open ground. We'll make them pay for every foot across that sonofabitch."

The cigar returned to its customary place. He almost chewed it in two. "Colonel Sydnor will give the final target briefing."

He strode down the aisle and left the theater as the men

once again stood and exploded with their approval and willingness to go.

Like Bull Simons, Pappy Kittleson used words sparingly. It was their generation, their warrior breed, that valued action over word. "You know," he opined in all earnestness, "I'd hate to have had this go down and wake up tomorrow to find I hadn't been a part of it."

CHAPTER 52

Normally, 90 percent of those American airmen forced to bail out of their stricken warcraft over South Vietnam landed uninjured. Almost the opposite was true for downed pilots and crew during the bombing of North Vietnam. Parachuting from a fighter bomber over Hanoi was generally attempted at supersonic speeds of four hundred knots or faster. The plane was in a nose-down attitude or tumbling out of control and disintegrating before it ever screamed to an impact with earth. In addition, the pilot punched out into a nasty sky exploding with flak, missiles, and ground fire. If he were smoked over Hanoi his chances were better than 90 percent that he ended up either dead or in prison.

Air Force Major Elmo C. Baker was shot down over Hanoi on 23 August 1967 during his sixty-first mission. He broke his left femur during punch-out. Captured on the ground, he was taken by chopper to Hoa Lo Prison in Hanoi. Hoa Lo, "Devil's Island of Southeast Asia," had been built by the French during their hegemony in Indochina. American inmates renamed it "Hanoi Hilton." It stank of forty years' accumulation of vomit, blood, urine, and feces. No talking, singing, or any other noise was permitted inside the walls. There was only silence and the padding of bony bare feet on dust. Political officers at the prison tortured Major Baker by twisting the foot on his broken leg.

On 24 May 1968, two and a half years before Colonel Bull Simons's raiders skyed up out of Eglin Air Force Base en route to somewhere in Asia, the POW camp at Son Tay became active. Prisoners were transferred by bus from Hoa Lo in two increments of twenty each on 24 May and 18 July and a final batch of fifteen on 28 November 1968. Among the first POWs moved to Son Tay were Air Force Major Irby Terrell, Jr., and airman Dave Ford. Major Elmo Baker showed up later to be celled with them.

"Used to I couldn't stand rice," Ford remarked with a thin chuckle. "I gave away my first rice. Now, I love rice. It's one of my favorite dishes."

That was because it was virtually the only dish served at Son Tay—and in very small quantities at that.

"Where are we?" Baker asked.

"You're at Cape Hope, near Son Tay Citadel," Terrell responded. "It's isolated as hell out here."

"Even if our guys are looking," Ford added, "they'd never think to search for us here."

Although escape from Son Tay seemed improbable, the fifty-five captives within its stone walls devised clever ways for communicating their presence to surveillance flights. They stomped out on the ground in ingenious hieroglyphics the message *55 POWS Here*. They arranged their laundry to spell *SAR*.

They waited. And nobody ever came.

CHAPTER 53

The American armada flew low through the darkness of enemy airspace. Like most of the other Green Berets in the HH-3 chopper's belly, Master Sergeant Pappy Kittleson had napped fitfully since taking off from Thailand, nodding off in the canvas below the port window where his M-60 machine gun was mounted, blanking out his mind. Long ago in the Philippines he had learned it was better before combat not to think at all.

The other thirteen Special Forces of the Compound Assault element were either dozing or sitting wide-eyed in the red glow of the interior night lights, waiting—like Kittleson, trying to blank out everything except this one moment in time. They wore green jungle fatigues and their faces were blackened with camouflage paint. The Air Force crew chief, a lanky tech sergeant named Leroy Wright, raised his head from where he dozed in his canvas jump seat. He looked at Kittleson across the aircraft. Then his neutral gaze shifted to Lieutenant George Petrie sitting next to the right door. The door was still closed, but Petrie's mounted M-60 was ready to rotate into the door to chew up things during that mad minute before they crash-landed inside the Son Tay compound.

The other raiders all knew about the tall lieutenant's personal grudge against North Vietnam. Nearly three years earlier, Petrie had been a Special Forces sergeant with the CIDG program in the central highlands of Vietnam. After being wounded and slicked out of a tight spot, he happened to read in *Stars & Stripes* that his cousin, U.S. Navy Lieutenant Commander Jim Henderson, had been shot down during a bombing mission over North Vietnam. He was still listed as MIA—either dead or a POW. Petrie and Henderson had grown up together, more like brothers than cousins.

"If we ever go up north to get those guys," Petrie had vowed, "I swear I will be there. I will damned sure be the first man on the ground."

He was disappointed that he wasn't to be the first man out tonight. That honor befell Captain Dick Meadows with his bullhorn. But what difference did a few seconds make? He would be right there behind Meadows un-assing the crashed chopper with all the others, like ants fleeing a flame.

Kittleson braced himself on the web seating and stood up. Pat St. Clair and Lorenzo Robbins stirred in their seats between Captain McKinney and Sergeant Tapley. Their eyes caught the red interior glow, reflecting out of their fierce camouflaged faces.

The little sergeant stretched cramped muscles and looked out the window. He had to piss, but he put it off just to prove he could. When a man reached his age, having to take a leak didn't necessarily mean he was nervous. Pissing was something a forty-six-year-old man had to do more often, was all.

Pappy wondered if fifty-one-year-old Bull Simons in the Command chopper, *Apple One*, had to take a leak.

Three hours was an eternity to sit in cold red-tinted air anticipating action. No one talked inside the aircraft, partly because it was hard to talk above engine noise, partly because each soldier confronted himself in his own way. They had all known when they volunteered that this night, or something like this night, would have to come.

Pappy's round face underneath his patrol cap as he looked out the window into the North Vietnam night was a kindly, benevolent face that belied the bloody conflicts he had seen in Vietnam and, before that, World War II. A number of raiders had not seen prior action. To their way of looking at it, Pappy Kittleson had been *around*, he had seen some *shit*.

The little armada screaming through the night, twisting and turning at low levels, consisted of a specially equipped C-130 Combat Talon spearheading a tight flying group of five HH-53 Super Jollies and the one smaller HH-3 carrying the Compound Assault force. The Talon was equipped with new precision navigation equipment and forward-looking infrared, never before used until tonight. This equipment helped calculate and provide all turning points along the route to prevent detection by enemy radar. A second Rescue C-130 had air-refueled the choppers over Laos, then turned back. The armada was now on its own.

Normal cruise speed for the Talon at low altitude was 250 knots. The HH-3's upper speed boundary was 105 knots, ten knots below stall speed for the C-130's four big engines. To compensate for the difference, the small helicopter sat tucked in underneath the Talon's wing, sucked along in its vacuum to gain necessary speed and conserve fuel. The Talon's broad wing cast a protective hawk's shadow over the helicopter. The five Super Jolly Green Giants flew in formation on either side.

An hour after the armada left Udorn, Thailand, a third Combat Talon and a flight of A-1 fighters took off to rendezvous with fighter planes from the aircraft carriers *Oriskany*, *Ranger*, and *Hancock* to form Flight Task Force 77, the largest night operation ever flown over North Vietnam. None of the aircraft was armed with real ordnance. What they had were pyrotechnics to *simulate* bombings and ground fights. Exactly twenty minutes before raiders crashed into Son Tay prison, the task force would stage diversionary mock raids all over Hanoi. All show and fury with no substance. All staged to cover the prison raid.

A quarter-moon ran aircraft shadows across the ground. Kittleson saw rice paddies, lines of dark jungle, and roads. Occasionally, a light burned in the black and alien landscape. Word passed back mouth to mouth from the two pilots in the cockpit.

Twenty minutes!

Following Colonel Simons's historic briefing at the theater that finally revealed the secret of their destination, the men returned to their barracks in an afterglow of excitement to prepare for departure. They had already signed wills, powers of attorney, and other legal documents. Kittleson stripped the sheets off his bunk and stored his few personal effects in his wall locker. He looked for a long, sober moment at the snapshot he always carried in his wallet. Darlene looked back at him.

The woman had endured a lot during an army career that bounced them from place to place like nomads while rearing two sons.

Some of the other men wrote last letters to wives, mothers, and girlfriends. Kittleson had never been much good at letters. He promised he would say to Darlene personally, afterwards, all that she meant to him over the years. Maybe he *would* try to give her that rose garden. He stuffed the wallet into his locker and was ready.

He snatched up his CAR-15, .45 Colt pistol, and LBE harness and headed for the door. Robbins fell in behind, along with the twenty-year-old Terry Buckler. The others followed in twos and threes, laden with weapons and equipment. The fifty-six raiders, not counting pilots and air crew, were heavily armed with an impressive arsenal.

Twenty minutes!

Pappy couldn't put it off any longer. He made his way aft to the piss tube, stepping on mattresses spread on the floor as padding for the crash landing. He steadied himself on the heads and shoulders of other raiders.

St. Clair looked up. "Pappy?"

"Yeah?"

"Nothing. Just, Pappy . . ."

Like he needed to hear a voice other than the little nagging one alone inside his head. Just a lanky kid, he and Buckler both. Kittleson had to remind himself that he was only twenty when he made the Cabanatuan raid.

Pappy clamped a thick hand on the kid's shoulder. "You'll do fine, Pat."

St. Clair returned a confident grin. A word like that from Pappy Kittleson was *the* word. The soft-spoken little Iowan carried a big reputation. St. Clair had merely stared the first time he met the diminutive warrior.

"Jesus. He was *there* when they rescued the Bataan Death March survivors."

The piss tube had frozen at altitude over Thailand and had not thawed once the armada dropped to low level over North Vietnam. Pappy took his leak and felt better, but urine ran over onto Lieutenant Petrie's webgear lying underneath. Petrie sniffed when he drew it on, getting ready.

"Pappy pissed on my gear," he murmured, but it was only a thought and it meant nothing. He returned to his station at the door. It was still closed, but Wright the crew chief stood by ready to open it.

By Pappy's synchronized watch, it was 0200 hours, 21 November 1970. Kittleson braced himself on his machine gun, taking up the shock of the rough low-level flying in his knees. He checked the gun a final time. Its feed and the belt of 7.62 ammo coiled inside the box hung on the weapon's feed tray. He ran his hand alongside the cold steel, feeling the safety, the ejection port, the trigger; focusing his thoughts.

Each man was merely a part of the whole—but the whole succeeded only on the shoulders of each man.

The men were shadows silent and waiting in the belly of the HH-3 as the armada hurtled through hostile airspace toward an enemy POW camp within sight of North Vietnam's capital.

They were deep, *deep* inside enemy country.

Word came back from up front: *Get ready!*

Kittleson removed the window and swiveled his gun barrel into the open space. Wind howled past. He watched the black shadow of the Combat Talon on the ground separate from the six chopper shadows and claw for altitude. It would launch its own flares and ground battle simulators.

The choppers continued flying so low that leaves on palms rattled like old bones. Blade wash rippled the surface of rice paddy water. They buzzed over a North Vietnam Army convoy halted on a road. Kittleson glimpsed a driver's face craning out the window of one of the little French-made trucks. He was smoking a cigarette.

It would have been easy to shoot him.

Master Sergeant Galen Kittleson braced himself at his gun.

Two minutes!

He bowed his head and prayed silently for the lives and souls of operation Kingpin and the POWs in the compound. Prayer was something Pappy Kittleson never forgot.

The two spare Jolly Greens peeled off to climb to fifteen hundred feet. They were backup in case something went wrong. The other four blasted ahead toward the prison.

CHAPTER 54

The lights of Hanoi sparkled beautifully toward the northeast. Most cities were beautiful when night covered their scars and scabs and warts. Haiphong Harbor out where the city met the South China Sea was even more spectacular tonight; U.S. Navy warplanes lit up the sky and harbor gloriously with pyrotechnics, like the greatest Fourth of July fireworks show ever. From the sound and the fury it could have been an invasion. The commies wouldn't know right away that no real damage was being done. They certainly had more to think about than a few helicopters attacking a small prison camp.

Kittleson picked out the Song Con River and the scattered lights of Son Tay Citadel, the village, on the other side. Then the chopper banked, cutting off that view. The next thing he saw, startling and confusing him, was the compound looming directly ahead. It lay in darkness except for dim lights shining through the windows of a long barracks-like building. An armed guard glanced up. The chopper flew so low Kittleson looked directly into the sentry's eyes.

He pinned the guard in the sights of his M-60 but held his fire. He swiveled his gun, frantically searching for his target—the southwest guard tower. It was dark, but not dark enough to hide main features. Not at this low altitude.

Something was wrong. There were no guard towers. The buildings looked different. And where the hell was the river? Barbara had it looping back sharply on itself and virtually lapping against the compound's west wall.

Jesus! They were crash-landing into the wrong compound!

Up in the cockpit, Lieutenant Colonel Herb Zehnder and Major Herb Kalen, the pilots, realized their mistake at almost the same instant. About four hundred yards south of Son Tay compound lay what had been dubbed the "secondary school" during raid planning and preparations. It was almost exactly the size and shape of the target, except it was only partly walled. The rest of it was wire net fencing.

Kalen shot power to the ship. The helicopter bolted on into the night, leaving the surprised sentry with only a glimpse and a fragment of reality, like what was left of a nightmare once you awoke.

Kittleson caught his breath in relief.

The chopper made a big swing to the northeast. Pappy spotted the river again, dark and serpentine, running between rice paddies on one bank and the village on the other. Electric lights burned here and there in the hamlet even at this late hour. Scattered clouds in a thin veil hung over Hanoi's Red River Valley. The scent of a recent rainfall blowing through the open chopper window reminded Pappy incongruously of mornings back on the farm in Iowa.

There was the bridge ahead, coming up fast, the way it did simulated back at Eglin. Firefight simulators dropped by C-130s were going off now to the south and east of Son Tay City, adding to the confusion of the "invasion" in Haiphong Harbor. A flare as brilliant as a miniature sun lit up the terrain. Poor commies probably didn't know what the hell was going on.

Major Marty Donahue, pilot of the leading gunship radio code-named *Apple Three*, also initially mistook the "secondary school" for the target. He corrected himself almost immediately when he detected Son Tay ahead with its towers lit up by flares. He soared down toward the camp, pulled up collective to gain more blade bite and eased off on the throttle. He spoke calmly through the intercom to his three gunners, Staff Sergeants Jim Rogers, Angus Sowell, and Aron Hodges.

"Okay. Ten seconds—then open fire."

The helicopter glided over the trees in the prison courtyard.

"Ready—*Fire!*"

The ship's three mounted miniguns—7.62-caliber Gatling-like six-barreled cannons—opened up simultaneously, pouring streams of red tracers into the northwest guard tower. The tower and the guards in it crashed to the ground.

"We got 'em! We got 'em! They're out!" the gunners radioed.

Donahue shoved in full throttle to get out of the way of the next helicopter in the assault line. He turned north toward a small rice paddy east of Finger Lake where he would set down in a holding area, monitor the radios now that mission silence had been broken, and wait until the released prisoners were ready to be extracted.

Banana One, the radio sign for Dick Meadows's Compound Assault HH-3, came in hard and close behind Donahue's *Apple Three*. Pilots Zehnder and Kalen pulled its nose down heavily and charged in a fast glide toward the southwest guard tower and the courtyard where it would crash-land. Kittleson saw the bridge over the Song Con sweep underneath and away. The flare illuminated the stone wall, and Kittleson made out each of the buildings. Looking at the compound was almost exactly like looking at Barbara.

He swung the muzzle of his M-60. He stood on the canvas seat and thrust his head and shoulders out the window for a better view. Wind whistled past his goggles.

He found the guard tower in his sights. It was on long

pole legs with an open-sided, thatched-roof shelter on top and another hootch built into the base of its legs. Movement inside said it was occupied. Kittleson squeezed his trigger gently and rejoiced in the smooth hydraulic-like recoil.

Apple Two with Sydnor's ground force aboard barreled directly toward the target, its pilots, Lieutenant Colonel John Allison and Major Jay Strayer, undistracted by the "secondary school." The Jolly Green rode hard into battle behind *Banana One* and made for its touchdown on the outside of the south wall.

Colonel Simons's *Apple One* brought up the rear. Like two of the three chopper pilots ahead, Lieutenant Colonel Warner Britton misidentified the target. An instant before Donahue's miniguns opened up on the real prison tower, which would have clued Britton to his error, he set *Apple One* down outside the barbed wire fence of the "secondary school."

It was no school. It was an ants' nest crawling with about two hundred army officer candidates.

Murphy's Law: Anything that can go wrong, will.

CHAPTER 55

Men tumbled out of the helicopter exactly as rehearsed in Florida. Britton bounced his Jolly Green back into the air to fly to his own holding area. Behind and below, he heard the immediate crack and thump of small arms discharge as raiders opened up on half-dressed enemy officer candidates bursting from their quarters. They scrambled about in confusion, like swamp mice kicked out of a nest. Bull Simons's heavily armed raiders began mowing them down. From somewhere, from nowhere, these demons had descended to spew fire, destruction, and death.

A North Vietnamese wearing only skivvies popped up from a sandbagged emplacement near the compound's southeast corner. He was naked from the waist up. Uncomprehending, he looked directly at Bull Simons. The colonel stitched the man across the chest with his CAR. The guy screamed once and fell back into his foxhole.

Bull Simons realized almost as soon as his twenty-two soldiers unassed the helicopter that they were in trouble. The place looked and sounded like what he'd expected of the prison camp—except, where was *Banana One*, with Dick

Meadows's voice booming through the bullhorn? And who the hell were all these goddamned people?

"It's the wrong fucking place!" Simons bellowed as his raiders continued to cut the surprised enemy to pieces.

It was a turkey shoot with the enemy running and howling in terror and dropping everywhere against the furious crescendo of firearms rattle.

"Get on the radio and get that fucking chopper back in here!" Simons ordered his radio operator, Staff Sergeant Walt Miller. "Get Sydnor and tell him to go to *Plan Green*."

He turned to Nickerson, his other communications specialist. "Turn on your strobe light. Mark the fucking LZ."

Bull's soldiers somehow breached the compound's south fence and streaked inside to continue their tidal wave of destruction. Red tracers streaked and skipped in dizzy, violent patterns. A fuel storage shed detonated in a brilliant fireball that rose and hovered, momentarily flushing the scene in a hellish red glow. Burning gas ignited other buildings. Flames licked at the night sky. Bodies littered the courtyard.

By this time three firefights raged within three kilometers of the POW compound: Simons's inside the "secondary school," the assault already begun on the real prison, and the fake firefights to the south and east.

Within five minutes after the American landing, the "secondary school" lay in blazing ruins. Simons's honed warriors mowed down more than one hundred enemy soldiers. Resistance quickly subsided into an occasional spatter of rifle shots against holdouts. Bull Simons's cavernous voice echoed above the turmoil.

"Withdraw! It's the wrong fucking place! We're pulling out!"

In the meantime, Colonel Britton had realized his mistake and turned back even before acknowledging the desperate message from Simons's radio operator. The camp looked like a giant bonfire. He spotted the soldier with the strobe outside the walls and skidded down for a landing. It was like setting down in a burning ammunition dump. Bull Simons crowded nearby. He demanded a head count from squad and team leaders as men disengaged through the breached south fence, firing tracers back into the conflagration as they withdrew.

Britton dropped his tail ramp. Men swarmed up it. Simons looked around to make sure no one was left behind, then leaped aboard. The chopper sprang into the air.

"Revert back to basic plan," Simons radioed Sydnor as *Apple One* screamed toward the south wall of the Son Tay compound where it was supposed to be.

Eight minutes after the assault began, Simons's men unloaded in a second air assault outside the Son Tay compound. For pilot Britton, it was a new record: three combat sorties in less than ten minutes.

Landing outside the wrong courtyard may in fact have been a fortunate blunder. The raiders had eliminated the raid's primary threat only four hundred yards away. Not one of Simons's men had been killed or wounded.

"Get our POWs and get out!" Bull ordered as his force split into teams and rushed along the outside wall to take out the guard quarters and support buildings by the main gate. "We got sixteen minutes left to get 'em and get out!"

CHAPTER 56

Pappy Kittleson swayed with the gun and used it for balance as blade downwash bounced off ground clutter and the ride roughened. He adjusted fire and kept hosing streams of tracers into the tower. Burning phosphorus on the 7.62 rounds sparked on impact, so that the tower lit up like a huge Christmas tree linked to the chopper by long cords of red light.

There was no return fire.

"We're going in!" came a shout.

The attacking helicopter skimmed over trees. The trees were much taller than those depicted on Barbara or with which they had rehearsed in the Eglin mockup. Pappy stayed on the gun until the last moment and continued pouring tracers into the tower and hootch below it on the ground. Aft from his position at the other window on the same side, Lorenzo Robbins emptied a thirty-round clip of 5.56 into the tower with his CAR-15.

The helicopter hovered for an instant, positioning itself. Then the bottom fell out. Tremendous vibrations all but shook Kittleson off his gun. He hung on. Suddenly, a tornado of leaves and tree branches and kicked-up earth vortexed around the night bird as it plummeted straight down through the trees. Its blades cut and ripped ten-inch limbs.

Captain Dick Meadows and Kittleson's team leader, Captain Dan McKinney, threw themselves faces down on mattresses near the tail ramp, as did Tapley and St. Clair. Lieutenant George Petrie held on at the open starboard door but remained on his feet. Tom Kemmer sprawled on a mattress directly at the door.

The chopper struck ground with such a solid jolt Kittleson felt like he was driven down into his boots and through the floor of the bird. Then he bounced and only his grip on the machine gun prevented his being thrown across the cabin like a pebble in a tin can.

A fire extinguisher torn loose from its mounting flew across the cabin and slammed into Air Force crew chief Leroy Wright, breaking his ankle.

Robbins's head struck the ceiling, stunning him for an instant. He landed on the floor in the midst of a pile of scrambling bodies. He quickly disentangled himself and broke toward the tail of the aircraft.

Lieutenant George Petrie, who had opened the side door on approach, was firing out at the main gate tower with his carbine when the bird crashed. The violence of the landing threw him out the door. He hit hard on his face and belly. He tasted North Vietnam soil wet from the recent rain. He was the first man on the ground after all.

Pilots Zehnder and Kalen cut engines. Blades—already tangled in limbs, trees, and a clothesline strung across the compound—stopped immediately. The tornado lost power. The tail ramp fell with a resounding thud. Debris still in the air rained down on the heads of troops as they charged out of the bird's belly behind Dick Meadows and his bullhorn.

The impact of the crash almost knocked St. Clair unconscious. Robbins jerked the tall kid to his feet and half dragged him down the ramp into the night. The flares had expired like dying suns, but *Apple Three*'s miniguns had left the crumpled northwest tower in flames, providing some

illumination, and Kittleson's southwest tower was smoldering and trying to burn.

Meadows went to one knee about fifteen yards from the
chopper and pressed the trigger of his bullhorn. His ampli-
fied voice resonated throughout the enclosure: *"We're
Americans. Keep your heads down. We're Americans. This is
a rescue. We're here to get you out. Keep your heads down.
Get on the floor. We'll be in your cells in a minute."*

His radio operator got on Colonel Simons's personal net.
Using team call signs, he radioed, "Wildroot, this is Blueboy. We're in."

Simons was in the heat of the brief battle at the "secondary school" and failed to hear him.

The first thing Robbins did when his feet touched solid
earth was to dart over and toss a concussion grenade into the
still-standing southwest guard tower. The thatched roof
popped off its walls by three feet, then settled again, lop-
sided, like a hat worn at a jaunty angle. Bright flames licked
around its edges, providing further illumination for the work
ahead.

Kittleson, his CAR-15 at the ready, hesitated a moment to
orient himself after the crash. He heard no nearby shooting.
Fires burning in the west guard towers sheened dimly off the
front of the long, low building in the center of the compound
that was his team's first assignment. Captain McKinney
shouted something and waved his arms. His team ran to him.
Adrenalin pumping, Kittleson and McKinney led the way
running toward the left half of the long center building.

"We're Americans come to take you home!" St. Clair
shouted. That was his rehearsed duty. "Americans, you're
going home!"

Sergeant Kenneth McMullin's job was to take up position
outside the crashed helicopter to provide cover for the teams
searching the buildings. Entangled in branches knocked
down during the landing, he scrambled through them to a
radish garden precisely eight paces to the northeast, exactly
where he was supposed to be. He had only to shift a little

ahead and to the right to obtain clear fields of fire around a fallen branch.

Lieutenant George Petrie and his two sergeants, Tom Kemmer and Pete Wingrove, streaked past McMullin, heading toward the front gate. Their task was to clear the gate, take out the guard tower and search the tall southeast corner building. Captain Jaeger's team had responsibility for the right half of McKinney's building.

A blast of AK-47 fire chattered from near the gate. Before raiders could return fire, a North Viet soldier ran out of the compound. Petrie heard him shooting again outside the wall as Colonel Sydnor's security platoon took up positions. A little firefight was going on outside as Petrie and his men took cover in trees at the foot of the main guard tower.

The tower was some thirty-five feet high with a concrete base about eighteen feet across, upon which sat a small tin building. The shack was empty. Petrie looked up at the tower; he expected it to be much lower to the ground.

"I can't throw a grenade that high," he exclaimed.

"Throw it anyhow," Kemmer encouraged.

Petrie stretched back like a major league pitcher and lobbed the little hand bomb. To his surprise and relief, it sailed directly through the side opening in the tower's guard shack. The flash-bang explosion cut short the guard's scream inside. The confused bastard must have been trying to hide.

Captain McKinney's building was stucco with a covered walkway along its entire front length. The front door hung slightly ajar. Surprised, Kittleson flattened himself against the wall to one side of the door, rifle prepared, while McKinney took the other side. Both switched on miners' lamps attached to their fighting harnesses.

Ready, Kittleson sprang back and stiff-legged the door wide. It flew open with a bang against the inside wall. St. Clair surged in low to the left, Robbins and Tapley to the right while Pappy and the captain covered for them. Beams from miners' lamps darted in the blackened room like dueling lasers.

Inside, Pappy expected to encounter a scene like that from Cabanatuan—wide-eyed, half-starved skeletons huddling cloaked in rags, terror, and confusion.

Instead, he found one large, open room. He turned in a circle to spray light into every corner. Trash and other debris littered the floor—old boxes, pieces of paper, a broken bunk frame, a Vietnamese sleeping mat. The room emitted a stale, long-unused odor.

Robbins's disappointed voice echoed in the otherwise empty room. "They're gone! They're fucking not here!"

"Try the other buildings," McKinney ordered.

The team scooted out of the long building in a rush just as Sydnor's men set off the satchel charge to blow a hole through the south wall. Americans scrambled inside through the breach.

McKinney and Kittleson led the way around the end of the building and behind, exactly as rehearsed. The burning crump of the fallen northwest guard tower silhouetted four Viets with rifles springing across the courtyard toward the front gate. Kittleson swung on them, but they disappeared before he could shoot.

"They're coming around!" somebody at the front gate yelled.

Kemmer dropped to his belly. Petrie remained standing. Four figures in a close stampede dashed into sight from behind the building. The Americans lay on their triggers and stopped the stampede, piling up the four bodies. Kemmer pumped a final burst into the heap of flesh, making blood and meat splatter.

"Get the POWs out," Petrie ordered as he took cover to one side of the open front gate.

An enemy soldier fully dressed and carrying a rifle ran past the outside of the gate toward the cluster of buildings in front, apparently pursued by Green Berets dumped outside

the south wall by *Apple One* and *Apple Two*. He was gone
before Petrie drew a bead.

The next two weren't so fortunate; Petrie was ready for
them. He tumbled both, pulling off carefully aimed shots on
semiautomatic. The gooks fell and did not move again.

By this time, Sydnor's and Simons's men had engaged
enemy troops in the barracks and admin buildings and were
in a hot firefight. Two Viets in a small concrete hootch about
twenty yards outside the gate pinged a few shots at Petrie.
The tall lieutenant held fire until he spotted muzzle flashes
in the hootch window. He switched to full auto and blazed
away at them. That ended the duel. Four American troopers
scurried by to clear out the building. "Good shootin'!" one
of them shouted.

An M-60 machine gun chattered angrily among the
buildings. Tracers waved and arced and ricocheted as they
ate up targets. A few enemy poured out the back of the little
settlement and headed for the bridge over the river.

McKinney's POW team burst into the small buildings
against the north wall. They were also empty, nothing in
them except trash and debris.

"Can you fuckin' believe this shit!" Robbins roared.
"What the hell have they done with our boys?"

Kittleson and Robbins took a look behind the buildings,
between them and the wall, just in case guards had had advance warning and executed or hidden the prisoners. There
was no one there either. Something arced over the wall and
landed within a few feet of the troopers. The fuse popped,
but the grenade failed to detonate.

"One of us is living right," Robbins said.

Anger and helplessness at finding the hole empty
tempted Pappy to join the heated firefight going on at the
front gate. However, rehearsals had drilled into every man
the importance of his being at a particular point at a precise
time. Deviating from the plan meant likely disaster. Captain
McKinney quickly assembled his disappointed fighters and

withdrew by the same route they had come. Captain Meadows was helping the chopper crew rig explosives to blow the disabled bird. He heard the bad news first from Pappy.

"Cap, the camp's been evacuated. There's nobody here."

Meadows looked stricken. "Are you certain?"

"There was nobody in our sector. *Nobody*. Maybe the other guys found something."

"Oh, Jesus. Okay. Get out through the hole in the wall and set up security on the LZ. The choppers'll be on their way back."

He banged his palm hard against the skin of the fallen HH-3. "*Jesus H. Christ!*"

Sergeants Kemmer and Wingrove burst into the tall southeast corner building, using their miners' lamps. *"We're Americans! We're here to rescue you! You're going home!"*

The only response was the echo of their own voices and the hollow stomping of their boots as they raced down a long hallway with cells opening off either side of it. The doors had iron bars, but the wall dividers were bamboo. The doors were all ajar, the cells empty except for old litter. Some of the cells appeared recently whitewashed and repaired with patches of fresh cement. An office space near the door stank of *Nuoc mam*—rotted fish sauce.

Kemmer exited the building and ran toward Petrie, who had remained stationed at the front gate. Petrie wheeled and threw his carbine to his shoulder. He blasted a round past the sergeant's face. Kemmer felt the heat blast.

"What the hell are you doing, Petrie?"

Petrie nodded toward the pile of gooks they had stacked up minutes before. One of them had not been dead after all. He was pulling himself up to brace himself against the wall for a shot with his AK-47 when the lieutenant noticed and nailed him. This time he was dead. He slumped forward, leaving blood stains on the wall.

Kemmer pumped another burst into the corpse to make sure.

Captain Meadows ran up. "Don't overkill, Tom," he said.

"The cellblocks are empty," Kemmer reported, his voice tense and edged with disappointment.

Meadows had already received the same disheartening news from both McKinney's and Jaeger's search teams. Petrie stared at the sergeant as though he failed to comprehend.

"There is nobody in the cellblocks," Kemmer repeated.

Petrie found his voice. "Are you sure?"

"There's nobody there."

Petrie did not want to accept it, any more than did Meadows. "Recheck the buildings."

Kemmer ran off. Meadows waited with Petrie until the sergeant returned. The firefight outside the gate was almost over.

"They're empty, sure enough," Kemmer confirmed. "It looks like no one's been there for a long time."

Meadows reluctantly radioed Colonel Simons at his command post outside the south wall. It was the hardest thing he had ever done. They were ten minutes into the raid when Meadows's voice delivered the news Simons neither expected nor wanted.

"Wildroot, this is Blueboy. Search complete. Negative items. I repeat, *negative items*."

A long air pause followed. Finally, Simons's voice dragged itself into the airspace.

"Roger that, Blueboy. Negative items. Prepare to withdraw to LZ for extraction. Set up LZ security. Blueboy and Redwine (Sydnor's platoon) exit on first extraction helicopter."

The raiders were going home empty-handed.

CHAPTER 57

Disappointment swept through raider ranks as the word spread. Son Tay was a dry hole. Kittleson felt numb, but he had little time to nurse his letdown. Although the assault *into* the POW camp had gone well, if not flawlessly, raiders still had to get *out*.

Twenty-eight minutes had elapsed by the time Kittleson's search team walked out through the hole blown in the south wall. The little sergeant glimpsed Colonel Simons busily directing the withdrawal. He was shouting at his signal specialist, who fired off a flare as a directional aid to guide *Apple One*'s return. In the background, U.S. Navy A-1 jets strafed the bridge over the Song Con River, which enemy vehicles were attempting to cross to reach the compound. Their nose guns crackled and spat streaks of flame, like exploding electricity, as the fast movers screamed in low, then swooped back into the sky for a second pass.

The enemy could not be held off indefinitely. Action inside and around the compound itself had ceased into an eerie silence. The U.S. "attack" on Haiphong Harbor and "firefights" elsewhere continued to sow confusion, preventing

Hanoi from organizing any kind of effective defense, but the attempt to send troops across the river indicated the enemy was at least beginning to react.

Colonel Britton's Jolly Green *Apple One* appeared like a hovering shadow, flared dramatically and set down quickly. The rear ramp was already open. Simons waved into the helicopter Captain Meadows's Compound Assault group, plus the two pilots and crew chief of the crashed *Banana One*, and most of Colonel Sydnor's element with the exception of a small security group, his pathfinders, and the Marshaling Area Control Officer (MACO). Meadows stayed behind to detonate explosive charges planted inside the crashed HH-3. The MACO, Captain James McClam, personally counted men as they boarded the helicopter to make sure no one was left behind. *Apple Two* was already buzzing toward the compound to pick up Simons and the remaining raiders.

Even before Kittleson buckled himself into the web seating, the Jolly Green jerked the raiders into the black night. A single rifle shot cracked *inside* the chopper's bay. All eyes snapped forward where Doc Cataldo had accidentally discharged his rifle, sending a round into the ceiling. Fortunately, the bullet caused no serious damage.

"It's only the Mad Doc," someone excused him.

The poor Doc ducked his head in embarrassment. Pappy bellowed orders for all weapons to be checked for SAFE.

Apple Two snatched the remaining raiders from the compound and the two helicopters barreled toward Laos. In the excitement of the getaway, Major Monty Donahue in *Apple Three* failed to receive the word to depart his holding area for nearly a half-hour after the other two choppers left. He sat idling on his darkened rice paddy, rotor blades turning for what seemed an eternity, one minigun on the lowered ramp covering the ground behind.

Donahue and his second pilot, Captain Tom Waldron, listened to the action over the radio net. They had heard Meadows's report of "Negative items at this time," followed minutes later by "Search complete. Negative items."

Donahue turned to Waldron. "Did you hear that?"

"I heard it, but I don't believe it. Let's wait to make sure. It *can't* be right."

It *was* right. They heard Simons's coded message calling in *Apple One* and *Apple Two* to make the extractions. More traffic followed and *Apple Four* and *Apple Five* lifted off from their holding pads. *Apple Three* was supposed to be the "cleanup ship," the last one out. It would tuck in on the tail of the five-bird procession as it headed balls to the wall for the Laotian border one hundred miles away.

Still, the "bug out" word failed to come. Donahue and Waldron waited, apprehension growing by the minute. In the darkness, they watched the shadows of about thirty people wandering around fifty yards away apparently searching for the noisy helicopters that had landed somewhere in the vicinity.

Inside *Apple One* and *Two,* the atmosphere was crushed, subdued. Kittleson leaned forward on his rifle, head down, staring between his boots. He felt the aircraft straining underneath his feet as it fought to whip every horse out of its engine. Someone had smuggled aboard a bottle of Scotch in anticipation of a victory celebration. It rattled unopened on the metal floor.

Still, there was little time at the moment to dwell on the mission's failure.

The chopper crew chief lying belly-down on the open tail ramp splashed more cold water on the atmosphere with his sudden panicked alarm: "*SAM! SAM!*"

Everyone had been conditioned to accept possible medium antiaircraft fire on takeoff—but not surface-to-air missiles.

Toward the rear of the aircraft, Sergeant Ken McMullin watched in fascinated horror as two bright red lights lifted off the ground and streaked toward the HH-53, growing larger and larger as they approached. They climbed and leveled off above the rice fields and turned into flying telephone poles.

We're dead, he thought.

At the last moment, Britton all but turned the chopper upside down on its rotors as he thrust collective full forward and almost shoved the Jolly into the rice paddies. The bird seemed to fall out from underneath Kittleson; he experienced momentary zero gravity. He held on, expecting to be shot out of the night sky.

The pair of SAMs streaked past.

Three more red lights flared and took off, barreling toward the escaping choppers. Foothills suddenly rose out of the rice paddies eight miles west of the camp. Britton in *Apple One* and Colonel John Allison in *Apple Two* popped their birds high, then plunged them behind the first ridge. The pursuing SAMs exploded into the side of the upcropping in brilliant flashes of searing light. The fleeing helicopters kept the mountains between them and the SAM sites around Hanoi as the other two *Apples* linked up with them and bolted for the border.

Still on the ground, Donahue and Waldron watched missiles going off all around, webbing across the night sky like a meteor storm. They counted eighteen of them, four of which were close enough to the escaping choppers to cause concern. After the fleeing helicopters passed over the mountain range, it got very quiet and lonely on *Apple Three's* rice paddy. The radio signals the pilots monitored grew weaker and weaker. No orders came to release them. Had someone forgotten to send the bug-out message to the last five Americans to leave North Vietnam that night?

Or had something else gone wrong?

Only one man—SFC Joe Murray—had been wounded during the raid, if you didn't count Sergeant Wright's broken ankle. (Murray suffered a superficial flesh wound to the inner thigh.) But as Donahue and Waldron listened to the diminishing radio traffic, they detected another budding crisis. There was some confusion over the head count. Only twenty-five raiders had boarded *Apple One*; there were supposed to be twenty-six.

The count went around and around inside the chopper cabins. *One . . . two . . . three . . .*

There were only twenty-five aboard. Kittleson stood up and made a personal count.

A man was missing. Someone remembered that one of the raiders had forgotten to cut hot wires to a power transmission tower he blew. He'd jumped off *Apple One* at the last minute to take care of it. Had he been inadvertently left behind, another contribution to the Hanoi Hilton? Simons's voice was thin and sharp as he demanded—"*Goddamnit!*"— an accurate count from both choppers.

The count passed back and forth, with the outcome still unclear. Donahue used his longer-range UHF set and volunteered to return to the compound to "police up the stray." The response soon came that *Apple One*'s missing man had boarded *Apple Two* after attending to his task. At least, that was how Donahue read it. He radioed one of the A-1 pilots in the clear.

"Did I read it right? Count correct?" he asked.

"That's an affirmative," the A-1 pilot responded. "It's all clear. There's nothing left to clean up. Get the hell out of there, *Apple Three*."

Donahue needed no further encouragement. The NVA searchers were moving closer to the sitting chopper. Staff Sergeant Jim Rogers nervously fingered the trigger of his minigun mounted in the open tail ramp. Any moment now the North Vietnamese were bound to spot them.

Donahue slammed in power and lifted the HH-53 into the air. A shot or two cracked at them in their wake.

Even at full throttle, it took *Apple Three* a half-hour to catch up with the other helicopters. Together now, heading for home, raiders settled down for the swift flight to the border, each nursing his personal disappointment. Even considering the mistaken flaredown at the "secondary school," the assault teams and pilots had performed marvelously. Surprise was total. The landings had been fast and violent, the search swift, firepower precise, reactions steady, the extraction smooth. It would probably take the North Vietnamese months to figure out what it was all about.

Someone had attacked an officer candidate school at one

compound, killing a bunch of future officers. Another batch of raiders had assaulted an empty camp, killing another fifty soldiers. Attackers had apparently landed all over the terrain and waged fierce firefights without ever actually engaging NVA troops, blew up a remote command center, strafed a bridge, deliberately crashed a helicopter, and raided Haiphong Harbor with *flares*. How could the commies ever make sense of it all?

It was all beautiful. Only one thing was wrong. The silence inside the choppers, the stone-frozen, well-deep, despairing silence, bespoke of what it was. The largest-scale raid in the history of attempting to free prisoners of war was returning home empty-handed. A failure. Not a single POW had been rescued. The Son Tay POWs had been moved weeks ago, judging from the appearances of the empty cells. The months of preparation, the drills at Eglin, the rehearsals, the elaborate planning—all for nothing. The Son Tay POWs, wherever they were, remained captives, peering into the skies and still waiting for rescue or release while hope slowly withered.

Master Sergeant Galen Kittleson shifted positions in the canvas seating, but his eyes remained as riveted on the helicopter's floor as the steel bolts that secured the metal plating. He was only a common soldier, a grunt, and not one of the men of the Big Picture who moved armies and manipulated history's great events. Yet, it had been his honor and privilege during his warrior's lifetime to have participated in great events. The raid to free the Bataan Death March survivors in 1945 and the Son Tay raid tonight were the two largest operations ever conducted by warring forces in attempts to repatriate prisoners of war. No less noble had been the Oransbari operation to free civilian POWs or the attempt to find and bust out Nick Rowe. Such efforts said something about America and the men who fought for her: It said no American was common, no American was expendable. *We're going to get you out*, it said. *God willing and if it's humanly possible.*

Two for four, Pappy Kittleson thought. No other Ameri-

can in history had participated directly in so many POW rescue missions. Two had been successful, liberating 594 captives—but two were failures, liberating no one. *Two for four.*
Not a bad ratio if you didn't happen to be a prisoner on the
zero side of the equation.

Pappy could not shake from his mind the haunted faces of
the skeletons the 6th Rangers and the Alamo Scouts had
extracted those many years ago from Cabanatuan. Those
same faces, those same eyes pursued him tonight all the way
back from North Vietnam.

He bowed his head inside the helicopter, this reverent,
unassuming little man from the cornfields of Iowa who
would have blanched at the suggestion of his being called a
hero, and he thanked God for the safe deliverance of those
brave men around him who had at least *tried.*

"God," he said, whispering, but the words thundered inside his head. "God, please let me be on it if there's ever another try at freeing those poor men from captivity . . ."

EPILOGUE

On Saturday, 21 November 1970, Darlene Kittleson went shopping in Fayetteville, North Carolina, home of Fort Bragg and U.S. Army Special Forces. For all she knew, her Green Beret husband was still at Eglin Air Force Base in Florida. She was driving home in traffic with the autumn sun bright and warm through the windshield when an announcement interrupted the easy-listening music on her car radio. A chill like a falling icicle slithered down her spine.

"It has been learned from sources at the Pentagon that the United States has made a daring raid outside Hanoi in an attempt to rescue American prisoners of war. It is unknown at this time how many POWs were rescued or if any were recovered. Stay tuned as this important story unfolds . . ."

Darlene didn't have to be told whether her husband was involved. She whipped the car toward a pay telephone booth. She jumped out and with trembling hands dialed two numbers—one to son Lance in college in Iowa and the second to Bruce at the family home in Fayetteville. She didn't want to have to wait until she arrived home to let them know what she knew instinctively.

"Turn on the television," she cried. "Your father has done it again!"

The Kittleson family spent the rest of the day and evening either on the telephone, since Lance was in Iowa, or huddled in front of their TVs. Gradually, details of the failed raid were made public. Darlene felt deep sorrow that no POWs were found in Son Tay. She also knew that however great her sorrow, it could not compare to her husband's own disappointment. Her personal relief at learning that none of the raiders had been lost—Galen was safe!—helped alleviate some of her disappointment.

When Galen telephoned to confirm that he was safe and that only one raider had been wounded by gunfire, Darlene collapsed into a chair. Tears brimmed in her eyes.

"Thank God," she said.

"Yes," Master Sergeant Kittleson agreed. "Honey, you think when I get home we might have some homemade bread . . . ?"

Public and congressional reaction to the raid was swift and not entirely unpredictable, considering the antiwar climate in the United States. Dark rumors of gross intelligence failures were circulated as various agencies sought to explain why they had not known in advance that the POW camp was empty. Senator J. William Fulbright called the raid "a major escalation of the war." Senator Birch Bayh referred to it critically as a "John Wayne approach." Representative Robert Leggett scoffed that the operation "must have been planned by the Saigon army, or perhaps by the script writer of a Grade C war movie . . . a first magnitude blunder from the very beginning."

Not all reaction, however, was negative; here and there, people approved of the effort. Senator Henry M. Jackson believed the raid to be "sound, prudent, and sensible." House Republican Leader Gerald Ford termed it a "great effort." Senator Bob Dole, himself a wounded and partially disabled WWII veteran, said, "It was a bold effort by courageous men who would do it again, and I hope they do. How many men must die in prison camps, how many women must be

told they're widows, how many children must be told they're
fatherless before we make some response?"

Despite the widespread criticism of the raid, almost none
was leveled at the brave men who went on it. They were
America's heroes. The army recognized the raiders' valor by
awarding four Distinguished Service Crosses and fifty Silver
Stars. It was Pappy Kittleson's third Silver Star for valor.

During the awards ceremony, Defense Secretary Melvin
Laird admitted that he knew there was "a chance of disap-
pointment—and even of failure. If a similar chance to save
Americans were to arise tomorrow," he added, "I would act
just as I did in approving and supporting the effort at Son
Tay."

As for the raiders, they had mixed feelings—disappointment that the raid had failed to free even one POW, but firm
in their belief that the raid had been the right thing to do.

Said Sergeant First Class Tyrone J. Adderly, the M-79
grenadier from Colonel Sydnor's Command Group, "It's
every soldier's responsibility if the situation presents itself
to go ahead and try to take advantage of it. Many times, opportunity knocks, and a lot of people complain about the
noise. If there were an opportunity to get back some of our
men, I would do it again."

"If there had been only one American there," said
Sergeant First Class Joe Murray, the only man wounded in
the action, "we would have gotten him out. It would have
been worthwhile. I guess it was still worthwhile because we
let the North Vietnamese know there are people in the U.S.
who would give just about anything to get our prisoners of
war out. . . ."

Master Sergeant Galen "Pappy" Kittleson told
Newsweek: "I remembered how happy the prisoners were
we got out in World War II. That's what bothered me most. It
was a big letdown. I felt too disappointed to speak. . . ."

Bull Simons, back in his office at Fort Bragg, was typically matter-of-fact when he rumbled, "I'm surprised people
think this was such a remarkable thing to do. The history of
the United States has a million things in it like this and this

doesn't seem to be so extraordinary. Maybe it is in contemporary days, but it's not unusual in history at all."

A total of 629 Americans survived POW captivity from the Vietnam War: 566 released in 1973; thirty-seven released by the Vietcong before 1973; two who escaped from the Pathet Lao; and twenty-four, including Nick Rowe, who escaped from the Vietcong. At least seventy-two Americans were known to have died in captivity, while more than seven hundred are still listed as missing in action.

About a year after North Vietnam released what it claimed to be the last 566 American prisoners held in the North, the former POWs were asked to complete a survey of "returned prisoners of war." In one part of the survey, they were asked how certain events affected their morale while in prison. Two events aided morale most: the Son Tay POW raid in 1970 and the bombing of Hanoi in 1972.

The senior U.S. officer in the Hanoi Hilton, Colonel John P. Flynn, called the Son Tay raid "the most magnificent operation of the war . . . There was a wave of exuberance. Our morale soared." Commander Dick Stratton, then a prisoner for almost four years, remembered how "heartened" he was at the news. "We had not been completely forgotten." All former POWs made similar comments.

Dr. Roger Shields, Deputy Assistant Secretary of Defense and the man coordinating POW/MIA activities, summed up the impact the Son Tay raid had on POWs: "[The raid] *did* succeed. There is just no question whatsoever about it. After the Son Tay raid, [the POWs] were all brought back to Hanoi. There, they were able to get together and organize, to mount some kind of common defense against their captors . . . The men could communicate, organize and support each other and care for the sick and wounded. Not only that, the morale boost that these men received was great. Some of them had been held incommunicado for years and didn't know what was going on. They were tremendously boosted to know that their country cared for them.

"I would hate to see the day when Americans feel that we have to have a one hundred percent guarantee of success before we try something like this. That would mean if we didn't have the guarantee, we just wouldn't try, we wouldn't do anything. There is a chance of failure in everything we do."

A political cartoon by R. B. Crockett of *The Washington Star*, appearing the day after news of the raid broke, expressed best the sentiments of POWs. It depicted a gaunt POW, ragged and bearded, ankles shackled, looking up with misty eyes while U.S. helicopters faded into the distance. The caption below read simply, "Thanks for trying."

The Son Tay raid proved to be the last in which Galen "Pappy" Kittleson was to participate in a distinguished military career that spanned nearly three generations of soldiers. On 31 July 1978, two weeks shy of his fifty-fourth birthday, Kittleson, wearing the highest enlisted rank in the U.S. Army, retired as Command Sergeant Major of the 7th Special Forces Group. In a fitting tribute to his roots, he returned to Iowa where he took up the farming he had first abandoned nearly four decades earlier.

Today, Pappy and Darlene Kittleson live in the two-story house in which Darlene was born, and in which the Kittlesons were married. It sits quietly and modestly on a street corner in tiny Toeterville, a town surrounded by cornfields and so small that it celebrated its centennial in 1998 with a "stand-still parade." The parade parked on the block-long main street in front of the post office and spectators came and walked around it.

Unassuming as ever, Pappy Kittleson tends a herd of fine Hereford cattle and, typically, rarely speaks of his unique honor of having been the only American soldier to participate in four separate POW rescue operations. It is what a man *does*, he believes, not what he *says* that constitutes the measure of any man.